THE YEAR WE
(Nearly)
WON THE LEAGUE

THE YEAR WE
(Nearly)
WON THE LEAGUE
STOKE CITY
AND THE 1974/75 SEASON

JONATHAN BAKER

For my cousin

Jeremy Le Poidevin

First published by Pitch Publishing, 2022

Pitch Publishing
A2 Yeoman Gate
Yeoman Way
Worthing
Sussex
BN13 3QZ
www.pitchpublishing.co.uk
info@pitchpublishing.co.uk

A CIP catalogue record is available for this book
from the British Library.

ISBN 978 1 80150 054 8

Typesetting and origination by Pitch Publishing
Printed and bound in Great Britain by TJ Books, Padstow

CONTENTS

FOREWORD

MANY BOOKS have been written about Stoke City Football Club. I can understand the fascination. We are the oldest league club in the world. Our history and heritage are rich. The likes of Stanley Matthews, Neil Franklin and Freddie Steele were household names. Imagine nowadays, three such players coming from one local area, fulfilling their dreams by playing for the club they had idolised as they grew up. It would not happen in today's game. Ironically, Matthews took a little bit longer than the others, as he was a Port Vale fan before joining the ground staff at Stoke City. The three all played for England. They inspired thousands of youngsters to follow their dreams, culminating in four local Stoke boys playing in the League Cup Final at Wembley in 1972.

What happened in the past is pure theatre. Take 1961, when the club were struggling in the old Second Division, and Tony Waddington was persuaded to bring Matthews back from Blackpool, where he was languishing in the reserve team. Considering that Matthews was approaching his 47th birthday, most people inside and outside the game thought Waddo was off his rocker. Crowds were down to 8,000. It was crisis time. The fee was £3,500, and immediately that was repaid because in Stan's first game back, the crowd swelled to 36,000. History will tell you that promotion soon followed.

Three 1966 World Cup heroes have graced the Victoria Ground: Gordon Banks, George Eastham and Geoff Hurst. Seven months after beating the mighty Chelsea at Wembley came the tragic accident in which Banks lost his eye. That would cost us in 1974/75, when we should have won the league, as this book describes. Had Banksy still been playing, there is no doubt in my mind that we would have become champions. Then, to rub salt in the wounds, came the collapse of the Butler Street Stand and the break-up of the team that would have gained further honours. Decline quickly followed.

These stories and more are told in this book, many of them described by some of the players who were in the title-chasing team that Tony Waddington built. You will read about how he did it, and how that team so nearly won the greatest prize. It's a great ride. Enjoy it.

Terry Conroy
August 2021

1

STUCK WITH STOKE

THE RACE for the First Division title in 1974/75 was one of the tightest there has ever been. The lead at the top of the table changed hands more than 20 times over the course of the season. At the beginning of April, six teams still had a genuine chance of winning, and only a single point covered the top three. The eventual winning points total was the lowest for more than two decades. It was a dynamic and pulsating campaign from start to finish.

Of those top six still battling it out at the death, only Stoke City had never won the championship before. And, as the title of this book suggests, they were destined to come up short once again. In the view of most Stoke fans of any vintage, the team that came so close in the spring of 1975 was the best in the club's history. In the previous couple of years, that team had won one cup – the club's first major trophy – and twice come close to winning another. Now it was involved in a serious tilt at the biggest prize in English football. But after failing narrowly to reach the summit, the descent would be swift and pitiless. Within two years, the architect of the team had gone and many of the players had gone too. Relegation swiftly followed. It was a classic tale of rise and fall.

In following the twists and turns of the 1974/75 season, this book tells several stories. It recounts the tale of Tony Waddington, the manager who revived an unfashionable provincial club that was dying on its feet, and built a team capable of winning trophies and – nearly! – winning the league. It reflects on the last hurrah of that team, their final thrilling full season together before a freak of nature and financial overstretch sent the club into free-fall. It details a nerve-jangling race to the finish line, with six runners more or less in line abreast as they entered the final straight. And it recalls a vintage era of footballers and of football – well within memory, but light years away from the game we know today.

This book is not just for Stokies. It is for every fan of a 'nearly' club – one that has never risen to the heights of being named English champions. By my reckoning, that embraces supporters of no fewer than 68 of the 92 clubs that currently sit in the four top tiers of English football. In the 93 seasons of the old First Division, there were only 23 different winners. The Premier League has been even more of a closed shop. In 30 years, there have been just seven different names on the trophy.

That means that nearly four in five league clubs and their supporters have never known what they can only imagine to be the giddy joys of winning the title. The experiences they *have* all shared, and continue to share, are depressingly familiar ones: hope and disappointment; occasional joy and more frequent despair; anger, frustration and shattered dreams; but always, always, affection and loyalty; and never, never, the smallest suggestion that allegiances might be abandoned or transferred elsewhere.

It was not written in the stars that I would spend my own footballing life as one of this large and permanently exasperated majority following the also-rans. As far as football went, I grew up in a divided household. My mother came from Leek, not far from the Potteries, and we were told that our grandfather had played in goal for Leek FC. His team was Stoke City. The family later moved to Uttoxeter, located at the midway point between Stoke-on-Trent and Derby, and right on the border between Staffordshire and Derbyshire. I was born in Derby, but brought up in Uttoxeter, on the Staffordshire side.

On the other side of the family, my grandmother came from Chellaston, five miles from Derby, and moved with my grandfather to Uttoxeter at about the time my father was born, a century ago. This grandfather was a Londoner, from Dulwich: I don't like to think about who he might have supported. But my father grew up as a Derby County man.

We might have been a house divided, but there was no real tension involved: no one of that generation in either family was all that interested in football, still less obsessed by it. I was about ten years old when Stanley Matthews helped Stoke City win promotion back to the First Division. It was a massive story that must surely have had the red and white households of Uttoxeter buzzing for months. Yet I have no memory of it.

I came late to the party. The first match I remember attending was on 30 December 1967, when I was already 14. It was Stoke City against Nottingham Forest at the Victoria Ground, and there were 20,948 of us there. The reverse fixture had taken place four days earlier, on Boxing Day, and Forest had won it 3-0. It must have been my father who took my cousin and me to the game, since my 'Stoke' grandfather, the goalkeeper, had died by this time. Why did my dad take us to see Stoke, and not his own team, Derby County? I suppose it might have been that Derby were in the Second Division at that time, and not faring too well. Whatever it was, my father must surely have known he was making a fateful decision, and that he would be setting us both on a course for life. Every football fan knows that your first team is your only team, and once you are stuck with it there is no escape.

So, from then on, I was Stuck with Stoke – even though they lost 3-1 that day, even though Forest had a striker with the same surname as me, and Baker scored. It didn't matter. It was already too late. To compound matters, I had a friend at school who was a Stoke City fanatic. Sensing a new recruit to the cause, he fatally infected me with his enthusiasm. From then on it was always Stoke, and to be honest, in spite of everything, I really wouldn't have had it any other way. That's another feeling all fans are familiar with, which is why I address this account of heroic failure to them, and not just to my fellow sufferers among the Stoke faithful. The team may often be useless, but they're *our* useless. They are our children. However disappointingly they turn out, we never give up on them.

Visits to the Vic were fitful in the early days of this growing attachment. It was a while before my cousin and I were considered old enough to go to games on our own. At first, we caught the train from Uttoxeter to Stoke, and took the half-hour walk to the ground. But the station was often full of opposing fans, and the atmosphere there, and on the way to the ground, was not always pleasant. So we switched to the Stevenson's football bus from Uttoxeter – 'Stevenson's Rocket' as it was known – which dropped us in the car park right next to the ground but took an eternity to get out of it once the game was over. Later still, we went by car. We parked up outside a pub and walked a mile or so through the streets of back-to-back houses to the ground.

Our first vantage point was the Juniors' Enclosure, until we were too old to be eligible for entry and switched instead to the Stoke End – a standing terrace open to the elements and facing the Boothen End, where the diehard faithful gathered.

We didn't go to many away games, but when we did they were memorable. An FA Cup third-round tie against Liverpool at Anfield, described later in this book, was one. The atmosphere was so partisan that we were terrified for our welfare if we won, and were almost relieved to go down 2-0 and to get home unscathed. I was working in Liverpool by that stage as a young newspaper reporter, and was witnessing daily a level of football fanaticism way beyond anything I had seen before. It was fuelled by the ferocious rivalry between the red and the blue areas of the city, at a time when both Liverpool and Everton were strong and often vying with each other for the top prizes. Both were in the mix as the 1974/75 season reached its climax.

Of greater significance for us was a trip to Sheffield Wednesday's Hillsborough for the FA Cup semi-final against Arsenal in March 1971. It was the furthest Stoke had advanced in the competition since 1899, and we were beside ourselves with excitement. We were the first ones into the ground when it opened at midday, a full three hours before a kick-off we thought would never arrive. Stoke surged into a two-goal lead, missed two glorious chances to settle the tie, and were then pegged back to 2-2 by a controversial last-gasp penalty. There would be a replay, but we knew the chance had gone. It was at once the most memorable and most heartbreaking day of my football life. It was also my 18th birthday.

The fun of following Stoke, going to the games and discussing the ups and downs that are a part of any football fan's life, was all the more enjoyable because I had someone with whom to share them. My cousin Jeremy was just over a year younger than me, and we had many enthusiasms in common, for The Beatles, for books and for Bob Dylan, and above all for the growing strength and success of the Stoke team at the start of the 1970s. Our joy was unconfined when the goals went in – especially if they were from the boot of Jimmy Greenhoff, our hero – and we consoled each other when they didn't. Even in the lean decades that followed the downfall of 'our' team, when we saw fewer games and much less of each other, we were always keen to catch up on the latest

Stoke gossip, recall the halcyon days and speculate about the possibility of their return. We celebrated Stoke's promotion to the Premier League in 2008. And there was one glorious final flourish, a sun-soaked day at Wembley in the spring of 2011. Forty years after we had endured the heartbreak of Arsenal at Hillsborough, we were at another FA Cup semi-final, against Bolton Wanderers. This time there was to be no last-minute slip-up as the Potters powered to a scarcely believable 5-0 victory, the largest in a post-war semi-final.

Once we had come back down to earth from this astonishing outcome, a process that took some time, Jeremy took the view that the experience could never be surpassed, and that the final itself would be an anti-climax. I suspected that he was right, but felt that as it had taken the club 150 years to reach the final, this would be a once-in-a-lifetime experience that I could not afford to miss. So I went, and he didn't. We went down 1-0 in an undistinguished match against Manchester City, but both of us were happy we had made the right decision.

We went to only a couple of matches together after that, although we still exchanged Stoke lore at regular intervals. We were still stuck with Stoke. His sad and premature death brought an end to this 50-year conversation. For me, much of the thrill of following the team through good times and bad has gone with him. So many memories, once shared and repeatedly returned to, are now mine alone. As I recall those heady days for you, so I dedicate this book to him.

2

THEN AND NOW

TO ANYONE whose memories of the beautiful game extend
no further back than the founding of the Premier League
in 1992, the world described in this book may feel like an
alien landscape. The English Football League, founded in
1888, is the oldest in the world. The way football is played
and organised has always evolved, but the adjustments and
modifications of the last half-century have made profound
changes to the nature of the game. True, there are still 11
players on either side, all trying to keep the ball out of one goal
and hoof it into the other. That is the simplicity and purity
that gives the game its universal appeal. Apart from that, just
about the only thing to have survived untouched is the theme
music to BBC Radio 5 Live's *Sports Report* at five o'clock on a
Saturday afternoon.

In 1974, when our story is set, the Football League in
England comprised four divisions – the First, Second, Third
and Fourth. It had been that way since 1958, when regional
Third Divisions were abolished. There were 22 teams in each
of the top three divisions, and 24 in the bottom tier. What
was then the First Division is today called the Premier League,
now made up of only 20 teams, while the old Second Division

is now known as the Championship. Today's League One and League Two are the old Third and Fourth Divisions of the Football League.

The bottom two teams in each division were relegated at the end of the season and the top two in the division below were promoted. Three down and three up was not introduced until 1973/74 – just before the events described in this book. Play-offs to decide the third club to be promoted did not start until 1986/87.

Before 1976, clubs finishing with the same number of points were separated according to goal average, which was calculated by dividing the number of goals scored by the number conceded. This was not something you could easily work out in your head, especially as goal averages would be calculated to three decimal places. Stoke City's figure in 1974/75 was 1.333. Was that good? I'm not sure. Apart from being unnecessarily complicated, this system was seen by those who understood it to encourage defensive rather than attacking play, and the much simpler goal difference that we know today was brought in. In the case of an identical goal difference, preference is given to the team that has scored more goals. In 1989 this rule actually decided the title, with Arsenal scoring the crucial goal in the last minute of the last game of the season.

Another fundamental change came in 1981, again designed to encourage more attacking football. Prior to that year, for almost a century, teams had been awarded two points for a win and one for a draw. But from now on, a win would be worth three points. Before the change, teams were usually happy enough with a draw, because it meant they lost little ground on their rivals. In 1974/75, Everton drew ten of their first 15 games and sat in third place. Under the three-point rule, they would have been way down in the middle of the table.

Substitutes were introduced only in 1965, and at first subs could come on only in the case of injury. That was soon relaxed, but managers were slow to see the potential of tactical changes. It was not unusual for the sub not to be used at all. In Stoke's 42 league games in 1974/75, they used their sub only 25 times. Only one could be named, a sort of 12th man, so it would often be a utility player who could cover several positions in the event of injury. If the goalkeeper was hurt, one of the outfield players would have to pull on the jersey and play in goal, and there were many stories of makeshift keepers performing heroics between the sticks. A second sub was allowed in 1987, and there have been gradual increases at intervals since then.

The idea of a large playing squad, squad numbers and squad rotation lay well in the future. The players did not have personal numbers allocated to them or wear their names on their shirts. The only thing on their backs was a number between one and 11, and those numbers indicated not their identities, but where they were going to play in the formation. Clubs had more than 11 senior professionals but nothing like as many as today. Consequently, players played more games and with shorter breaks between them. In October 1974, Stoke played eight times in 24 days. Over Easter, the top clubs played three games in four days. In 1975, Stoke had a tough Easter schedule of successive away trips to West Ham and Arsenal on Friday and Saturday, followed by a home match against league leaders Liverpool on Easter Monday. Stoke fielded the same 11 for the first two, and there was a single injury-enforced change for the third. Because of their involvement in several cup competitions, Stoke played a total of 70 matches in the 1971/72 season – and full-back John Marsh missed only one of them. Imagine how today's managers, with 30 or more players to choose from, would rant about such a programme.

One consequence of this was that players often turned out when they were well below full fitness. This was in part a throwback to the days before wages had improved, and poorly paid players depended on their appearance money and win bonuses just to make ends meet. They would be very reluctant to miss a game, and managers would be reluctant to drop them just because of a niggle. If you were 80 per cent fit, you were fit. If you were in pain, a cortisone injection would sort you out. This practice was widespread and probably caused further long-term damage. Cartilages were whipped out with abandon to sort out knee injuries. Nowadays the talk is all about the long-term brain damage caused by heading the old lace-up leather balls made heavy by moisture, but there are also plenty of ex-players now in their 60s and 70s who are hobbling about with walking sticks as a permanent legacy of playing when they should have been on the treatment table.

The Stoke manager Tony Waddington was probably no better or worse than any of his peers when it came to coaxing his walking wounded out on the pitch. If they declared themselves unfit, his inevitable response would be, 'Let's have a look at you.' A cursory inspection would often determine that they were not as crocked as they thought they were and were able to play after all. The manager's diagnosis would be, 'You look all right to me,' and out they went. Much faith was also placed in the magic sponge – a douche of cold water – if you picked up a knock during play.

Tough but injury-prone defender Denis Smith was subjected to these primitive fitness tests on numerous occasions, perhaps most notoriously on the night of an FA Cup replay against Manchester United. Smith was desperate to play, and his manager was desperate to have him, but a back spasm had left him barely able to walk. He went down to the Victoria Ground to watch the game from the stands, although so stooped was he by the pain that his wife had to drive him there.

As he got out of the car to go in and wish the team luck, something in his back clicked and he was able to move a little more freely. He made the mistake of telling Tony Waddington this when he arrived in the dressing room. Smith takes up the story in his autobiography, '"Step up on the bench," said the manager. I stepped up, and Waddo and his coaching staff looked at my back intently. They poked and prodded and asked me how it felt before Waddo declared, "You look all right." That was my fitness test. Before I knew it, I was having another injection, hearing my name announced and walking down the tunnel.'

Smith had enjoyed a meal of steak and chips before leaving home, secure in the knowledge that he wasn't playing. His manager assured him that he would quickly 'run it off'. No one was more surprised to see him trot on to the field than Mrs Smith, who was by then sitting in the stand waiting for him to join her. She watched her husband score a late equaliser and Stoke went on to win the tie in extra time.

It was a different game in other respects too. Managers tended to be appointed for the long term, and were not summarily sacked after a couple of poor results. In the modern era, Sir Alex Ferguson and Arsène Wenger, with their long reigns at Manchester United and Arsenal, are regarded as exceptional. Back in the day, it was quite common for managers to spend a decade or more at the helm. Tony Waddington's 17-year stay at Stoke City was among the lengthier tenures, but other mighty figures also served long terms: Sir Matt Busby was at Manchester United for 24 years, Bill Nicholson at Spurs for 16, Bill Shankly at Liverpool for 15, Joe Harvey at Newcastle for 13, Ron Greenwood at West Ham for 13 (and his successor John Lyall for 15), Harry Catterick at Everton for 12, and Bertie Mee at Arsenal for ten. These men were giants of the game, as well known as any of their players, and they wielded much more power than their modern-day counterparts – controlling transfer policy, for example. And all of them were British: there were no foreign managers, and very few foreign players either.

It was not unusual for players to spend their entire careers at one, or perhaps two clubs, rather than moving on every couple of years as is the fashion today. In reality, they had little choice. The £20-a-week maximum wage had been quashed in 1961 and Johnny Haynes of Fulham would soon be the first player to earn £100 a week. But the clubs still held the whip hand. If a player was under contract, he was not automatically free to move when that deal ran out. The club could hold on to him and demand a transfer fee. They could even stop paying him. The Bosman ruling, which scrapped this system, was still nearly 20 years in the future.

The wages of the players were not public knowledge, as they are today, and their bargaining power was slight. Few of them had an agent. 'I never knew what other players' salaries were,' says Stoke's Terry Conroy. 'I wasn't interested, as long as I was happy with what I got. The money wasn't big, and you knew that there was no freedom of contract. So you couldn't think, "I'll see my contract out and move on." That wasn't in your mindset. Every two years when your contract came up for renewal, you were always looking for more than you got, but in the end you always signed. You'd really no option. You were thinking about a rise of maybe £15 a week and they'd knock you down to ten. This never cropped up in conversation with other players. Even in the press they were never anxious to know what players were earning. It was never part of the agenda.'

When rival clubs tried to buy them, the players might not even be made aware of it. Having established himself as a top defender, Denis Smith began to attract attention from other clubs. Leeds United offered what would have been a world-record fee for a defender of £250,000. Manchester United wanted him, and were even prepared to consider letting George Best go the other way to secure him. After Smith's performance against Ajax in the UEFA Cup ties of 1974, there were inquiries from abroad too.

Smith knew nothing of any of this and found out about it only much later. He was certainly never consulted, 'Tony Waddington's answer to all of these flattering inquiries from major clubs was to just tell them all in no uncertain terms to "get lost". I was never any the wiser until long after the event. That was how it was then. I was a Stoke City player. They owned me, and I could not make any decisions as to my own future.'

As it happened, he was happy enough at Stoke, but not everyone was so lucky. Some were unsettled or stuck with clubs that no longer wanted them. Others reported for training as usual, only to be informed that they had been sold. They had no say. It was all wrong of course, although it did mean that money, and talk of money, did not dominate the game to the interminable and stultifying degree that it does now.

If you wanted to see your team in action, you had to go to the game and stand on the terraces. Very few matches were televised, and only the FA Cup Final was shown live. The BBC's *Match of the Day*, which was first broadcast in 1964, was exactly that – extended highlights of a single game. The ITV regions each covered a game on their patch every week, and showed the highlights on Sunday afternoons. Fans of Stoke City and other Midlands teams fondly remember *Star Soccer* and the voice of commentator Hugh Johns. So if you didn't actually go to the games, you might see highlights of your team's games no more than eight to ten times a season. If your team was not in the First Division, you would not see them in action at all.

Watching the matches in the flesh was a different experience for fans in the days before all-seater stadiums. Grounds were converted to seating only in the 1990s as a result of the Hillsborough disaster, the major crush before the FA Cup semi-final between Liverpool and Nottingham Forest which led to the deaths of 97 supporters. Before that, although grounds had an official capacity, the terraces often felt dangerously overcrowded. Imagine being one of the 84,569 people squashed into Maine Road in March 1934 for an FA Cup tie between Manchester City and Stoke – still the highest attendance at an English game. I once stood on Liverpool's famous Kop and found it a terrifying experience. If Liverpool were attacking the Kop end, the fans would crane forward to see the action and might surge down 20 or 30 steps into a massive pile-up at the bottom before climbing back up when the moment passed. Today's spectators have a sedate experience by comparison.

The least attractive aspect of football in the 1970s was widespread hooliganism, and violent clashes between rival fans. Football hooliganism was to disfigure the game for at least the next couple of decades, and although it has never been completely eradicated, it exists at a much lower level today. The conversion to all-seater stadiums, while prompted by safety considerations, also helped with the segregation of fans and more orderly behaviour – inside the ground at least. Going to the matches in the late 1960s, when we were in our early teens, my cousin and I would stand in the Juniors' Enclosure and never saw or experienced much trouble, apart from one unpleasant encounter with West Brom fans at Stoke station. But by the early 1970s, organised 'firms' of fans intent on confronting opposition supporters – especially on derby days – led to violent incidents at grounds up and down the country. Stoke City were not immune, and a small section of their support was a part of the problem. Attendances fell, with many fans staying away for fear of being caught up in violence before or after the game. You would think twice before organising a family outing to the match, something which is commonplace today.

As for the football itself, today's referees are tougher on foul play than they were then, and issue yellow and red cards much more readily than they did. As a flying winger, Terry

Conroy talks about facing knee-high tackles from defenders he describes as professional assassins, 'They would be trying to nobble you and put you out of the game, or at least keep you quiet.' Tougher refereeing has tilted the balance back a little way in favour of the skilful attacker.

Mike Pejic – himself one of the toughest defenders of that or any era – agrees. In his *Sentinel* newspaper column, he painted a terrifying picture of the physical dangers of playing the game in those days, when a career-ending tackle was always just round the corner. 'We really didn't talk about hard men back in the day, because it was a given. If you weren't hard, you simply didn't last. Johnny Giles of Leeds was a silent assassin. He was certainly one of the more ruthless and cynical players around. He'd quite happily touch the ball just ahead of him, so you'd be tempted to come in, then find a set of studs going down your shin. As a full-back, you'd often find six studs going down your leg from someone as you cleared the ball up the line.

'There was no somersaulting through the air to try and win a free kick though, because the ref would look the other way and everyone else would probably have laughed at you. With no rules to protect you from tackles from behind, and no TV cameras to capture everything from every angle, all kinds of things went on.

'The secret was to make sure the officials weren't looking and that's when you'd get an elbow in the face, or one in the kidneys, and your toes stamped on. Show any hurt and you were labelled a coward or soft, or even a cheat.

'It was a battle out there, a war at times, and one you had to win, in between trying to play some football. The skill was not just on the ball, but trying to avoid a challenge that could end your game.'

Geoff Salmons, who joined Stoke in the summer of 1974, agrees. 'It was more dangerous playing then,' he says. 'High tackles. You used to take 'em. If someone kicked you, they'd know they'd get it back. Not like today, lie screaming on the floor holding your leg. You had to look after yourself.'

Conroy also notes that today's footballs are a completely different proposition from the old leather lace-up variety. If you want to win a few quid in the pub, tell your mates that footballs are the same weight today as they always were, and wait for them to bet you that you're talking through your hat. It is a myth that today's balls are much lighter – at least at kick-off. But they are different, because the material used today does not absorb water, and so their weight remains constant, whereas the old balls would get heavier as they got wetter. The aerodynamics of today's balls are also affected by their smoother surface, which is why they can now be hit further and faster than before.

Finally, and probably most significantly, there is the state of the pitches. In the days of which we speak, even the top grounds would look like park pitches by November, with a broad strip of mud extending from one goalmouth to the other, and a couple of narrow green strips down the wings. These days, the pitches are like billiard tables from August to April. In past eras, winter games were played on mud baths. Conroy describes the pitch at the Victoria Ground as 'a sludge pit', and there are those who would say this was far too complimentary. Nowhere was immune – prestige grounds like Stamford Bridge and Old Trafford were often as bad as anywhere else. By common consent, the worst surface in the old First Division was Derby County's then home, the Baseball Ground. You don't have to take my word for it. Go online and search for Derby County v Stoke City in March 1975 and you'll have some idea of what would be regarded as standard winter conditions in those days (you'll also see two cracking Stoke goals in defiance of the swamp, but that is not the point). If you are younger than 60, you will be shocked. To admire the Victoria Ground in its winter plumage, search for Stoke City v Manchester City in February 1975 (where the bonus is four cracking Stoke goals; but never mind that – look at the state of the pitch).

Long-serving defender Alan Dodd reckons the pitches were far from perfect even at the start of the season, and that this was an obstacle to good football, 'We were a footballing side. We just didn't bash the ball long into the opponents' area, we did play a bit of football and the pitches weren't really suitable for that. I remember the first match of the 1974/75 season, when we beat Leeds. Obviously, that's when the football pitches should have been immaculate. The pitch at the Victoria Ground *looked* immaculate that day, but the ball was bobbling all over the place. And that was the first match of the season! That was the standard of football pitches at the time.'

Geoff Salmons echoes this. 'We were a good side,' he says. 'The only thing that let us down were the pitches. They were diabolical when you look back now. When you look at what we played with and what they've got today – it's unbelievable. It was bad at Stoke too. Denis Smith once put a ball back to Peter Shilton, and Shilts went to kick it and it bobbled over his foot and into the net!'

Eric Skeels underlines all these points, 'Nowadays you can't really tackle a bloke because you'll be booked straight away. Not like in our day. If the weather was bad or it was icy, you'd be sliding in, and you couldn't stop. The referee realised it was awkward and let you go on, or might give you a warning or maybe book you. Nowadays they send you off. Our game was more physical.

'The game's changed altogether now, it's not as robust as it was. Now it's more technical – pass, pass, pass. On our pitches you couldn't do that. If the ball dropped in front of you on a muddy pitch, it wouldn't bounce up at you – it would stick in the mud. But the pitches now are fabulous. The ball's like a balloon; you can kick it from one end to the other. Gordon Banks on a wet pitch could just about get a goal kick over the halfway line.'

One idiosyncrasy of the game up until the 1970s was peculiar to Stoke City. Most league matches were on a Saturday afternoon, and they all started at the same time – 3pm. Except at Stoke. Kick-off for home games at the Victoria Ground was at 3.15pm to allow workers at the local potteries to get to the ground at the end of their Saturday shifts. The later starts were introduced after the war by manager Bob McGrory to help maximise gates. They had a further unexpected benefit for others too, since in those days pubs closed at three o'clock on a Saturday afternoon. The late start meant drinkers at the pubs around the Stoke ground could be supping right up until closing time and still be in their places by kick-off.

If you were not there in person though, and were reliant on the radio for news of the result – as we often were in those days before mobile phones – the delayed starts at Stoke were a nightmare. At five o'clock you would be hanging on every word of John Webster or James Alexander Gordon, the men who intoned the results, only to hear the dread words, 'Stoke City against Derby County – late kick-off.' Then you had to wait until they remembered to tell you the final score later in the programme. It was agony.

You are now ready to be transported back in time to the game as it was. Not necessarily better – but very different from today. Let's not even get started on VAR.

3

THE DARK AGES

STOKE CITY did not win the Football League championship in the spring of 1975. This would not have come as a huge surprise to their supporters, since they had failed to do so in any of the previous 43 seasons they had spent in the First Division since the Football League's inaugural competition of 1888/89. Stoke were members of the first league, and in that launch season they finished bottom. That set the tone for much of what was to follow.

Founded in 1863, Stoke have a claim to be the oldest club in the top four tiers of English football. That is a proud distinction. But it also means their followers have waited longer than any others for their team to win the greatest prize. They are waiting still. And in the current environment it seems likely that the wait will be indefinite, and that their three consecutive ninth-place finishes in the early years of the 21st century may represent the best they can reasonably hope for in an era when a handful of super-rich clubs dominate the Premier League.

All the more reason to celebrate the near miss of 1974/75 – a much more democratic era in which many teams could harbour realistic dreams of becoming champions. When Leicester City won the Premier League in 2016, their starting odds of 5,000/1 did not, at the time, seem unreasonable. Their triumph was rightly hailed as something extraordinary, almost miraculous. But in pre-Premier League days money was less of a determinant of success, and was generally more evenly distributed. Leicester and a host of other provincial clubs would always think they had a shot at winning the First Division title if they could put a decent team together. The odds on Leicester then would have been much shorter. Derby County, Burnley, Nottingham Forest, Ipswich Town, West Bromwich Albion, Portsmouth – they have all won the league in their time. None looks likely to repeat the feat in the foreseeable future. The playing field was much more level before the Premier League established an elite into which it was hard to break without spending many millions.

Stoke's tilt at the top prize in 1974/75, and their narrow failure – largely due, literally, to a series of bad breaks – was not even the closest they had come to winning the title in almost a century of trying. In the first season after the Second World War, 1946/47, they were within one result of doing so. Victory in their final game would have seen them crowned champions. The reason they failed stemmed less from their football, and more from the fact that the two most important people at the club detested each other.

The Stoke manager was Bob McGrory, a tough Scot who had joined the club in 1921 as a player, and notched up more than 500 appearances as an uncompromising defender. You can tell he was an uncompromising defender just by looking at his picture. You wouldn't fancy coming up against him in Stoke on a wet Saturday afternoon in November. In his final season, although by then past 40, he had not missed a game. As soon as he retired he became manager, a job he was to hold for 17 years. In his first season, Stoke finished fourth. And in 1946/47, he could so easily have taken them all the way.

McGrory's prime asset was another long-serving Stoke player, the great Stanley Matthews. Stan was 30 at the end of the war and had lost what, with any ordinary mortal, would have been considered the years of his footballing prime. But his skills were undiminished. Even in a pre-television, pre-internet age, his genius on the right wing was legendary throughout the world. Known variously as 'The Magician' or 'The Wizard of Dribble', his fame was based on explosive speed from a standing start, and on tight control of the ball even when running at full tilt. Few full-backs could live with him, and although he scored goals himself, his main value was in creating them for others – beating his full-back on the outside and sending over accurate crosses for the big men in the middle.

McGrory had built a strong side for this first season after the wartime break of seven years, and as perhaps the most famous player on the planet, Matthews was its undisputed star. But the relationship between the two former team-mates was sour. In part, it dated back to a pre-war dispute over McGrory's refusal to pay Matthews a bonus to which he believed himself entitled. The Stoke fans were appalled to hear that Matthews had responded by putting in a transfer request. A host of clubs immediately queued up to sign him. There were mass 'Matthews Must Not Go' demonstrations in the Potteries, and a tense stand-off. The row was eventually patched up and Matthews got his money. The transfer request was withdrawn, but the rancour engendered by the incident never really went away.

Matthews believed his manager disliked him for two reasons: one, that when he had first been brought into the Stoke first team as a 17-year-old wunderkind, it had been at the expense of McGrory's best friend, Billy Liddle; and two, simple jealousy. Matthews thought McGrory was envious of all that he had gone on to achieve in the game.

The ill feeling surfaced again early in the 1946/47 season. Matthews missed seven of the first ten games with injuries, and Stoke made a poor start. When the winger recovered, his manager suggested he had a run-out with the reserves before returning to the first team. Matthews insisted he was fully fit and ready to come straight back in. He declined to turn out for the reserves and was not picked for the next game.

Such was Matthews's profile that what might seem like a minor spat became a big story for the newspapers. It was reported that the other first-team players thought Matthews had become too big for his boots and had actually requested that he should not be picked. This was publicly denied by the captain, Matthews's fellow England international Neil Franklin. 'It was rubbish to say Stan was not popular,' said Franklin later. 'He was a man loved and admired by us all.' After a few days the row was smoothed over again, and things returned to normal. Matthews was restored to the team, and Stoke embarked on a strong run that lifted them into title contention.

One of the coldest winters ever recorded now set in. There was no football for ten weeks, and the season was extended into June. When play resumed, the enmity between the manager and his star player reared its head once again.

In those days, the Easter programme was even more packed than it is now. There were games on Good Friday, on the Saturday and on Easter Monday – three in four days. The schedule of 1947 meant a long journey from Grimsby back to Stoke between the first and second of them. Matthews was due to play for England the following week, and thought that four games in eight days, the last of them an international, would be too taxing. He asked the manager to rest him for the first match, and McGrory agreed, on condition that he played in the other two.

On Good Friday, Stoke won comfortably at Grimsby without him, and Matthews half expected McGrory to retain a winning team the following day. But on the Saturday morning, McGrory told him he was playing. Less than an hour before kick-off, with Matthews already changed into his kit, the manager pulled him out the dressing room and said he had changed his mind. He wasn't playing after all. Matthews accepted the decision, though annoyed about its lateness. Stoke won again, and Matthews wasn't picked for the Monday game either.

All this created a bad atmosphere, and everything came to a head when Matthews returned from international duty a week later. McGrory told him he was back in the team for the next match. Stoke won it, and Matthews was among the goalscorers. But after the game, he happened to pick up a matchday programme – which had been sent to the printers the day before. His name was not on the team sheet. It occurred to him that McGrory had not intended to play him, and that he had been brought in only as a late replacement because another player had sustained an injury. Neil Franklin confirmed these suspicions. As he drove home that night, Matthews resolved to leave. He no longer trusted his manager, and felt that if he was to make a move at all, he had better do it now while he still had a few more seasons in his legs.

With the season nearing its climax, and Stoke still right in the hunt, Matthews went to the board and requested a transfer. He knew exactly where he wanted to go. During the war he had served as a physical training instructor in the RAF, and been based in Blackpool. He loved living by the sea, and the main part of his training regime was daily runs on the beach. When the war ended, he and his wife had bought a small hotel and made their home in Blackpool. He trained on his own or with the Blackpool players during the week, and drove the 85 miles to Stoke only for full training sessions and home matches. He told the Stoke board he wanted to leave and play for Blackpool – a rare instance of a player selecting the club he wanted to join. After failing to dissuade him, the board agreed that he could go, but not until the end of the season. In the meantime, everyone agreed that the arrangement would be kept top secret. The next morning, the papers were full of it.

There followed an unsavoury period of negotiations over the fee. Stoke wanted a record £20,000 for their star man, but Blackpool would not offer more than £11,500. Matthews thought his age – and McGrory's determination to be rid of him – were behind Stoke's eventual acceptance of the offer. 'At the time of my move to Blackpool, there were a number of people who thought I was finished then, and I firmly believe Bob McGrory was one of them,' he wrote later in his autobiography. 'Bob wanted me to go, of that there is little doubt. At 32, he obviously thought the £11,500 being offered by Blackpool, even though it fell short of Stoke's asking price, was too good to turn down.'

While all this was going on, Matthews was still turning out for a title-chasing team. He played in away victories against Blackburn Rovers and Leeds United – scoring in the first of them. But then it was over. It was clearly no longer tenable for him to remain until the end of the season. Stoke's most famous son, one of the finest players ever to grace a football field, left for Blackpool with three games still to be played and his team still right in the title race. It is hard to imagine a greater act of self-harm by a club on the brink of bringing home the first title in its history.

Stoke did not collapse in his absence, though on the day of the move they could manage only a goalless draw at home to Sunderland. A 1-0 win at Aston Villa followed, leaving only an away visit to Sheffield United. This was a game in hand, postponed during the big freeze. All their major challengers had completed their fixtures. The excitement was great: the title would be decided by the very last match of the season. And the tension had plenty of time to build, because there was a two-week gap before that fixture was to be played. Liverpool topped the table, two points ahead of Stoke with all their games played, but with an inferior goal average. A win at Bramall Lane would bring the title to the Potteries for the first time.

In goal for Stoke in that final match was Dennis Herod. When invited to choose the 'Match of My Life' for a book of that name by Simon Lowe, this was the one he chose. It was an odd choice, because Stoke lost it 2-1, and with it the championship. Not only that, but Herod made the mistake that enabled Sheffield United to take the lead after only two minutes. Stoke quickly equalised and battered the Blades' goal for the rest of the match, but a breakaway goal and some heroic home defending on a muddy pitch saw them succumb.

Herod chose that match because so much was at stake. 'It meant everything,' he said. He blamed himself for the opening goal, but he blamed the sale of Matthews for the loss of the title. As he asked in that book, 'If you had to win three matches to win the league title, would you sell the best player in the world?' It is a question many asked at the time, and it is still being asked today. In an interview in 1999, Herod summarised it bluntly: 'Bob McGrory's jealousy of Stan's fame cost Stoke their best chance of the First Division title. Before our last game at Sheffield United, he sold a world-class player, and we lost that match without him. It was folly to leave Stan out, and the decision to sell the best forward in the world to Blackpool was sheer stupidity.' Herod died in 2009, the last survivor of that gallant team that fell only at the final hurdle.

And what of Matthews? He will reappear in our story later, to dramatic effect. When he arrived at Blackpool, he recalled that the manager, Joe Smith, said to him, 'You're 32. Do you think you can do a job for us for another two years?' Matthews replied, 'At least two years. The way I'm playing and the way I feel, I think I could go on for another five at least.'

It turned out to be a conservative estimate. Matthews was to play on for 14 years at Blackpool, securing an FA Cup winners' medal in the celebrated 'Matthews Final' of 1953. He turned out for them more than 400 times, until he was well into his 40s. And even then, he was far from finished.

The 1946/47 campaign represented the pinnacle of Stoke's achievements until the early 1970s, when the team that is the subject of this book also came close to winning the title. That later team also established a reputation as a formidable cup side, reaching FA Cup semi-finals in successive years, and in 1972 lifting the League Cup – still the club's only major honour.

But as for the years between 1863 and 1947 – they did not, it has to be said, add up to an unbroken record of success. Rather, the story is for the most part one of underachievement and failure, relegations or near-relegations, applications for re-election and even, at the nadir of their fortunes, liquidation and forced withdrawal from the league. There were occasional flashes of hope, and even more occasional promotions. But they were just that, flashes, sporadic pinpoints of light in the prevailing gloom.

Given this unimpressive record, it is perhaps not surprising that there is not even a definitive date for the foundation of the club. Most official records say Stoke were founded in 1863, and indeed they celebrated their centenary in the promotion year of 1963. That made them the second most senior club after Notts County, usually regarded as the oldest professional association football club in the world. When Notts County dropped down into the National League in 2019, Stoke could lay claim to being the oldest club in the top four divisions of English football.

But are they? Stoke City historians Wade Martin and Tony Matthews have investigated the popular view that a group of former pupils of Charterhouse School founded a team in Stoke in 1863 when they were working as apprentices at the North Staffordshire Railway Works. We even have the names of four of them. Unfortunately, research failed to find any of these names in the Charterhouse register of former pupils. Soccer was certainly being played in Stoke around that time, but there is no solid evidence of any organised matches taking place.

The first recorded game was not until fully five years later, in October 1868, when Stoke Ramblers played out a 1-1 draw with E.W. May's Fifteen. Stoke City's lineage cannot reliably be traced back to anything before that date. Captaining the Ramblers was Henry Almond. He was indeed an Old Boy of Charterhouse, but he had only just left school and come to Stoke when the Ramblers took to the field in 1868. A report in *The Field* magazine in September 1868 informed its rapt readership: 'At Stoke-upon-Trent, a new club has been formed for the practice of the Association Rules, under the charge of HJ Almond, one of the most prominent performers in the Charterhouse School Eleven of last year.' Since Almond can only have been about 18 at the time, and yet was captain of the team on its first outing, it seems fair to assume that he was a leading light in its formation.

The 'Association Rules' referred to in *The Field* did not bear much comparison to the game we know today. As we have seen, the first Ramblers game was played against EW May's Fifteen. A football team in those days could number anything from 12 to 15 players, and was frequently a mixture of football and rugby – indeed, it was sometimes played with a rugby ball. Association Football, played mainly with the feet, was known as 'the dribbling code'. The rules were not fixed, and might vary from game to game. The legal use of the hand to control the ball did not die out until the formation of the Rugby Football Union in 1871, after which the two games became distinct.

Within a couple of years, 'Ramblers' was dropped from the name and the club were simply known as Stoke, or Stoke-on-Trent. They were not known as Stoke City until the 1920s.

Football was developing rapidly in this period, and the FA

Cup was already a prestigious competition. By 1885, Stoke were playing at the Victoria Ground, which would be their home for more than a century, and the players had turned professional, paid five shillings a game. International matches were being played, and three locally born Stoke players were in the England team – goalkeeper Billy Rowley and full-backs Tommy Clare and Alf Underwood.

Although the FA Cup, the world's oldest national football competition, had been going since 1871, there was frustration among many clubs that once you were knocked out then that was in effect the end of your season, and it was back to meaningless friendly games. From this frustration was born the Football League, a single division formed of 12 teams in the summer of 1888. Stoke were founder members, and their secretary Harry Lockett became secretary of the new league.

Stoke's first fixture was a home match against West Bromwich Albion. There was enough interest in the new venture to attract a crowd of 4,500 to the Victoria Ground and prompt the *Evening Sentinel* to publish a special edition with a report of the game. The special's 'Stop Press' column also recorded a new murder in London carried out by the serial killer known as Jack the Ripper. This would have been rather more gripping than the match report, since Stoke lost 2-0 and finished the season at the bottom of the league. They won only four of their 22 games. Coming bottom meant they had to apply for re-election for the following season – there was no Second Division into which to drop down. This they did successfully, only to come bottom again, now with only three wins. This time they were not re-elected, and went off to play in the Football Alliance, made up of 12 teams from the Midlands and the north of England. They won that, and when the Football League was expanded to 14 teams for the 1891/2 season Stoke were readmitted. They didn't come bottom this time, but did badly enough to have to rely on re-election once again.

By 1894/95 the Second Division had been added, with relegation and promotion decided by a series of Test Matches played between the bottom three in the First Division and the top three in the Second Division. Needless to say, Stoke were involved in those first play-offs, but managed to hold on to their status in the top flight. Two years later, it was the Test Matches again, and again they survived. After that, automatic relegation and promotion were introduced.

By the dismal standards of these early years, 1898/99 looks like a vintage season. Stoke finished 12th out of what was now a league of 18 clubs, and advanced to the semi-final of the FA Cup, where they were beaten by Derby County. It would be another 72 years before they next progressed to that stage of the competition, and more than 100 before they featured in a final.

After that, it was back to a succession of dour battles against relegation and a deepening financial crisis. There were some false dawns – late in 1903 they sat fourth with four games to go, and with a mathematical chance of winning the title. But fourth is where they finished. They won the first five games of the 1905/06 season and were attracting crowds of 12,000 and more. But form fell away, and they finished tenth. The next season brought one relegation battle too many, and Stoke were back in the Second Division.

They took only one point from their first four games in the lower tier, and although things improved after that, the club's finances were now in a critical state. Players were sold, the crowds stayed away, and eventually they had to withdraw from the league. It was the end of the line. The club went into liquidation.

It took the efforts of a dozen local businessmen and former players to rescue the situation by raising £2,000 to take over the club and its remaining assets. In June 1908, they formed Stoke Football Club (1908) Ltd. They kept the club alive, but there was no way back into the Football League, so they compensated by taking part in two other leagues at the same time: the Birmingham and District League, and the Southern League Division Two (Western Division). In 1910/11 they won the Birmingham and District League and were promoted from the Southern League Division Two. This had involved playing a total of 59 games, two of them on the same day. They played 19 games in eight weeks.

Leaving the Birmingham and District League to concentrate on the Southern League proved a false move, because relegation back to Division Two followed. They fared better there, and when top-class football was suspended because of the Great War, Stoke applied successfully for readmission to the Football League when it resumed. They would have to wait another four years to take up their place.

At first, their fortunes post-war were no better than before, but that all changed in 1921/22 when, buoyed by 25 goals from Jimmy Broad, a signing from Millwall, they were runners-up and so won promotion back to the First Division.

This season also saw the arrival of full-back Bob McGrory from Burnley. McGrory is one of the towering figures in the club's history. He would stay with Stoke as player and manager for 31 years, a stalwart of the defence into his 40s, turning out more than 500 times. As manager, he relied heavily on local talent, often fielding an entire team of Potteries-born players. This was also a sound financial policy since they had cost him nothing more than the basic £10 signing-on fee. They were known as 'Bob McGrory's £10 team'. Trainer Vic Shaw cost even less – McGrory somehow persuaded him to do the job for nothing.

We have already seen how McGrory's various fallings-out with Stanley Matthews might well have cost Stoke their first title in 1947. Many Stoke fans were reluctant to forgive him for the loss of Matthews at such a critical time. But his contribution and service to the club over such a long period certainly deserve respect.

The return to the top flight did not last long, as the club embarked on a period of seesawing fortunes:

1922/23 – relegated in their first season back.

1925/26 – relegated again, to the Third Division North. The club was renamed Stoke City FC after Stoke-on-Trent was granted city status.

1926/27 – back up to the Second Division at the first attempt, thanks in large part to 25 goals by Charlie Wilson, a recruit from Huddersfield Town .

1931/32 – third in the division, missing promotion by two points.

1932/33 – Stanley Matthews made his debut at the age of 17, and was quickly recognised as a precocious and prodigious talent. Stoke won the Second Division championship and were back in the top tier.

And in the First Division they were to stay until the suspension of football because of the Second World War. There was a good FA Cup run in 1934, which ended in a 1-0 defeat at Manchester City in the sixth round – a match notable for a record crowd for a club game of 84,569, and a whopping £5,426 in gate receipts.

In 1936/37, McGrory's first year as manager, Stoke finished fourth. At the end of that season they provided the entire England forward line for a match against Scotland at Hampden Park in Glasgow that was watched by 149,000 people. Freddie Steele and Joe Johnson were picked alongside Matthews, and Steele got England's goal in a 3-1 defeat. In 1938, Stoke had faded after heading the table early on, and needed to beat Liverpool in the last match to stave off relegation. Steele got married on the morning of the game, then hurried from the church to the Victoria Ground to pull on his boots and score the second goal in a 2-0 win that guaranteed safety.

All told, it is the kind of rollercoaster ride with which most football supporters are familiar: a continuous cycle of triumph and – more often – despair, the constant clinging hope that things will improve and the sinking fear that they won't. It is the eternal lot of the football supporter. And yet somehow the game never completely loses its grip: nearly 30 years later, things were no different for the fans anxiously tracking the progress of Stoke's 1974/75 vintage. The title would elude them that year too. But what a shot they gave it.

4

TONY AND STANLEY

LIKE MANY top-class managers, Tony Waddington had an unremarkable career as a player. He was good enough to be offered amateur terms by Manchester United in his early teens, and even played for the first team at the age of only 16. But this was 1941. League football had been suspended because of the war. Waddington's further progress was frustrated, first by war service and then by injury.

The teenage Waddington was called up by the Royal Navy and served as a radio telegraphist aboard HMS *Hound*, a minesweeper that would take part in the Russian convoys and the D-Day landings. Playing football for the Navy, he injured his knee and had a cartilage operation that was only partially successful. A few days after the end of the war, he went to see a consultant to ask about his prospects for picking up his career where he had left off. He was told he would never play professional football again. He was not yet 21.

Manchester United's new manager Matt Busby released Waddington and wished him well, and that seemed to be that. But after he turned out for Crewe Alexandra in a friendly match, he was offered a professional contract. He nursed his dodgy knees through seven seasons with Crewe in the Third

Division North, making nearly 200 appearances for them as a wing-half. Then he had to admit defeat. Both cartilages had been removed from one knee, and there had been several operations on the other. He finally heeded the advice the consultant had given him seven years earlier, and started looking for a job in coaching or management.

He had already done some coaching with Crewe's reserves and with youth teams in Cheshire. His former boss at Crewe, Arthur Turner, was now managing Stoke City, 15 miles down the road, and he offered Waddington a job as youth-team coach. He agreed to a pay cut to take up the job, which, he later recalled, entailed plenty of menial tasks. 'Apart from my coaching duties with the reserves, the schoolboys on two evenings and the A team on Saturdays, I also had to help scrub out the dressing rooms, blow up the lace-up footballs – which was an art in itself – and clean and cobble the boots, that were leather-studded in those days. I also washed the stockings, as they tended to run when sent away to be washed. And all for £11 per week!'

But he was on the managerial ladder, albeit its lowest rung. Stoke were a First Division club – for the time being – and as we have seen, they had come close to winning the title only a few years previously. His timing was off, though. It was obvious that those heady days had gone, not to return any time soon. A year after Waddington's arrival at the Victoria Ground, Stoke were relegated to the Second Division.

The club was clearly on the slide, but Waddington was smitten. When Turner moved on again, to take over at Birmingham City, he invited Waddington to go with him as assistant manager. Waddington declined. 'My heart was at Stoke,' he said later. And at Stoke he, and his heart, were to remain.

The club's fortunes fluctuated in the Second Division under new boss Frank Taylor. Three times they finished as high as fifth, but mostly they were down in the bottom half of the table. Taylor suffered poor health, and after he was incapacitated for a while with heart problems in 1957, Waddington had a stint as caretaker manager. He took the opportunity to make the first of the eye-catching signings that would become his trademark.

Dennis Wilshaw was past 30, but he had won the First Division title with Wolves and had a dozen England caps. He was a versatile and free-scoring forward of the type Stoke badly needed. And by good fortune, in those days of amateur and part-time players, he lived and worked in Stoke as a schoolteacher. Waddington persuaded him to step down a division and join his hometown club. Before a broken leg ended his career four years later, Wilshaw played nearly 100 times for Stoke with the high return of a goal every two games.

When Taylor resumed his managerial duties, Waddington was rewarded for having kept the seat warm by promotion to assistant manager. But in spite of the efforts of Wilshaw, and the emergence of promising young players like Tony Allen and Bill Asprey, the club's fortunes continued to slide. In the spring of 1960 they lost ten games in a row and missed relegation only by a whisker. Taylor's contract was not renewed, and in June 1960, at the age of 35, Tony Waddington was appointed manager of Stoke City Football Club.

It was a bold move by the club and quite a feather in the cap of the ambitious but still young and completely untested manager. Waddington was barely a year older than Wilshaw, his star player. And the task ahead of him was immense. The club was in the doldrums, and badly needed an injection of energy – and new players – if it was not to fall into the third tier of English football for the first time since the 1920s. The facilities at the Victoria Ground were in an equal state of tiredness and disrepair. When he had first walked into the dressing room in 1952, Waddington had noted the spartan nature of the facilities. 'There was a huge stove in the centre of the dressing room and coke was constantly shovelled in, resulting in fumes all over the place. The stove supplied the hot water for the communal bath. Sometimes the water was not changed for a week.' The same stove was still belching out those fumes when he took over as manager eight years later.

The rest of the infrastructure was not much better. 'The ground was a disgrace. Plaster was peeling off the visitors' dressing room, and I was ashamed to ask them to change there. There was a plan to build the Boothen Stand in three stages, but the money had run out after constructing the centre piece, which stood out like a pigeon loft.'

The kitty was empty – in fact, the club was running an overdraft of £100,000, a crippling burden in those days. There was no money for players: any spare cash would go towards completing the construction of the Boothen Stand. And when the new manager's gaze shifted from the unfinished shell of the stand to the pitch, it would alight on a flock of sheep – the property of one of his eccentric directors, who insisted on his right to graze them there. The overall impression was of a down-at-heel provincial club that had seen better days, and had little prospect of seeing them again. No wonder the crowds in what had once been a football-mad city had dwindled to the low thousands.

He might have been dispirited, but the ebullient new manager was not daunted. He was up for the challenge, and straight away set about the task of reversing the decline. His options were limited: like all managers in such a position before and since, the way forward was to bring on some of his promising younger players, and go hunting in the bargain basement of the transfer market. He adopted a pragmatic and practical approach to transfer dealings from the start, and it was one that was to characterise his early years in charge.

Since his team had shipped 83 goals in the previous season, finding a new goalkeeper was an obvious place to start. This would have been his instinct anyway: a striking and abiding feature of Tony Waddington's managerial career was an almost obsessive belief in the desirability of having a top-class goalkeeper. He was almost permanently fixated with the necessity of having the very best keeper available – and in years to come, he would put his money where his mouth was more than once. The reasoning was simple: a top-class keeper might save 15 to 20 shots a season that a less-talented stopper might let in. That, in Waddington's eyes, was the equivalent of having a striker who would score you 15 to 20 goals a season. It wasn't exactly quantum mechanics, but it was not a fashionable view at the time.

In 1960, the goalkeeper he had his eyes on was Jimmy O'Neill of Everton. A Dubliner, O'Neill had been with the Toffees for a decade, making more than 200 appearances for the club, and another 17 for the Republic of Ireland. His handling was sound, and one of his strengths was his ability to deal with high crosses. He was experienced, but still only 28 – young for a goalkeeper. Within a few weeks of taking over as manager, Waddington had secured his first recruit.

In front of O'Neill, Waddington built a powerful back line to defend the Stoke goal against all comers. So extensive and unyielding was it that it was soon nicknamed 'Waddington's Wall', and although the 1960/61 season was a struggle, and the football was not beautiful, the team did concede far fewer goals. O'Neill later joked that the Stoke formation that year was essentially 1-9-1, with a phalanx of defenders to protect the goal, and scoring opportunities only available on the break, through an isolated striker such as Dennis Wilshaw or Johnny King. Into this wall, Waddington gradually introduced some young, homegrown talent who between them would eventually register more than 1,500 appearances in a Stoke shirt: Tony

Allen, Eric Skeels and Alan Bloor. Skeels and Bloor were still regulars in 1974. Eccles-born Skeels had made his debut as a 20-year-old in 1960, and holds the record for most appearances for the club.

SIGNING FOR STOKE: ERIC SKEELS

'I played for Eccles Schoolboys and the town team, and from there I went to Adelphi Boys in Salford, one of the main amateur clubs. I did a bit of training and played one or two games with them. I was only there six months if that, and then I decided just to play local football with players I knew. I was playing locally in Eccles and a scout came along and asked me if I fancied going with another lad for a trial at Birmingham City. I was 18. So we went to Birmingham and played in their A team a few times. After the games I had to get the train back from Birmingham to Manchester and then the coach to Eccles.

'After maybe five games Birmingham sacked their manager, Arthur Turner, who had been the Stoke manager before that. I hadn't signed anything by then. Nothing happened. The same scout said, "Do you fancy going to Stoke City? I can get you a trial there." I went to Stoke and played a game with the A team on the old training ground near the main ground. I enjoyed myself and they just let me do what I wanted. In those days I was an inside-forward and was scoring a few goals.

'After the game Tony Waddington, who was then assistant manager, came up to me and introduced himself. He was a good talker, very down to earth. He just said to me, "I like the way you're playing. We've got a few more trials to play – we'd like you to come and have another couple of games." And I said, "Well that sounds great – but I've got to get to Manchester and get a bus to Eccles!" He said, "We'll pay your expenses." So I did that a few times and then they asked me if I'd sign. So I did! I was inquiring where I would live, and they said, "We'll sort all that out, we just want you to sign. And we'll give you £10 a week and a £20 signing-on fee." I thought that was great – at that stage I was working for only a few pounds a week. And that's how my football career started.'

Eric Skeels was worried that Stoke would consider him too old to take on, so kept quiet about his age and told his new employers he had lost his birth certificate. He recalled: 'The scout said, "If they don't ask you anything, don't say anything." I played the game, they didn't ask me any questions so that was down to them. It was only after I'd signed that the story came out.' By this time, he had already appeared for the club in an FA Youth Cup game against Wolves, even though at 20 he was two years too old to be eligible. 'He had not liked to tell us his real age in case we thought he was too old,' Waddington recalled later. 'We lost the game, which was fortunate!' It was not the most auspicious start for the man who would go on to become one of the club's greatest servants.

Waddington moved Skeels from inside-forward to half-back, which turned out to be the perfect position for him. 'I was always a fit lad, played up front, scored a few goals, was always chasing people,' says Skeels. 'Tony Waddington asked me if I would play wing-half. That still meant doing a lot of running and chasing, so it didn't bother me at all, and that's how it started. That became my set-up position. I was young, and Stoke's team was getting old, so I was doing a lot of running around! I was good with both feet. So I'd be playing right-half and then the left-half was injured and he'd say, "Switch over to left-half," and I'd do that and as the seasons went on eventually I played in every position bar goalkeeper.'

The team was still struggling in the lower reaches of the Second Division, but as the 1960/61 season neared its end, the defence was no longer the main issue. Jimmy O'Neill and the Wall in front of him would concede 59 goals that year – only four teams gave away fewer. The problem now was at the other end, and it became urgent when one of the few sources of goals, Dennis Wilshaw, broke his leg at Newcastle. With relegation still a possibility, Waddington had to find a proven goalscorer, and quickly.

His search took him to Blackpool, where he homed in on the seasoned Scottish international Jackie Mudie. Mudie had joined the Seasiders at the same time as Stanley Matthews in 1947 and been in the side that reached two FA Cup finals, winning one of them – the famous 'Matthews Final' of 1953. He was now 30, and although Blackpool were reluctant to part with him – and Stoke were hard-pressed to afford him – a deal was done in time for Mudie to play the last dozen matches of the season. He scored within five minutes on his debut and helped the team stave off relegation. Short of stature, but a good header of the ball with keen positional sense and an eye for goal, he would be a key member of the team for the next two momentous years.

Waddington's Wall had worked – just. Stoke finished 18th in the Second Division, his first season in charge, three points clear of the drop. It was one place lower than the season before, but it was safety. The only way from there would be up.

The signing of Mudie was a portent of things to come. One of Waddington's principal strengths as a manager was his ability to spot quality and pedigree – and continued potential – in those regarded by others as being past their prime. This was an era in which players were often seen as being over the hill well before they were 30, and Waddington was ready to pounce whenever he heard of someone with class who had suddenly become surplus to requirements. As he explained to the *Sentinel* in a series of interviews in his retirement, their age did not bother him if the quality was there. 'The art of signing experienced players of calibre was based purely on pedigree. Players who had performed at the highest level could step down a shade and produce something. A player's legs tend to go in their mid-30s. Yet even at that stage, the class players can make the ball do the work, and do not need to do quite so much running.' In his efforts to turn things around at Stoke, this view became every bit as enduring a pillar of his managerial strategy as his obsession with exceptional goalkeepers.

It was an approach that satisfied another ambition and need of the manager. As well as reviving the fortunes of the club on the pitch, he wanted to put Stoke back on the wider footballing map. He wanted his team talked about, and he wanted the supporters to flock to see them again. Persuading a top-class player like Mudie to drop a division and come to Stoke had made a few headlines. Now Waddington was greedy for more – an even bigger name that would alert the footballing world to the fact that Stoke were on the way back: what today we would call a marquee signing.

His attention turned first to the England legend Tom Finney, who would certainly fit the bill. Negotiations progressed for a while before foundering on a technicality. Waddington had to think again. Prompted by Wilshaw and Mudie, his thoughts led him to another giant of the English game, and one guaranteed to fire the interest of the Stoke supporters, the country and, as it turned out, the whole football world. The young manager was about to pull off one of the most sensational and celebrated transfer deals in English football history.

SIGNING FOR STOKE: STANLEY MATTHEWS

There are various accounts of how the wheels that led to the return of Stanley Matthews to Stoke City were set in motion. The Mudie connection was clearly important. Mudie had just made the same journey from Blackpool to Stoke, and he and Matthews were close friends after playing together for more than a decade. Dennis Wilshaw was also involved: after his career-ending injury, he had stayed on at the club as a scout and coach. It was even suggested that the idea came to Waddington and his chairman Albert Henshall when they were on a trip to Turkey and had an encounter with a fortune teller. She foresaw much success for them, with the help of 'an old man from the sea'. Waddington later said there had been talk about Matthews coming back for as long as he had been at Stoke. Whatever the truth of it, by the autumn of 1961, negotiations for the return of the prodigal son were well advanced.

The move spoke irresistibly to the theatrical impresario in Waddington, whose managerial career would be punctuated by eye-catching signings that seized the imagination of the football world. He saw it as a headline-grabbing move that would, at a stroke, energise the team and bring back the fans. It would be a huge public relations coup for him and for Stoke.

It would also be a colossal gamble. Matthews was now 46, more than a decade past the age when most players hung up their boots. He had enjoyed 14 highly successful years at Blackpool, winning his long-coveted FA Cup winners' medal in 1953 and challenging for the title more than once. Now, though, he could no longer command an automatic place in the first team. A lifelong fitness fanatic, he was still in great shape: he never smoked or drank and – unusually for that era – took a close interest in his diet. He fasted on Mondays. He would even wear lead-lined shoes when walking to the ground, so that his football boots would feel featherlight by comparison when he put them on.

The regime was one that meant he was fitter than many players 15 years his junior. Dennis Wilshaw said he could pass for 30. But he had a troublesome knee, and could no longer rely on one of his key weapons – the explosive pace over ten yards that had been the beating of so many despairing full-backs down the years. The manager who had brought him to Blackpool, Joe Smith, had departed, and his successor Ron Suart could hardly be blamed for thinking that the end of what was already an extraordinarily long career must be in sight.

Suart wasn't alone. When the news filtered out that Matthews was contemplating a return to his home town, there were plenty of armchair experts ready to denounce the idea as lunacy. The old man's glittering career would end in ridicule and ignominy. The headline above an article by *Daily Express* sports reporter Desmond Hackett summed up the mood: 'Don't Do It, Stan. Retire with Pride – Now!'

Stan was not remotely interested in retiring as long as there was still a chance of kicking a ball around. Playing the game was all he had ever wanted to do, and the urge was as strong now as it had been when he was a kid in the Potteries in the 1920s. He was strongly attracted by the idea of returning home, and finally dispelling the cloud that had hung over him since his acrimonious departure 14 years earlier. He was undeterred by Stoke's lowly position, or that they were, as he put it in his autobiography, 'wandering up and down the nether regions of the Second Division like a dog that had lost the scent'. As for Waddington, the more publicity the proposed move generated, the more he liked it. He revelled in all the attention.

But things did not go smoothly. Blackpool had been expected to recognise Matthews's long service over more than 400 appearances by giving him a free transfer. Instead, they demanded a fee of £3,500. Matthews was not impressed, and was even more disgruntled when he learned that Blackpool had not told Stoke about his persistent knee troubles, 'To ask a fee for a player who had given 14 years' loyal service to the club and who was now 46 years old, with a dodgy knee, seemed a bit rich to me.'

Personal terms were more easily arranged – the only issue was that Matthews complained that they were too generous! In his autobiography, he recalled, 'I'd talked to Waddington for half an hour and asked him to make me an offer. He suggested £50 a week with £25 appearance money and a two-year contract.' He'd been on £25 at Blackpool. Matthews was less convinced than Waddington about his long-term playing future., 'I said, "No, make it a year, two years might boomerang on you."' He also declined the appearance money. 'My motivation in going was not money but the fact that I just wanted to keep playing, that I loved the game.' Stoke reluctantly agreed to Blackpool's price, and the deal was done. The *Daily Mail* did not share the scepticism of the rival *Daily Express*. 'Stoke City have pulled off the biggest short-term transfer bargain in history,' it reported.

With his masterstroke in the bag, Waddington was determined to surf the resultant wave of publicity. He arranged for Matthews to complete the move live on television on the BBC's midweek sports programme, *Sportsview*. As the cameras prepared to roll, there was an unexpected hitch. One of the Blackpool directors took Waddington to one side and told him, 'We are making a mistake. We have decided to keep him.' In one of his later interviews Waddington said he replied, 'It's too late. Stan signed before the programme.' He admitted, 'That was not strictly true.' In fact it wasn't at all true. 'He had only agreed verbally,' Waddington said. 'The signing actually took place in front of the cameras.' His rapid sidestep worked. As Matthews signed, Waddington leaned over him and said, 'Welcome home Stan. For years this club has been going nowhere. Now we're on our way.'

Ever the showman, Waddington now set about masterminding the old maestro's second debut for Stoke City. The next fixture was away at Plymouth Argyle. Waddington had no intention of throwing away his big moment on a wet October afternoon in South Devon, nearly 250 miles from the Victoria Ground. It was not a journey many of the fans would be making. He held Matthews back for a home debut against Huddersfield a week later. Matthews was happy to go with the flow. 'It was a great marketing ploy on his part,' Matthews recalled. 'By delaying my debut until Stoke's next home match, Tony hoped to attract many stay-away supporters who, he believed, would turn up not only to see me play, but for the additional reason that for the rest of their lives they could say "I was there" when Stanley Matthews made his return debut for Stoke.'

In the week before the game, excited anticipation built in the Potteries and way beyond. As the lord mayor of Stoke was to say, 'Matthews has given the team and the city a new pride. Everywhere people are talking about Stoke.' The Huddersfield Town players were probably the least excited by the move. They waited without enthusiasm to play what they knew would be a supporting role in the drama of the homecoming. They would certainly never be forgiven if they rained on Stan's parade. There was particular pressure on Ray Wilson, later a World Cup winner with England, who would have the responsibility of marking the returning hero.

In his biography of Matthews, David Miller quotes Wilson's recollections of that week, 'The atmosphere was electric. The build-up, even over here in Huddersfield, was receiving more attention than we'd get for a quarter-final in the cup. National newspaper photographers, and all that.'

And when the big day came, 'I'd never seen him [Matthews] on the field until that moment. I really did worry about it the week before. I only had my name taken once in my career, for arguing, so I wasn't going to clatter him, to try and bend him and then be the big bad wolf. There was no talk in our dressing room beforehand, but as soon as we got outside on the pitch, I felt we were intimidated. The Stoke guys were really fired up, they had nothing to lose.'

Wilson's fears that he and Huddersfield were on a hiding to nothing were soon realised, 'Whenever the ball came to him the crowd erupted. Once, I slid in quick, got the ball off his feet, never touched him. The whistle went. A foul! As we came off at the end I jokingly said to him, "I coughed twice in the second half and nearly got booked!"'

The day did not disappoint. The previous home game, a 1-1 draw against Preston North End, had left Stoke 19th in the table and heading for another grinding battle to stay up. A paltry 8,409 spectators had watched that game. For

Huddersfield – or rather, for Stan – that number quadrupled to 35,974 – more than enough to wipe out the cost of his transfer from Blackpool. Matthews led many of the supporters there himself, walking from his hotel to the ground like a Pied Piper, with excited fans trailing in his wake.

As the occasion demanded, Stoke had a relatively comfortable 3-0 win to ease their relegation worries. Matthews had a quiet game, but had a hand in one of the goals, and the effect of his very presence on the rest of the team was clear. The whole atmosphere around the club and in the dressing room was lifted. Matthews brought calm and experience to the pitch, and those around him raised their game accordingly.

Eric Skeels played in that game, the day after his 22nd birthday. 'After playing in front of a few thousand, all of a sudden it felt frightening actually running out on the pitch! It was fantastic, exciting. The pitch was so tight then – when you were on the touchline you could hear what the crowd were saying. Our orders were: when you get the ball try to give it to Stan and let him get on with it. He was surprising for his age – over the first six or seven yards he was faster than me! From a standing start! It was unreal. And once he was past his man, he was on his way – gets to the byline and across it comes. In that game he played really well. He didn't chase back like everyone does nowadays – he ambled his way back and was waiting for the next time we could give him the ball. Fabulous, it was.'

The momentum was maintained. As Skeels puts it, 'Everything in Stoke-on-Trent was buzzing.' The big crowds kept coming at home, and the Matthews effect doubled the average gates at away fixtures too, at Swansea, Middlesbrough and Rotherham. Results began to improve, and Stoke embarked on a run of eight games unbeaten, losing only four of their remaining 17 games after the Huddersfield match. There was no talk of relegation now. The former Chelsea player Willie Russell, now living in the Potteries, reflected, 'Before

Matthews came back, this place was a cemetery with electric lights. The old man has worked a bloody miracle. When he was signed by Stoke, I thought it was a ridiculous stunt. I was so wrong.' Russell and Desmond Hackett both. And quite a few others too.

As the results and gates improved, and with them the club's financial position, Waddington was not slow to use the new-found interest in Stoke as leverage in the transfer market. As Matthews himself recalled, 'He exploited my appeal to the maximum, not only for publicity and eye-catching headlines but in persuading other players to join the club. I didn't mind this one bit. In fact, I felt flattered to think one of the reasons players wanted to sign for Stoke was for the opportunity of playing alongside me.'

A case in point was the next big-name recruit, the Manchester United forward Dennis Viollet. As a son of Manchester, a former United player and a friend of Matt Busby, Waddington kept a close eye on the fortunes of his former club. In December 1961 he noticed that Viollet – for so long one of United's star forwards – had lost his place in the first team at Old Trafford. Waddington's antennae began twitching at once. Viollet had exactly the sort of pedigree he was looking for. A survivor of the Munich air crash, he was a prolific centre-forward, who had been a regular 20-goals-a-season man throughout the late 1950s. In 1959/60, he scored 32 goals in 36 appearances, a club record. In all he scored 178 goals for United in fewer than 300 games. His speed and stealth around goal were well known. He was still only 28. If he were to become available, Waddington would want him at Stoke.

Busby was unwilling to sell, but after much nagging he eventually gave Waddington permission to talk to Viollet. This opened the door for the Stoke boss to give full play to his legendary skills of persuasion. Many of the players he signed for Stoke during his long period in charge were not initially eager to join him. The question, 'Fancy coming to Stoke?' was seldom met with the instant response, 'Where do I sign?' But once Waddington turned on the charm, it did not take him long to persuade them that this was the place for them.

Waddington and Viollet talked late into the night, and parted with Viollet agreeing to come and see Stoke's next home game, an FA Cup replay against Leicester, before making up his mind. Stoke won 5-2 and Viollet was convinced. Matthews had scored first to begin the rout, and was clearly a factor in Viollet's decision to sign up. Waddington says Viollet turned to him after the match and said, 'I don't know what you need me for! But if I can play alongside that man, it's a great moment in my career. I've always had an ambition to play with Stan. If he is in your team, that's good enough for me.'

Waddington had some trouble persuading the board that Viollet was worth the £23,500 asking price, but was later to consider it one of the best and most significant signings he ever made. Viollet would retain his goal touch at Stoke, scoring at a rate of one in every three games. And when he lost some of his pace in attack, Waddington turned him into a creative force in midfield.

The recruitment of Viollet – even though he was still in his prime – played into the growing narrative that Waddington's policy was to snap up seasoned old pros whose legs were going and giving them a last hurrah in the Potteries. If there was any truth in it, Waddington could afford himself the last laugh, because he barely made a false move in the market, and all the experienced players he brought to Stoke in these years did a great job for him. In his *Sentinel* interviews he reflected on his success with some satisfaction. 'Ever since the Busby Babes, the cry in soccer was for youngsters,' he said. 'The vogue left me free to exploit the market. People were writing off players at 28. I cleaned up.'

Even so, he was careful about his targets, 'My approach to signing players was always whether they would blend into the team. I often feel that clubs who have money to spend heavily just sign players without deciding how they are going to fit them in.' As true today as it was then.

'I don't sign old players,' he said on another occasion. 'I sign thoroughbreds.' He was an astute judge of a player and knew how to get the most out of them on the pitch by giving them their heads. There was no micro-managing or over-elaborate coaching. Waddington's view was that if you put class players together in the right combination, they would work out a way to play.

He continued to ignore the jibes about signing old crocks. At the end of a season that saw Stoke finish a respectable eighth, he brought in Eddie Stuart and Eddie Clamp, two members of the great Wolverhampton Wanderers side that had won three league titles and the FA Cup in the 1950s. Stuart was a reliable defender who was made club captain. Clamp, jovial off the pitch, was a brutal enforcer on it, a full-back of the they-shall-not-pass school, nicknamed 'Chopper'. Part of his role was to protect Matthews against young full-backs trying to make a name for themselves by flattening the legendary winger. Clamp was always in trouble with referees, and, having been pulled up yet again in a game against Chelsea, delivered what Matthews said was one of the best lines he ever heard on a football pitch. 'The trouble with you referees,' Clamp told the official, 'is that you don't care which side wins.'

Waddington now had a team that seemed capable of taking Stoke back into the First Division, and after a dreadful start to the 1962 campaign left them without a win in six games, everything suddenly came together. An 18-match unbeaten run took them almost to Christmas, before – just as in their title-chasing season of 1946/47 – winter set in with a vengeance. After Boxing Day, there was to be no more football until the beginning of March.

Waddington used the time to good effect. He had spotted another top-class player who seemed to be at odds with his club. This time his gimlet eye had fallen on Burnley's Northern Ireland international Jimmy McIlroy.

McIlroy's standing at Burnley was not far short of that of Matthews at Stoke. He was an idol at Turf Moor. There is still a stand named after him there. A subtle inside-forward, McIlroy had appeared in the claret and blue almost 500 times, and won more than 50 caps for his country. He had helped Burnley win the title and reach the FA Cup Final, and was worshipped by the home support. And suddenly – mysteriously – he was out of favour.

McIlroy was puzzled to find himself on the transfer list, and the Burnley fans were beside themselves with rage. If there was more to it than met the eye, no one ever found out what 'it' was. After some hard bargaining, McIlroy joined Stoke for £25,000 in time for the resumption of football and the climax of their tilt at the Second Division title. Waddington now believed he had the final piece in his jigsaw. And although McIlroy's debut ended in a 6-0 drubbing at Norwich, things soon began to fall into place.

By now, the youngsters in the team had got over their awe of Matthews, and had learned how to play with him. It was a counter-intuitive process.

David Miller wrote, 'One of the changes to which the Stoke players had to adjust was getting used to passing the ball to Stanley *when he was marked*. Most of them were accustomed to playing the ball away from a tightly marked colleague. They had never met someone who could control the ball with a single touch and then take on his marker. This would be, just as it had been for the past 30 years, Stanley's value to his team: that he drew opponents to him without surrendering the ball, thereby putting them out of play while he remained in it.'

McIlroy saw those Matthews qualities for himself when he arrived to bolster the title challenge. 'His confidence was unbelievable for 48. He was unique. By the time I was 36 it was my concentration that was going, not my physique. Stanley still had total concentration at 50.'

Waddington himself had every right to be pleased with the way his dramatic coup had worked out. He had never doubted that Matthews could still turn it on, even though most of his contemporaries had retired more than ten years earlier. 'Even at 46, he still killed the ball stone dead without looking at it,' said the manager. 'He never gave it to a player in a bad position. People tend to think of him as a dribbler not a passer, yet he had such vision he could see everyone, all the time.'

Waddington did what he could to help his ageing superstar. Mindful of that troublesome knee, he went out of his way to make sure that the going was always soft at the Victoria Ground. Sometimes that meant enlisting the help of the fire brigade to pump thousands of gallons of water from the nearby River Trent on to the pitch, to help protect that valuable knee from the hardness of the ground. It was a ploy he was to use repeatedly in later years, long after it was no longer necessary to worry about Matthews. Teams visiting the Victoria Ground after a prolonged dry spell would be baffled by the softness of the playing surface.

After McIlroy's disastrous debut, Stoke embarked on a run of six consecutive victories, scoring 16 goals and conceding only two. They wobbled during the run-in but by the penultimate game of the season, and the last at home, they knew that a win would send them back up into the First Division.

So far, the Matthews fairy tale had followed the script to the letter, and the 33,644 people who were jammed into the Victoria Ground were desperate to see a happy ending. The opponents were Luton Town, who were battling relegation and had plenty to play for. Mudie put Stoke ahead, but the important second goal eluded them, and Luton began to play with more confidence. Then, with 15 minutes left, McIlroy picked up the ball. He said, 'Out of the corner of my eye I noticed Matthews, streaking towards goal. So I whipped the ball over the full-back's head. I put Stan in the clear and he just waltzed past the keeper and tapped it into the net.'

Not surprisingly, Matthews himself had an equally clear memory of the moment, which he recalled in his autobiography: 'Having beaten one Luton defender, I headed straight for goal, the tell-tale click-clack of boots running through mud telling me two or three defenders were in hot pursuit. I took to my toes as the Luton goalkeeper Roy Baynham came out of his goal to narrow the angle. It was a simple job of feinting one way so he committed himself, and going the other. Taking the ball wide of Roy, I took a moment to glance up and see the open goal before side-footing the ball into the net.'

It was the perfect ending to the fairy tale. In their centenary year, Stoke were going back up as Second Division champions, and it was Stanley Matthews who had scored the goal that had sealed the title. It was the only goal he scored that season, and no one could fault his timing or sense of occasion. Matthews had been named the inaugural Football Writers' Association Footballer of the Year after his first season at Blackpool, and now he won the honour again – a rare recognition for a Second Division player. And for Waddington it was a triumphant vindication, not only of his decision to bring Matthews home, but also of his policy of signing veteran players with a few years left in their legs and the class to revitalise a moribund club.

He knew, of course, that his problems were only just beginning. Having reached the top flight he had to stay there, and those veterans who had served him so well would have to be replaced sooner rather than later. Even the mighty Wizard of Dribble would have to call it a day at some point.

That point came early in 1965 when, five days after his 50th birthday, the great man made a final appearance at home to Fulham. Six weeks earlier he had been knighted, the only time the honour had ever been granted to a footballer who had not yet retired. By February 1965, he had not played in the first team for a year, and had only appeared nine times since the club's return to the top division. But he still set up the first goal in a 3-1 win, and the Potteries wished him a fond, and this time final, farewell.

Tony Waddington had already moved on. He was working on the foundations of another team – one he hoped would first establish itself in the First Division and then lay low the spectre of 1947's agonising near miss, and bring Stoke City a maiden league title.

5

BANKS AND BALLET

HAVING PROPELLED Stoke City back into the First Division, Waddington set about dismantling the team that had got them there – an inevitable consequence of his strategy of signing class players who were nearing the end of their careers. In the unforgiving way of football management and the march of time, he had extracted what he needed from them; some now had little more to give. He needed to build a new team to consolidate the club's position in the top flight.

Characteristically, he began by looking at the wearer of the green jersey. We have already noted how vital he considered the last line of defence to be in any team. We will have cause to do so again. In his time at Stoke, Waddington signed a dozen goalkeepers, most of them of international pedigree. One of them was the best in the world.

Although Jimmy O'Neill had been an ever-present during the promotion run, he soon found himself third choice after the arrival of two other established keepers. Bobby Irvine, who would win eight caps for Northern Ireland, was brought over from Linfield within a few weeks of promotion. He was joined four months later by Lawrie Leslie from West Ham, who would play five times for Scotland. A couple of years later, Waddington signed the legendary Manchester United goalkeeper Harry Gregg. He really was at the end of his career and made only two appearances for the Potters.

Irvine and Leslie shared the goalkeeping jersey for the first couple of seasons in the First Division. Leslie seemed to be the first choice, playing 25 games in his first season and 41 the next. Then Irvine had a run between the posts before Waddington lost faith in him. In due course he broke with his usual habit, and decided to entrust the goalkeeper's jersey to John Farmer, a local lad who had come up through Stoke's youth teams and who was given his debut at the age of only 18.

Among the first of the seasoned pros to depart after promotion was Jackie Mudie, who had scored 20 goals in helping Stoke come up, but who now crossed the Potteries to Port Vale. His great friend Stanley Matthews was not long in following him out of the club, more than 30 years after the start of his Stoke career. Matthews managed nine games on his return to the First Division, but an injury in January put paid to his season. He had set his sights on playing until he was 50, and was content to spend his time with the reserves before fulfilling his ambition with that final appearance against Fulham.

Mudie and Matthews left big holes to fill, but Viollet and McIlroy were still there, and would remain so for a couple more seasons, offering further proof of Waddington's canny eye not only for class but also longevity. McIlroy made more than 100 appearances before leaving to become manager of Oldham Athletic, and Viollet retired with more than 200 Stoke City games and 66 goals under his belt – not too shabby for a player who had been seen as past his prime when he came to the club.

Although Waddington continued to keep an eye out for top players who had become disenchanted with their clubs, or were being prematurely discarded, the team that would consolidate Stoke's place in the top tier had a strong element of young homegrown talent, as well as new players who would be longer-term prospects. The defence had a strong local feel with Tony Allen and Alan Bloor now established as first-team regulars alongside Eric Skeels. The midfield was given extra bite by the arrival of Mike Bernard from Shrewsbury Town. Stoke established themselves as a mid-table First Division side, starting with a 17th-place finish in their first season back up, and then finishing successively 11th, tenth and 12th.

Part of their success was down to the discovery of a top-class – and this time youthful – centre-forward. It wasn't Waddington who discovered him; but with a typical bit of sharp practice, he managed to steal him from under the nose of the man who did.

SIGNING FOR STOKE: JOHN RITCHIE (Part 1)

John Ritchie was working in a shoe factory and turning out for his hometown team, Kettering Town, when he began to arouse the interest of clubs in the lower leagues. He scored 40 goals in two seasons and first caught the eye of Dave Bowen at Northampton Town when the two teams met in the FA Cup. When Bowen was temporarily absent with a health problem, the way was opened for Arthur Turner to step in and take the 21-year-old Ritchie to Oxford United. But there was a hitch. Kettering wanted £2,500 for him, and the Oxford board would not stump up more than £2,000.

Arthur Turner was friendly with Waddington from their time together at Crewe and Stoke. As they chatted one day, Turner enthused about the young striker he had found and bemoaned his failure to raise the money to buy him. The conversation alerted Waddington to a possible opportunity.

'I made a few phone calls,' Waddington later recalled, 'and built up a picture of this goalscoring centre-forward. I knew Arthur was a good judge of a player, and for £2,500 it was worth taking a chance.

'I persuaded the board to give me the £2,500 and so I went to Kettering and signed John Ritchie without ever seeing him play.

He was offered a one-year contract. He suggested he should have two years to give him time to adjust, and I agreed.'

The following day, Waddington had another call from his friend, with an update. Turner was bubbling. The Oxford board had relented and agreed to pay the full £2,500. Awkward.

Waddington says he replied, 'Sorry Arthur, he's my player now.' Turner's response is not recorded.

Stoke were about to be promoted back to the First Division and the Stanley Matthews story was running hot, but Ritchie said he didn't know too much about the manager who was about to pluck him from his workbench and the grasp of Oxford.

'I was working in the shoe factory. The Kettering secretary, who had cycled down to contact me, said Tony Waddington wanted to talk to me. My initial reaction was, Tony who? He'd heard I could score a few goals. But at £2,500, I wasn't really a major signing.'

It might not have been a major signing at the time, and probably passed relatively unnoticed amid all the brouhaha of promotion. But it proved to be a very sound investment. Promoted to the first team after Viollet was injured, Ritchie scored twice on his debut and embarked on a scoring run of 14 goals in nine games. These goals helped propel Stoke to the final of the relatively new League Cup competition, where they faced Leicester City. The final was not played at Wembley in those days, but was a two-legged affair, and it offered Stoke the chance to win their first major trophy in more than a century of trying. They went down 4-3 on aggregate.

Ritchie scored 25 league goals the following year, became a crowd favourite as his touch and heading ability improved, and he seemed fully established as part of the forward-looking team Waddington was building. He was scoring comfortably more than a goal every other game by 1965, when his serene progress to the ranks of the top strikers was halted by a sudden medical problem. He complained of chest pains and was diagnosed with tuberculosis. He took three months out to recover. When he returned, his goalscoring prowess continued, but Waddington thought he detected a loss of aggression, and was perhaps worried about longer-term health issues. Showing the same ruthlessness he had displayed in buying Ritchie in the first place, he now sold him, to Sheffield Wednesday.

'The £75,000 fee was a fair one at the time, so Ritchie journeyed to Sheffield taking his X-rays with him,' Waddington recalled. 'The Wednesday chairman was a respected medical man and there was never any attempt to disguise Ritchie's condition. But they had no qualms about his fitness and so the sale went through, although to fans in the Potteries there may not have seemed much logic to it.'

That was an understatement. The fans were outraged and bewildered in equal measure, and the *Sentinel* was full of letters from angry supporters. Waddington later admitted the sale of Ritchie had been one of his rare missteps in the transfer market. Luckily for him, he got the chance to correct it.

SIGNING FOR STOKE: JOHN RITCHIE (Part 2)

Ritchie carried on scoring freely for the Owls until the goals dried up in the 1968/69 season. His new manager Danny Williams decided, in that dreaded phrase, that his best days were behind him, although he was only 27. Waddington saw the chance to rectify his mistake.

'We were on our annual summer holiday in Bournemouth,' Ritchie later recalled. 'One of the hotel waiters came running on to the beach and told me the hotel manager needed to speak to me. I raced back and found him with his hand over the receiver whispering, "It's Tony Waddington, I think he wants to re-sign you."'

Waddington brought Ritchie back to Stoke for £28,000. He was to claim that the profit made this a shrewd piece of business, but he wasn't fooling anyone, least of all himself. Everyone knew he should never have sold him in the first place. Ritchie was leading the line again by the start of the 1969/70 season. His best years were actually still ahead of him: he went on to become Stoke's all-time record scorer with 171 goals in 343 appearances.

The first major recruit after promotion also offered a strong sign of Waddington's intention of building a team that would rely less on veterans. Peter Dobing had the class for which Waddington was always on the lookout, and at 25, he had already racked up almost 300 appearances for Blackburn Rovers and Manchester City. A combative but cultured inside-forward, he also had an impressive scoring record. Waddington broke the club transfer record when he paid £37,500 to sign him from newly relegated Manchester City.

Dobing became known for a habit that would be unthinkable in a top player today – he smoked a pipe. With his immaculate three-piece suits and a briar clamped between his teeth, he was dubbed 'the pipe-smoking gentleman of English football'. While he was no doubt avuncular enough when puffing away after a game, Dobing had a short fuse on the pitch, and served several suspensions during his ten years in the Potteries. But he played nearly 400 times as a creative and competitive inside-forward, and scored nearly 100 goals. He captained Stoke to their League Cup success in 1972, and retired the following year after breaking his leg.

On transfer deadline day in 1965, Dobing was joined by Roy Vernon and Harry Burrows. These were experienced players, but no old crocks. Vernon, who cost £40,000 from Everton, was a Welsh international of 27. A famously heavy smoker, he was much admired for his ability to keep a cigarette alight while taking a shower. He was also said to enjoy a flutter at the racetrack. Vernon was a class act, and his early form may have been a factor in Waddington's decision to sell Ritchie. But the later part of Vernon's five years at Stoke was dogged by injuries, and without Ritchie, goals were again hard to come by. The 24-year-old Burrows made up some of the shortfall. A £27,000 signing from Aston Villa, he had been a crowd favourite at Villa Park, and his signing enhanced Waddington's reputation as a shrewd dealer in the market. The Stoke fans took to Burrows as well, nicknaming him 'Cannonball' because of the ferocity of his shooting with his left foot. Although he could play in most forward positions, and was the taker of penalties, he was usually to be found on the left wing, where the crowd would urge him to unleash one of his celebrated thunderbolts at every opportunity. He too would stay with the club until given a free transfer in 1973.

Waddington's determination to keep Stoke in the spotlight was assisted by two big set-piece events. The club's centenary was celebrated – arguably five years prematurely – with the visit of the legendary Real Madrid, five-time winners of the European Cup. The timing was risky – towards the end of the promotion run-in of spring 1963. But it was another golden opportunity to seize the attention of the footballing world and fix it on Stoke-on-Trent. A crowd of 45,000 packed into the Victoria Ground to see the likes of Alfredo Di Stéfano and Puskás – just legendary names to most of the spectators, in the age before television cameras were at every ground for every game. Stoke went in at half-time a goal down, but then the provincial Second Division outfit from the Midlands shocked the Spanish aristocrats by going ahead through Viollet and McIlroy. They then conceded a penalty and in the end were content to hang on for a 2-2 draw.

The testimonial match for Stanley Matthews, two years later, was an even bigger event. An all-star Stanley Matthews XI took on a powerful Rest of the World team in a game that once again put Stoke-on-Trent in the footballing limelight. Di Stéfano and Puskás were back, as was the imposing figure of the Russian goalkeeper Lev Yashin, among a host of other top names. This time television was there to lend a hand, with the

BBC reporting that the game was watched by more than 100 million people around the world. You can still see extended highlights online. The Rest won an open and entertaining game 6-4, and Sir Stan finally hung up his boots for the last time.

In the summer of 1966, not even Waddington's nose for a public relations stunt was going to divert the spotlight from the World Cup. It was held in England for the first time and eventually won by the home nation in a Wembley final that is now part of our national story. But even as the nation worked itself into a fever of anticipation, Waddington's search for players who could strengthen his team did not let up. His next coup stemmed from something he overheard while visiting Arsenal, to watch them play West Bromwich Albion. 'At half-time I was having a cup of tea in the Highbury boardroom,' he recalled. 'George Eastham was playing for Arsenal that day, and I was astonished to hear the Arsenal contingent criticising him unmercifully.

'Football is about opinions. A manager must have confidence in his own judgement irrespective of conflicting points of view. My own opinion was that Eastham was the best player on the pitch.' He did not hesitate. 'I immediately made a move for him. Consequently, we signed one of the best midfield players in the game for just £30,000.'

Eastham was another player who fitted the Waddington brief to perfection. Experience? Check: 350 games for Newcastle United and Arsenal. Class? Check: 18 England caps and a member of the victorious 1966 World Cup squad. Still some miles in the tank? Check: he was still a month away from his 30th birthday. Potentially available? Check: Waddington had the evidence of his own ears that Eastham was out of favour at Highbury.

It was another great capture. Eastham stayed for eight years at Stoke, turned out for them nearly 250 times and scored the winning goal in the 1972 League Cup Final. He was awarded an OBE and succeeded Waddington as manager. His experience and calmness on the pitch became ever more valuable assets as younger players were introduced into the team.

Eastham did not play in the World Cup. Other England players wrote their names into the history books, with Bobby Charlton cementing his reputation as one of the all-time greats, and Geoff Hurst becoming the first man to score a hat-trick in a final. By the end of the tournament, Gordon Banks of Leicester City and England was acknowledged as the best goalkeeper in the world.

And yet, strangely, only 12 months later, Banks's future at Leicester seemed uncertain. The club had a new emerging talent in Peter Shilton, and it was becoming increasingly difficult to deny him first-team action. Banks was dropped, and his manager delivered the dreaded verdict that his best days were behind him.

This situation was meat and drink to Tony Waddington. A move for Banks would tick just about every box he could think of. First of all, given his obsession with goalkeepers, he would be signing the best there was. He had never been one to listen to talk of top-class players being past their prime. In any case, Banks would not turn 30 until the end of the year – no age for a goalkeeper. If Waddington could persuade Banks to come to Stoke, he would be making a powerful statement of his ambitions for the club, which went far beyond the comfort of mid-table finishes. And because of the reputation Banks enjoyed around the world, it would be another outstanding public relations coup – on a par with, perhaps even surpassing, the return of Matthews. Waddington steamed into action.

He had plenty of rivals in the chase, but the asking price of £50,000 was too steep for many of them. It was regarded as an excessive sum for a keeper. But it did nothing to daunt

Waddington, who put such a high value on quality between the sticks. He was prepared to pay, and with his customary sleight of hand overcame a last-minute hitch to seal the deal.

Banks recalled in his autobiography his astonishment at learning that Leicester were ready to let him go. Until that moment he had had no fears for his place in the team: he had that World Cup winners' medal, he was England's number one keeper and he was nowhere near the end of his career. But one day his manager Matt Gillies called him over for a chat after training. Banks takes up the story.

SIGNING FOR STOKE: GORDON BANKS

'"Gordon, the directors and I have been talking," said Matt. "Not to put too fine a point on it, we think your best days are behind you, and you should move on."

'I was speechless. Dumbfounded. Shell-shocked. It took a few moments to gather my thoughts. Even then all I could think of was to ask Matt to expand on his statement.

'"What are you saying gaffer? That I'm finished here?"

'"I think it's best for all concerned," he said.'

It soon became clear to Banks that what had prompted this bombshell was that young Peter Shilton, the second-string keeper and rising star, had given the club an ultimatum: either he played in the first team, or he was off. Banks didn't blame him, but he was surprised and not a little hurt that the club was so willing to comply. West Bromwich Albion, Manchester United, Liverpool and West Ham all showed interest in him but did not follow through. According to Banks, 'The lack of interest had, I believe, much to do with the fact that many managers still didn't fully appreciate the worth of a good goalkeeper to their team.' Tony Waddington, as we know, was not one of those people.

Banks continues, 'Matt Gillies called me into his office one morning in April 1967 to tell me he had received a firm offer for me, and that, as I had not asked for a transfer, he and the board would discuss the payment of a loyalty bonus in recognition of my seven years' service at the club.

'This was great news. Who had made this "firm offer"? He told me it was Stoke.

'Stoke City, a mid-table First Division side, were hardly the most fashionable club of the day, but I'd played against them often enough to know they were a good side, with the potential to be even better. Having discussed the matter with [wife] Ursula, I told Matt I was interested, and he immediately arranged for the Stoke manager Tony Waddington to come over to Filbert Street to discuss terms. I had no idea what wages Stoke City were offering, but as Leicester were known for the lowest pay in the First Division, I didn't think I was going to take a drop.

'Prior to meeting Tony Waddington, I had another meeting with Matt to discuss the proposed loyalty payment. It didn't go well.

'"Have you and the board reached a decision?" I asked.

'"We have."

'I settled back in my chair to await the good news.

'"We've decided not to pay you a penny," he said.

'I was flabbergasted and furious. I told him exactly what I thought of him and the directors, but he wouldn't be swayed.

'"There's to be no compensation payment and that's final," Matt said firmly.

'"Then the deal's off," I told him. "If it means me staying here and playing in the reserves then so be it. You and the board can sing for that 50 grand."

'I left Matt's office in a dark mood and found Tony Waddington sitting in the main foyer. "I'm sorry Mr Waddington, but the deal's off," I said with a shrug, and proceeded to tell him why.

'His face betrayed no emotion whatsoever, and he didn't say much. He simply stood up and said, "Leave this to me," before sweeping into Matt's office without knocking.

'Five minutes later he marched out. "Two grand all right?"

'I told him that would be fine by me.

'"Good!" he said. "Then let's do the deal and get out of here."

'We did the deal, and I became a Stoke City player there and then.'

But Waddington had not told Banks the full story of that five-minute meeting with Matt Gillies, and it was some time before he heard about it. 'A couple of years later, I was on Stoke City's pre-season tour of Holland, and one night in our hotel I got talking with Doc Crowe, a Stoke director. I told him how happy I was at Stoke, and the story of how my transfer would have fallen through if Tony Waddington hadn't persuaded Leicester to come up with the compensation payment.

'"Did they hell," he said. "We paid you that!"

'He went on to relate how Tony Waddington had found Matt Gillies as awkward and intransigent as I had. Having got nowhere with him, and afraid that the deal might fall through, Tony had simply walked out of Matt's office and plucked the £2,000 figure out of the air, knowing that his own directors would back his judgement, and that the Stoke board, already committed to paying £50,000, wouldn't baulk at parting with another couple of grand if that's what it would take to sign the current England goalkeeper.

'For two years, I'd had no inkling that the Stoke board had paid the compensation – the money had simply been credited to my bank account. It was typical of Tony Waddington; he was a great guy and one of the most underrated managers in football. Tony realised the importance of a good goalkeeper to a team, and I'd like to think he believed that his board's money was well spent. Later he said my efforts in goal saved Stoke City 20 goals a season. Whether that was truth or flattery, it was nice of him to say it.

'Some say that Tony was ahead of his time in recognising the value of a good goalkeeper. To my mind it was a case of other managers being behind the times. Whatever, I loved the man. He always tried to sign the gifted players who would entertain the supporters; always believed that football at its most inspirational and creative has a place in the best of all possible worlds. He never forgot how important the role of football was in the lives of working people.'

Gordon Banks quotes taken from *Banksy* – his 2002 autobiography.

Waddington's quick-thinking and spur-of-the-moment ploy of stumping up for the bonus on top of the fee had worked. A World Cup winner was on his way to the Victoria Ground. And, of course, Banks was very far from being finished. He made 250 appearances for Stoke, and would have made many more but for the car accident that cost him the sight of an eye and compelled him to retire in 1973. He won more England caps while with Stoke than he had at Leicester. And his World Cup wonder save from Pelé, regarded as one of the greatest ever, was still three years in the future.

It is tempting to see the joint signings of Banks and Eastham as a watershed moment of the Waddington years. Their arrival had an influential and consolidating effect on the second of the teams Waddington built – the one that fully established the club in the First Division. True, after a 12th-place finish in 1966/67, there were a couple of flirtations with relegation. But in 1969/70, Stoke finished with the highest points tally since their return – 45, good enough for ninth place. The signings of Banks and Eastham also marked the end of Waddington's strategy of snapping up good players who were in the latter stages of their careers. Consciously or not, he was now on the cusp of starting to build his third team, the one that would become doughty cup fighters in the new decade, and then credible challengers for the First Division title. From now on, he would be bringing on homegrown talent, especially in his back line, and signing players whose best years were in front of them, rather than behind: whose potential was yet to be realised. Neither Banks nor Eastham were part of the title-chasing team of 1974/75, though Banks might well have been but for his fateful accident.

There was a change of style in the air too. Although a pragmatist, Waddington also had a romantic streak, as evidenced in his penchant for grand gestures such as the signings of Matthews and Banks. Not only did he want Stoke talked about in England and far beyond, he wanted them to be talked about because of their stylish and attractive brand of football. The jibes about 'Waddington's Wall' might have been justified in the early 1960s, when his priority was first holding on to Second Division status and then making it back into the top tier. But it was an unwanted tag, as Waddington made clear in a celebrated and oft-quoted phrase he coined in 1967. This is how he described how it came about: 'The United States were attempting to introduce a footballing set-up similar to England. We were invited over for a tournament devised to introduce the game and educate the American sports enthusiasts. I wrote a booklet explaining the laws of the game and how we saw football at the time. I described football as "a working man's ballet".'

It was an attractive description and it stuck, as it deserved to. Alan Hudson liked it so much he made it the title of his autobiography. It was an elegant summary of the philosophy Waddington was to adopt as he set about taking the club into its next phase.

6

POTHUNTERS

WITH THE capture of a World Cup winner to join another member of the victorious 1966 squad, Stoke entered the 1967/68 season with the core of the team for the next five years. Banks and Eastham joined Dobing, Burrows, Ritchie, Skeels and Bloor in what was beginning to look like a seasoned and well-balanced squad. Of these seven, only Ritchie and Skeels survived in the team long enough to play any part in the title challenge of 1974/75. Banks would certainly have done so but for the injury that brought an early end to his career. So would Bloor, and indeed he was still playing as late as 1978. But a troublesome injury restricted him to only two appearances in 1974/75.

Slowly but surely, Waddington added new members to the squad and developed them into first-team players. He now wanted to shed his reputation for signing old crocks – proven performers still with a few seasons left in them. He wanted younger players with potential and flair. His thirst for big-name headline signings was temporarily slaked, and his transfer strategy now took a markedly different turn.

Two players who fitted perfectly into this new approach had been brought to his attention, and only a few days before he had signed Banks, he managed to snaffle both of them too, in the teeth of considerable competition. In the end, he nabbed the pair of them for a total outlay of less than £30,000, and they signed contracts with Stoke within hours of each other. Even compared to the sensational swoops he frequently made into the transfer market, securing the signature of Banks and pulling off these two lower-key pieces of business must be regarded as the best couple of weeks' work he ever did. The two lads would be at the heart of everything Stoke achieved over the next half a dozen seasons.

Terry Conroy was no one's idea of what a glamorous Swinging Sixties footballer should look like. 'He looked like a milk bottle,' says Denis Smith bluntly. Tall and gangly and with a shock of ginger hair and extravagant sideburns, Conroy's chalk-white matchstick legs looked as though they would snap in two at the first encounter with a Ron Harris or a Norman Hunter. Born in Dublin, Conroy had turned down offers from local League of Ireland teams in order to try his luck with Glentoran in Belfast, where he felt he had a better chance of being noticed by English clubs. He followed the English game closely, and knew all about some of Stoke's big names, past and present – Neil Franklin, Freddie Steele, and, of course, Stanley Matthews. The ten-year-old Conroy saw Matthews in action for the Football League at a game in Dublin, and dreamed that one day he too would be racing up and down the right wing with the number seven on his back. His admiration for Stanley Matthews and Stoke City would soon be a factor in deciding his future.

Conroy's move to Belfast plunged him into an increasingly threatening and violent Northern Ireland at the start of the Troubles. His life was further complicated by the fact that, while playing for Glentoran, he kept his job in the print business in Dublin, travelling between the two capitals by train. The twin demands on his time soon caused tensions, but an understanding manager at the print works helped him keep all the plates spinning. On the pitch, he soon attracted notice for his attacking play and all-round goalscoring ability. This was duly noted by George Eastham senior, the father of Stoke's recently acquired George junior, who was manager of another Northern Irish team, Ards. George senior told Tony Waddington that the coltish kid was tailor-made for the sort of team he was bent on producing – tough at the back, but free-flowing and creative in attack. Waddington was also alerted to the boy's potential by the father of one of Conroy's former school friends, whose work took him to Crewe on a regular basis. The bar of the hotel where he stayed happened to be Waddington's favourite watering hole, and the two spent many evenings putting the world to rights in the bar. Here Waddington heard further glowing reports about the brilliant prospect who had turned up in Glentoran.

But when the call came for Conroy, it wasn't from Stoke. Fulham manager Vic Buckingham had heard about him too, and travelled to Belfast to offer a tempting £10,000 for the youngster. It was the dream of every young Irish player to be spotted by an English First Division club – indeed, that was why Conroy had headed north in the first place. And it was big money for Glentoran too.

SIGNING FOR STOKE: TERRY CONROY

'Glentoran had played Derry City in the cup. It was 2-2 so we would have to go up to Derry on the following Wednesday for the replay. My normal routine after a game would be get changed, head over to Victoria Station in Belfast and get the train back to Dublin. As I was getting changed, Billy Ferguson, who was the secretary at Glentoran, said, "Terry, would you mind stepping into my office? There's someone who would like to meet you."

'I went in and sat down and in walked this man who was absolutely immaculate – he reminded me of Arthur Daley out of

Minder: the Crombie hat and cravat, very smart. He introduced himself as Vic Buckingham, the manager of Fulham. I was very surprised. He said, "Look Terry, we've agreed terms with the club to buy you. You're going to be a Fulham player. I'm looking to build a future around young players, and you fit the bill." The usual baloney! I was surprised. I said I'd have to discuss it with my father. In those days you needed parental consent if you were under the age of 21. He said, "I understand, you've got to talk to your parents. Once you've spoken, we'll get you over next week and we'll sign, and you'll become a Fulham player."

'I should have been elated, because that was my lifelong ambition – to become a professional footballer in England. And now it was happening. I got to the station and I got the paper, the *Belfast Telegraph* football special, and I saw the headline, "Conroy signs for Fulham". Apparently it was a done deal. This only served to make me more unsettled. On the way back down on the train to Dublin I was thinking about the move. Somehow it didn't excite me. It was the fact of London. It was daunting, and I just somehow didn't fancy going to live in London. I went home and spoke to my father and he said, "Whatever you want to do, son, it's okay by me. You make the decision." I had to let them know after the replay against Derry.

'Unbeknown to me, on that night George Eastham senior had rung Waddo. He'd seen the headlines too. He said, "Look Tony, this kid is going to be signing for Fulham. I've told you about him enough times. Get your backside over here on Wednesday night to watch him. I'm telling you, you should buy him."

'So, Wednesday morning, I headed back up to Belfast for the replay. As I got off the train and came through the gate, Billy Ferguson was waiting for me. He said the game had been called off.

'There had been snow overnight in Derry, and the game was postponed. Of course, there were no mobiles in those days, they'd had no way of contacting me. Billy said, "What are your thoughts about signing for Fulham?" I said it looked as though I'd be sitting down with them to discuss terms. It was left at that.

'As I'm heading back to go through the gate to Dublin, this character comes out from behind a pillar. It was like *Tinker Tailor Soldier Spy*! It was George Eastham senior. I'd met him a couple of times because I'd played against his team, Ards. He had been lying in wait for me ready to pounce when I arrived at the station, but had then been forced to hide to keep out of sight of Billy Ferguson.

'I said, "Hello Mr Eastham." He said, "I'd like to introduce you to Tony Waddington, manager of Stoke City." Then out of the shadows came a second figure, this time Waddo himself. "Hello Terry," Waddo said. "I came all the way over here to see you play, but the game has been postponed. Would you mind if I travelled back with you on the train to Dublin? There's something I'd like to discuss."

'The penny didn't drop immediately, but as we settled in for the journey back south it became apparent that Waddo had come to Ireland to convince me to join Stoke. He turned on the charm all the way home. Waddo was a very persuasive, sweet-talking, charming man, and within ten minutes he'd convinced me that I wasn't going to Fulham. I promise you, it was ten minutes. He said, "You're not a Fulham player, you're a Stoke player. You're going to sign for Stoke. It's the place for you. I'm building a young side at Stoke and you are going to be part of it." Almost exactly the same words as Vic Buckingham, but they were delivered in a very different way. Somehow you wanted to be with Waddo. He was such a charming man. And I knew the history of Stoke because of Stanley Matthews. I didn't know what the Potteries was like obviously, but I was well-versed in the history of Stoke.

'Waddo had actually seen me play once, but he wouldn't have remembered. When I played for Home Farm, my previous junior club, we played Stoke in a friendly in Dublin, I think in 1964. I'd have been 17 then, but he wouldn't have remembered me. So in effect he was signing me without seeing me play.

'I said, "Look, I've got to speak to my father. But I'm very happy. But what do I do about Glentoran?"

'What I had no idea about was that this was actually the classic old-style illegal tap-up! It was against the rules – he'd approached me before he'd approached the club. He said, "Leave that to me. I'll get in touch with them and make a counter bid of £10,000 and we'll sort out personal terms." I agreed.

'He accompanied me to my house and my father got the whiskey out, and the two of them drank half a bottle of whiskey between them. By the time that was done, he had my father eating out of his hand. "Whatever Terry wants to do is fine by me," he slurred. We ordered Waddo a taxi and he staggered into it – he was well-oiled too. His parting words were, "I'll see you on Saturday."

'So the next morning I get a call from Billy Ferguson; he said, "Terry, I've got a surprise for you: another club's come in for you." I said, "Oh!" I had to pretend ignorance. Arrangements were made for me to attend the Stoke City game against Liverpool at Anfield on the Saturday. We met the directors before the game and then we got the plane back to Dublin on the Saturday evening. And the following week I made my way over to Stoke and signed a contract.'

Conroy joined Stoke for a £10,000 fee, plus another £2,500 if he played more than ten first-team games (he ended up playing in more than 300) and a further £2,500 if he was capped by the Republic of Ireland (which he was, 27 times).

Waddington was never one to pass up the opportunity for some headlines. He unveiled his new discovery at a press conference with a powerful sales pitch.

'During the conversation with my father, Waddo had found out that I was the seventh son,' says Conroy. 'Now there are supposed to be some mystic powers attached to the seventh son of the seventh son. So at the press conference to introduce me, Waddo said, "There's something special about this kid. He's the seventh son of a seventh son." Now my father was the only boy in his family, so he wasn't the seventh son. He had two sisters! I'm listening to this and the press are latching on to it and saying, seventh son of a seventh son, that's remarkable, and I said to him, "Mr Waddington, I'm a seventh son, but my father was an only boy." He said, "Well you know that Terry, and I know that. But they don't!"'

Waddington was just warming up. 'He was coming out with all sorts of things,' says Conroy, 'and the press lapped it up.' He went on to portray the new boy as a stereotypical Irishman. The red hair helped, but the manager ladled it on. Conroy, he announced, loved the craic (true), loved a steak (not true) and loved a Guinness (not true either, he was teetotal, never touched the stuff).

'What's more,' said the manager, 'he's a great singer.' This was also news to the nervous 20-year-old subject of all this hype. Worse was to follow. 'He put me up on the stage! I couldn't refuse because they were all clamouring. So I sang "Danny Boy" which was probably the only song I knew at the time. Talk about thrust into the deep end! This is when I found out about the power of promotion, and keeping Stoke City in the limelight. Waddo was a great one for that.'

It all went down a storm, and Stoke fans could have been forgiven for thinking they had signed the new George Best – a flying winger with a taste for the high life. Waddington did try to feed up his new boy, perpetually worried about Conroy's habitual pallor. 'He would send me into hospital for check-ups all the time,' Conroy recalled. 'He thought I was anaemic. He gave me Guinness and steak to build me up.'

Waddington's second major capture, within a few hours of securing Conroy's signature, was Crewe Alexandra's John Mahoney. He was an inexperienced but promising midfielder who had already attracted the attention of other clubs, including Liverpool. Waddington's local connections enabled him to jump to the front of the queue.

SIGNING FOR STOKE: JOHN MAHONEY

John 'Josh' Mahoney was only a few days older than Conroy, and was playing for Crewe after a spell at non-league Ashton United. His potential was spotted by team-mate Johnny King – a former Stoke favourite who had begun his career at Crewe and was now ending it there after eight successful seasons at the Victoria Ground. This transfer was considerably less complicated than the Conroy saga.

'Johnny got in touch with Waddo about me, and he can't have said anything bad, because Waddo came in for me, and that was it,' says Mahoney. He had also been attracting interest from Liverpool. 'I found out about that because I had played in an under-23 international in Belfast, and Bill Shankly was on the plane on the way home,' says Mahoney. 'I didn't particularly want to go to Liverpool. But in any case Stoke came in. I joined within a couple of days of Terry, and we've been joined at the hip ever since.' Waddington nipped in ahead of Shankly to secure Mahoney's signature for £19,500.

Waddington developed Mahoney into a high-quality midfielder, but with Mike Bernard in the side, he could not always command a regular place – though he and Bernard did sometimes line up alongside each other. Mahoney's potential was spotted by Millwall manager Benny Fenton, who offered Stoke £50,000 for him, and held out to Mahoney himself the prospect of a regular place in the first team. Waddington wasn't interested, and neither was Mahoney. 'I decided I wanted to stay and fight for my place,' he said. But Fenton did not give up easily. 'We were waiting for the train back to Stoke after going to the Gordon Banks *This Is Your Life* programme,' said Mahoney. 'Benny Fenton pops out from behind a pillar all

Cockney-like and tries to persuade me to sign.' It was a stunt lifted straight from the Waddington playbook, but it didn't work for Fenton. 'I told him I didn't want to come to London.'

The Stoke careers of Conroy and Mahoney, who rapidly became room-mates and best friends, ran on remarkably parallel lines. Born less than a fortnight apart, and signed within hours of each other, they were key figures in the team for a decade. Most remarkably, they each recorded exactly the same number of appearances for the club – 336. Conroy says, 'We signed together and we were the same age and we just hit it off. We were inseparable for years.'

They were also the dressing-room jokers. 'Full of pranks,' says Smith ruefully. 'Some days your socks would go missing after training, or your shoelaces would be tied together. They loved getting up to mischief. TC [Conroy] was the character in the dressing room. He was a bloody nuisance! If you came in and something had gone on with your clothes, or your locker was locked – it'd be TC. Or Josh.'

A celebrated prank was played on Peter Shilton. When Shilton wasn't looking, Conroy put some weights into his kitbag, before he picked it up after training. When he didn't seem to notice, extra weights were added the next time. And so it went on. Shilton never reacted – he just slung the increasingly bulky bag over his shoulder and left. They never did find out if he genuinely hadn't noticed, or was refusing to give them the satisfaction of showing that he had. Conroy pleads guilty to being the team prankster, aided and abetted by Mahoney. 'We did get up to a little bit of skulduggery from time to time, some high jinks,' he grins.

On the pitch, Conroy and Mahoney were perfect for the sort of approach Waddington was now pursuing – young, raw, talented, ambitious, creative. Terry Conroy on the wing with his ginger mane and outrageous sideburns, dancing past defenders with a shimmy of those unnaturally white and skinny legs, became a defining image of the team in the late 1960s and early '70s. He was happy to try his luck on either flank, getting to the byline and sending over crosses, doing a little give-and-go, or cutting in from the wing and taking a shot. He chipped in with important and sometimes spectacular goals, twice getting into double figures for the season. Though plagued with knee injuries that kept him out for long periods, he was one of the talismen of the team.

Mahoney's contribution, though less flamboyant, was no less important. A midfield workhorse also capable of letting fly with his left foot from distance, Mahoney would link play from defence to attack, or break down opposition moves and spread the ball wide to the likes of Conroy or Jimmy Robertson. Understated and sometimes underrated, Mahoney was another wonderful servant to club and country, winning 51 caps for Wales.

Waddington's vision was that of all aspirational managers: attractive flowing and attacking football, built on a solid defence. Usually, the defence comes first. Any manager taking over a struggling team concentrates first on stopping that team from leaking goals. We've seen how Tony Waddington did just that when he first became manager, installing Jimmy O'Neill in goal and then building Waddington's Wall in front of him. He'd already repeated the first part of that trick by signing the best goalkeeper in the world. The Wall he was about to build in front of Gordon Banks would be every bit as effective as the version of a few years earlier, but would be based on a more conventional back four. In the late 1960s, a settled line of defence emerged that would be as good as any in the league. It was the rock on which all the spectacular cup successes and league form of the early '70s would be based. And, remarkably, it was all homegrown: four Stoke lads born and bred within not much more than a stone's throw of the Victoria Ground.

One member of the group was already in place. Alan Bloor had made his debut as a teenager as long ago as 1961, and was now in the middle of a 17-year career at the Victoria Ground. Only four Stoke players have surpassed his record of 484 appearances for the club, one of them his contemporary, wing-half Eric Skeels. A product of Queensbury Road School in the Potteries town of Longton, Bloor had represented Stoke Schoolboys and signed for Stoke on his 17th birthday. By the time he was 21, he had established himself as a first-choice left-sided centre-half. He was nicknamed 'Bluto' after the dark and extravagantly muscled character in the *Popeye* cartoons. Bloor had a powerful physique to justify the tag, and was everything you would want in a central defender: an aggressive and destructive tackler, resolute under the high ball, calm and reliable – and well versed too in some of the darker practices of the defender's art.

Bloor found his perfect partner and foil in another Potteries legend, hewn from the same rock. Like Bloor, Denis Smith hailed from Meir in Longton, the most southerly of the five towns (or six, depending on which ones you include) that make up the city of Stoke-on-Trent. Together they formed a solid partnership at the back that would be the bedrock of the team for several seasons, playing alongside each other nearly 200 times.

By the age of 11, Denis Smith had already decided he was going to be a professional footballer. And he knew who he was going to play for: Stoke City. As he wrote in his autobiography, *Just One of Seven* (a reference to the fact that he had six siblings), 'My dad took me down to watch the side in red and white stripes that had fallen on hard times in the 1950s, following an era in which they had been contenders for the League title and boasted the most famous footballer in the world among their ranks – Stanley Matthews. I first watched Stoke around the age of seven from the boys' enclosure in one of the paddocks on the side of the ground. Ever since I was first taken to see them as a boy, I was hooked by the speeds and sounds of the game, the intensity of the atmosphere, the ferocity of the tackling, the glory of the game.'

He turned down the chance to go to grammar school because they played rugby there, not football. Instead, he followed the same path Bloor had trodden a couple of years earlier, from Queensbury Road School through Stoke Schoolboys to the Victoria Ground. How he got there – recounted in *Just One of Seven* and in an interview for this book – was not the result of Waddington pursuing him, and deploying his usual blandishments. Rather the reverse.

SIGNING FOR STOKE: DENIS SMITH

'Stoke-on-Trent schoolboys at that time were run by Dennis Wilshaw, an ex-player who was very good. We won the English Schools Shield two years running, which was a massive thing. The first year I broke my leg in the first game, so I missed out. I was still only 14 then. But the following year we won it again.

'I was offered apprenticeships by Tottenham and by Portsmouth, who had got a good youth team. I was flattered, but this wasn't going to divert me from my chosen course. That, as far as I was concerned, was set. I didn't want to go to London or the south coast. I only wanted to play for Stoke. There is a kind of passion in all of us who are fans that drives us to play for our boyhood teams. I wouldn't dream of playing for any other club. I was a Stoke lad and Stoke supporter. It was Stoke or nothing.

'The issue was that Stoke City didn't seem that sold on me. They only took on so many full-time apprentices each season and I wasn't one of them. They only offered me amateur terms. One of the directors, Percy Axon, had a plumbing and building business so I went there as an apprentice plumber. That didn't work out. A couple of my brothers and my sister and brother in-law worked at Stone Lotus which was a shoe factory – Lotus Shoes. So they said, "Come and become a clicker," which is cutting shoes, and actually I was quite successful at it. It was piecework and I was still at training. But while I was earning 20 quid a week, the other lads were earning about five. The factory tried to get me to go into management, but I still wanted to be a footballer.

'I was playing for Stoke reserves – so I was playing ahead of people who were already under contract. Obviously they thought my style wouldn't fit. I played in goal for them, I played centre midfield, I played left-back. I preferred to be a centre-half, but I had a spell at centre-forward where I was scoring every week in the third team. So I played different positions but the one I wanted to play was centre-back.

'Waddo just didn't rate me. Naturally I thought I was good enough to earn a contract. I thought I was the best young player at the club. But it was now the start of the 1966/67 season, I was already 18 and I hadn't been signed. Being an amateur though gave me more rights back then because I had freedom to move. I decided to take the bull by the horns one day and present Waddo with an ultimatum.

'So I went and knocked on his door. I was no shrinking violet, I've got to be honest.

'He said, "What's your problem?"

'"I'm leaving," said this 18-year-old know-it-all.

'"What do you mean, you're leaving?"

'"I'm going somewhere else" – playing the only card available to me. I was always fairly to the point in conversations such as this. "You're not paying me, and you know I'm good enough. I'm going to sign somewhere else," I said. "I want to become a pro. I think I deserve to become a pro. I'm in the reserves in front of some of the other lads."

'This was a high-stakes strategy. If Waddo dismissed me out of hand, sending me off to sign for my mythical other club, I'd have no choice but to clear my locker and attempt to do just that.

'He looked me up and down for a moment and eventually said, "There might be a place in the game for a player like you." He went on, "But I can't pay you. What are you on?"

'"Twenty quid a week," I replied.

'"Well I can't pay you anywhere near that," he said flatly.

'"What can you pay?"

'"Twelve quid," said Waddo.

'"Done."

'So I signed professional terms, losing my job and taking a 40 per cent pay cut.'

Smith insists that although he and the other so-called hard men of the time were seen only as brutal stoppers, most of them could actually play a bit. 'In training I used to do skills as well as anybody else. I could pass as well with both feet over 20-25 yards. With my left foot I could drop them in there all day ten out of ten. With my right it might have been nine out of ten. It was just that my job was as a defender, so I learned to be as effective as I could be.'

By the time he came to Stoke, Smith had already broken his leg twice – the first in an astonishing catalogue of injuries and broken bones that by 1976 had earned him an unwanted place in the *Guinness Book of Records* as 'The Most Injured Man in Football'.

'I have had at least 28 breaks or major operations,' he wrote. 'And those are the ones I can remember. Not to mention having over 200 stitches in my face over my career. I have broken almost any bone you could mention, including both legs, ankles, knees, toes and fingers. I smashed my nose, cut my face to ribbons on numerous occasions, had my lips and ears slashed by flying boots, suffered debilitating back injuries, plus damaged ligaments and tendons and had a plate inserted into my neck, and one into my arm.'

As a teenager he was told he might have brittle bones. He favoured a less scientific explanation. 'I certainly didn't have brittle bones – I was just a blinking nutter.' He would often turn out for Stoke when a long way short of full fitness. None of this discouraged him from persisting with his wholehearted approach, which simply endeared him to the crowd even further.

With his new contract in the bag, he brought the same all-or-nothing attitude to training, but was eventually banned from practice games against the first team because he crocked so many of them with his ferocious tackling. But there was a silver lining, 'The first-teamers began to tell the manager I was difficult to cope with, and that they hated facing me so much I might be worth giving a go in the first team.'

After a couple of years being developed in the reserves, that opportunity duly came. With the team struggling at the start of the 1968/69 season, he was given his chance against Arsenal. He gave away a penalty in the first half, and although Banks saved it, Arsenal scored from the rebound and won 1-0. Two weeks later Smith conceded two more penalties at Ipswich and was dropped. It took him five months to earn another chance – but he fared little better then. An injury to Bloor gave him a place against Leeds, who were on their way to their first title. He was marking Mick Jones. Stoke lost 5-1 and Jones got a hat-trick. Further injuries to Bloor meant that he kept his place though, and notched up 14 appearances during the season. When Bloor came back, they were put together, and from that point on, the two of them became fixtures at the heart of the defence.

Bloor was the quiet one – Smith was vocal, a leader. No slouch himself when it came to keeping opposing attackers honest, Smith would become the symbol of the spirit, passion and never-say-die character of the team, a man who would run through a brick wall for the club. It was an attitude and commitment that was adored by the Stoke faithful, who relished every crunching tackle, and the way Smith put his body on the line in the Stoke cause. Even Leeds United's Norman 'Bites Yer Legs' Hunter, one of the fiercest defenders in the game, described Smith as 'the hardest man in football'. Given that this was the age of Ron Harris, Mike Doyle, Tommy Smith and Hunter himself, this was quite an accolade. Smith himself doesn't care for the word 'hard' and prefers 'brave'. Given his injury record, the word is certainly justified.

The strong defence on which Waddington would base his next team was taking shape. Top-class goalkeeper: done. Strong central defence: done. Now Stoke just needed a couple of class full-backs. Again, they did not have far to look.

John Marsh – usually known as 'Jackie' or 'Jo' – was another local boy, and a friend of Denis Smith's through their time together with Stoke Schoolboys. He recalled those early days in an interview with the retro football magazine *Backpass*.

SIGNING FOR STOKE: JOHN MARSH

'When I was at Queen's School in Fenton, I played inside-left. I used to train at Northwood Stadium in Hanley under Dennis Wilshaw. I was scoring goals for fun – I used to go past Smithy as if he wasn't there!

'But Dennis Wilshaw decided I wasn't a forward and would be better suited to right-back. If it hadn't been for him I might not have had a football career.

'Vale offered me an apprenticeship and there wasn't much between the two clubs then. But my heart was set on Stoke. I'd watched them since I was eight or nine when Robertson, Cairns, McCue, Coleman, Bowyer, King and Oscroft were in the side. To think I'd be in the same dressing room as Matthews, Mudie and McIlroy, even if it was just cleaning boots and picking up training kit, was fantastic.'

Smith recalls, 'Jackie was a kid from the rough end of town like me. Jackie and I would grow up in football together, winning trophies as we did so. He would become my room-mate for years at Stoke City. Although we were very different personalities and had totally different outlooks on life and being a professional footballer, the camaraderie we developed from the age of 11 kept us closely together and became a very important factor in the success of Stoke City's homegrown defence.'

A Stoke City fan as a boy, joining his hometown club was a dream come true for the young Marsh, who developed into an effective right-back and one of the jokers of the Stoke dressing room. Marsh was a compact 5ft 8in but with a turn of speed that belied a not obviously athletic build. Thrown in at the deep end with a debut away at Arsenal on the opening day of the 1967/68 campaign, he had to wait until the middle of the following season to reclaim the right-back berth. Once he had done that, he dropped anchor, and was another to join the 400 Club of appearances for Stoke, with 444 in all. He was adept at keeping opposing wingers quiet, and liked to get forward as well, overlapping and combining with Conroy, and delivering hard, low crosses into the box.

Completing a notably tough back four was Mike Pejic, arguably the toughest of the lot. Born in Newcastle-under-Lyme and the son of a Serbian immigrant, he was another who had supported Stoke as a boy.

SIGNING FOR STOKE: MIKE PEJIC

Naturally left-footed, Pejic played on the left wing for Newcastle Schools and England Schools. He came to the notice of a Stoke scouting machine determined to ensure that no local talent ever escaped its clutches. Even so, Pejic was initially rejected as a winger, and worked for a year driving a lorry before he was spotted in a trial game with as many as 70 juniors involved.

Tony Waddington later described his first sight of the combative Pejic, 'I first spotted him in our A team at Littleshall Road, playing on the left wing. Cliff Birks, who was in charge of our youth scouting system, had a good relationship with Mr Finch, headmaster of

Stoke St Peter's High School, who looked after the City Boys, and it was our proud boast that no Potteries boy left the area and went on to make it elsewhere.

'Pejic was not tall but I saw his strength, and decided he would make an ideal full-back. I promptly signed him on apprentice forms. I remember our late chairman, Tom Degg, remarking "whatsisname will never make a player" but Pejic proved me right and went on to play for England.

'Pejic never let us down. He never gave less than 100 per cent.'

By the age of 19, Pejic was helping Stoke keep a clean sheet on his debut against a West Ham side featuring Geoff Hurst and Martin Peters.

Pejic was one of the few to develop an interest outside the game. He ran a farm near Leek, about ten miles from Stoke, and preferred spending time there than mixing with the other players. Famously unsociable, and a member of the awkward squad if he felt professional standards were being allowed to slip, Pejic was something of an odd man out. 'Football was not something that dominated his life,' says Terry Conroy. 'After the game he'd rush off home and get back to his farm. He was happy enough in that environment – the football world, the social side never appealed to Pej in any way. If there were functions, he might not turn up – it just didn't interest him. He had very simple pleasures. He loved farming and the wild side of life. He used to come to training in an old Land Rover, and he'd have one of these Shetland jumpers on and wellington boots on and straw in his hair – I kid you not – and he'd have a Dulux dog, a sheepdog called Ben, sitting in the front while he was training.

'He was economical with the time he spent at the club – he had other things to interest him. He was intense, he spent as little time at the ground as possible. His routine was he'd get there at two minutes to ten on a training day, a Monday or a Tuesday, and get changed within two or three minutes and then he'd be away after a shower or a bath within five minutes and back home. Most of us after training we'd go to the social club and we'd have a sandwich and a chat and spend quite a bit of time in each other's company. He was a one-off in lots of ways.'

The hard-tackling Pejic was a fitness fanatic with exacting personal standards and he never left anything on the pitch. Opposing wingers rarely got any joy from him, and like Marsh he enjoyed foraging upfield to relive his days as a winger, and ping crosses into the box.

The homegrown back four of Marsh, Smith, Bloor and Pejic first played together in September 1969 in a 4-2 home win over Sunderland. They were the mainstays of the defence for more than seven years. Their joint confidence was boosted for much of that time by the presence of Banks behind them. Sadly for the purposes of this book, Bloor's role in 1974/75 was a peripheral one, because of the recurrent injury that restricted him to only two games that season.

As these players were arriving and gradually being introduced to the team, results were stubbornly disappointing. There were two successive flirtations with relegation towards the end of the 1960s. But gradually the new recruits found their feet, and with an improving defence aided by the skill and experience of Skeels, Eastham, Dobing and Burrows, things began to improve. Goals, however, were in short supply. Waddington made good his earlier error by buying back John Ritchie, and then started looking for a skilful inside-forward to play off him.

Once again, his instincts did not let him down. Waddington was never a hands-on coach. But his assessment of a player, and the vision to see which players would fit into his set-up, were among his strongest qualities as a manager. Very few of his investments over 17 years turned out to be duds, and he was skilled at getting the best out of a player. His judgement was as sound as ever when, in the summer of 1969, he broke Stoke's transfer record by splashing £100,000 on a young inside-forward from Birmingham City named Jimmy Greenhoff.

Most Stoke fans regard the team of the early 1970s as the finest the club ever assembled, so it is not surprising that nearly half a century on, so many of the players still enjoy legendary status with the Boothen End faithful. Even in this mighty pantheon, Greenhoff's name stands out. The fans adored him, and for those of a certain age he will always be their favourite player. Only Sir Stan himself, and perhaps Gordon Banks, could begin to match his popularity as an all-time great of the club. When he came to watch games after he retired, the fans would chant his name as soon as he was spotted taking his seat. After a while, the chants of 'Greenhoff, Greenhoff' began to distract the players on the pitch, and the modest Greenhoff found it an embarrassment – to the extent that he eventually stopped going. Greenhoff and Stoke City were a match made in heaven, and they enjoyed many years of mutual bliss before unforeseen events occasioned a sad divorce.

Greenhoff was a Yorkshireman, born in Barnsley. He showed early promise as a member of the Barnsley Schools side that won the English Schools Trophy in 1961, and he was apprenticed at Leeds United. After a period in decline, Leeds were on the way up under the managership of former player Don Revie, and would soon become, and remain, the powerhouse team in the First Division. Greenhoff was a regular member of the team that won promotion to the top tier in 1963/64 while he was still a teenager, and he played in the 1968 League Cup Final when Leeds beat Arsenal.

But he was often passed over in favour of Peter Lorimer. And after a time, as he told the Stoke fanzine *Duck*, he felt he had to make a move. 'I wanted to go. It wasn't a case of them wanting me to go. I wasn't getting enough game time and I was always the one who I felt wasn't definitely going to be in the team. So I felt it was time to go – I wanted regular football.' Perhaps rather impulsively, he moved in the summer of 1968 to the first club to come in with an offer, Second Division Birmingham City.

He played 36 times for Birmingham and scored 15 times, but 12 months after signing he was on the move again. He did not see eye to eye with manager Stan Cullis. 'He called me into his office first thing on a Monday morning,' he told *Duck*. 'I thought he was going to offer me a new contract to tie me up for a few more years, but he told me I wasn't scoring enough goals. I thought he was joking. He said, "Jimmy, when was the last time that you scored?" Don't forget that this was on a Monday and I said, "Er, Saturday against Huddersfield, boss!" As a wing-half I was never going to be prolific as a goalscorer. I'd chip in, but my role and my game was about far more than that.'

Since this conversation took place only seven games into the season, it is fair to assume that Cullis was not much impressed with his new recruit – nor Greenhoff with his new manager. A month later, Greenhoff scored four goals in a single game against Fulham, part of a run in which he scored nine in seven. But his failure to settle in at St Andrew's was not going unnoticed. And one of those who had noticed it was Tony Waddington.

SIGNING FOR STOKE: JIMMY GREENHOFF

'I was struck by Jimmy's positional sense when I saw him play for England under-23s against Wales at Wrexham,' Waddington recalled in his 1988 interviews for the *Sentinel*. 'It was John Mahoney's first appearance and I had really gone to The Racecourse to support him. One player stood out like a beacon, and talking to people I discovered that Jimmy wanted to leave Birmingham. I was told he had become unsettled, as his striking partner Fred Pickering was on a higher wage.

'At the same time I discovered that Tommy Docherty, then manager at Aston Villa, wanted him. Because of the rivalry that existed between the two clubs the Birmingham manager Stan Cullis said there was no chance of Greenhoff going "across the road". I couldn't really believe that Greenhoff was being made available. I had a chat with Maurice Lindley, then chief scout, at Leeds and asked him about the player. Maurice suggested he was lazy and would not put himself about. That was far from my personal view having watched the player closely. I backed my own judgement in the summer of 1969 even though it was Stoke's first six-figure transfer fee. Stan Cullis said, "This is a transfer I am making with regret. You will not find a better player." He was right.'

Aston Villa were not the only competition for Greenhoff's signature, but once again Waddington got his man. That he was successful in doing so owed much to Greenhoff's basic integrity. He shook hands with Waddington, and even when he heard of other interest he stuck to his word.

'I'd heard rumours about other clubs wanting me at the time in the papers,' said Greenhoff. 'Just before the season started, Waddo came over with Albert Henshall [the Stoke chairman] and I got the call to go to St Andrew's as there were a couple of fellas interested in signing me. I wasn't told who.

'So I went down. I must admit, Stoke weren't my first choice at the time, but we had a chat and I asked if he'd start to look at putting a younger team out at Stoke. I didn't want to be bought to do the running for other players. I wanted to play my own game. Waddo said that he would, and we shook hands on the deal.

'So I went back home and I'd only been in the house 20 minutes or so and the phone rang. It was a *Daily Mirror* reporter called Bob Russell, and he asked if I'd signed for Stoke. I told him "no" and he said, "Don't! Everton are coming in for you. They're on tour though." A bit later I got a call, and it was Alan Ball who also said Everton wanted me. Managers wouldn't call you themselves, they could get into trouble for that.

'I asked my wife and she told me to do what I wanted. I had already shaken hands with Waddo, so that was that.

'Everton went on to win the league that year, but the great thing about it was that I stuck to my word and Waddo stuck to his. The make-up of the team at Stoke immediately became much younger. Conroy, Mahoney, Pejic and others came into the team. It turned out to be the best move I ever made.'

Greenhoff's arrival coincided with the return of John Ritchie, and the effects were soon felt. They rapidly established a strong partnership up front, feeding off each other and bringing a new dimension to Stoke's play. Greenhoff also worked well with Conroy, exchanging one-twos that would send the winger hurtling towards the byline before looking for the head of Ritchie with his crosses. 'He proved to be the perfect foil for Big John,' wrote Conroy. 'Jimmy was a nippy forward who could feed off Ritchie, had an eye for goal and could hit a volley as well as I've ever seen anyone strike one.'

Greenhoff was a striking figure in more ways than one, with a shock of blond hair and a distinctive style, crouched over the ball to keep his balance even and to enable him to turn defenders. Though naturally right-footed, he could score with either foot, or with his head. His principal asset was that rare ability to time the ball sweetly on the volley, a skill that brought him a hatful of sensational goals. He practised volleying every day. 'Waddo purred about Jimmy every day in training,' says Conroy. 'He wanted the other players to model themselves on him.'

Greenhoff was a confidence player, and he responded well both to Waddington's injunction to 'just go out and play', and to the adoration of the supporters, whose admiration and warmth he is still feeling to this day.

He was also part of a much-improving team for which last-ditch relegation struggles were becoming a thing of the past. They now had Banks in goal, a young and durable back line getting stronger by the game, midfield ball-winners in Bernard and Mahoney, Conroy proving himself a handful on either wing, and the increasingly productive strike pairing of Ritchie and Greenhoff up front. With Dobing and Eastham pulling the strings, things looked rosier than for many a year. This was evidenced by two mid-table finishes as the 1970s dawned, and even more so by the team's sudden emergence as a force to be reckoned with in the cups. League form might dip, but it was more than compensated for by a series of extraordinary cup runs over the 1970/71 and 1971/72 seasons, culminating in the club's first major trophy in more than a century of endeavour.

There was little sign of what was to come when Stoke tamely surrendered to Millwall in a replay in the League Cup in September 1970. Four months later, they drew Millwall again, this time in the FA Cup, and overturned that first result with a 2-1 victory. It then took three attempts to overcome Huddersfield, after a 3-3 draw at home and a goalless replay. A goal by Greenhoff in the third game saw them squeeze through. That brought a home tie against Ipswich Town, and when that too ended 0-0, it looked like the end of the run. But a Smith goal was enough to win the replay at Portman Road, and to earn a tricky quarter-final away at Hull City. Stoke were the clear favourites, but on a bitterly cold and snowy March day they were soon two goals down and heading for the exit. A brilliant effort from Conroy offered a way back, and two second-half goals from Ritchie broke Hull hearts.

By now there was real excitement in the Potteries, especially when the semi-final draw pitted Stoke against Arsenal. The Gunners were having a fine season, but memories were still fresh of a 5-0 thrashing handed out at the Victoria Ground at the start of the campaign – the goals from which can still be relished online! Two of the strikes, by Ritchie and Conroy, featured in Goal of the Season competitions (Conroy thinks he scored several better ones). For Arsenal, that had been a low point. They had since been on a long unbeaten run, but Stoke were confident of turning them over a second time at the neutral venue of Hillsborough, Sheffield Wednesday's ground.

The match has passed into the folklore of the club. Stoke started in express mode and, enjoying a little luck, were soon two goals in front. A ricochet off Smith shot past a startled Bob Wilson, who was then rounded by Ritchie when a back pass sold him short. Greenhoff blazed over when through. Had he scored, that would surely have been that. As it was, Arsenal came back into the game with a Peter Storey goal. Stoke held on into injury time when Banks claimed to have been fouled as he dropped a cross. The referee didn't agree and awarded a corner. It led to a final Arsenal effort which was cleared off the line by Mahoney, using his hand. A penalty was awarded and with the last kick of the match, Storey stroked it home. The Stoke players were devastated and never hit the same heights in the replay. Arsenal won it 2-0 and went on to beat Liverpool at Wembley with a famous Charlie George goal that secured them a First Division and FA Cup double.

It was a bitter pill to swallow but Stoke came back even more strongly the following season, this time in both cups. Again, it started unremarkably, with an effortful 2-1 win over Southport in the League Cup, and victory over Oxford United only after a replay. The next round then delivered a really tough proposition – the league leaders, Manchester United, at Old Trafford. Stoke had arguably the best of a 1-1 draw, but the replay at Stoke was goalless. In the third game, Stoke went through 2-1 with goals by Dobing and Ritchie. The three games were watched by 130,000 people. Even more remarkably, Waddington got into conversation with George Best as the

United ace was waiting for the coach home, and suggested that he might like to join Stoke City. Waddington knew that for all his genius, Best was giving his manager problems, and he scouted the possibility of an exchange deal. The player United boss Frank O'Farrell wanted was Denis Smith. It is a measure of the regard in which he held his centre-half that Waddington said later, 'There was no way I was releasing Denis, not even for George Best.' The dialogue fizzled out. Bringing Best to Stoke would have topped anything else even Waddington managed, before or since. Perhaps he could have tamed the wayward genius in the way he was later to do with another wild child, Alan Hudson. Just another of football's millions of might-have-beens.

The Potters made easier work of Bristol Rovers in the League Cup quarter-final. A 4-2 win brought them up against West Ham United in the semi-final. It turned out to be another epic encounter, played out over four games, another tie that has become the stuff of legend in the Potteries. The *Daily Mail*'s top football writer, Jeff Powell, called the deciding match 'one of the greatest football nights of all time'.

The semis were played over two legs, and Stoke seemed to have let their chance slip when they lost the home tie 2-1. They fought back to lead 1-0 in the second leg, but again seemed to have lost the tie when they conceded a penalty three minutes from the end of extra time after Banks brought down West Ham's flying winger Harry Redknapp (yes, that Harry Redknapp).

Stepping up to take the kick was Geoff Hurst, England's hat-trick hero from 1966, who had already smashed home a penalty in the first match and had not missed from the spot in four years. Against him was Gordon Banks, still England's first-choice keeper at the age of 33. Hurst went for power, as he had with his previous effort, and blasted the ball towards the centre of goal. But Banks stood his ground and somehow got enough fingers, hands, wrists and arms on it to deflect it over the bar. It was one of the best of his many stupendous saves. The photograph of it was one of his favourites, and he chose it for the frontispiece of his autobiography.

Banks later told the *Duck* fanzine, 'Geoff says that my save from his penalty was better than the save off Pelé. I just remember his run-up ... it was massive. He rarely missed penalties, he was a great striker of a ball. He started from outside the area and when he started his run up, I knew he was going to put it to my right if anything, as from his body position I knew he couldn't rotate and put it to my left. He just absolutely walloped it, just right of centre. I looked up, and I'd pushed it over the bar. Then all I knew I was screaming at our players to stop jumping on me and start marking their players for the corner! I was pushing them off me!'

The replay required a neutral ground, and that meant a return to Hillsborough, ten months after the FA Cup heartbreak there against Arsenal. The match was a goalless draw, necessitating a second replay, this time at Old Trafford. This was the game eulogised by Jeff Powell. Things seemed to be tipping Stoke's way when the West Ham keeper Bobby Ferguson had to go off for 20 minutes after a collision with Conroy, and no less a figure than the England captain Bobby Moore took his place in goal. A few moments later, Stoke won a penalty. Mike Bernard stepped up – and Moore saved it! Thankfully for Stoke the ball rebounded to the mightily relieved Bernard, who knocked it in.

With a superhuman effort, the ten men of West Ham not only equalised, but actually took the lead when Ferguson returned to the action. Dobing levelled things up at 2-2 by half-time. The second half could hardly match up to the drama of the first, and the tie was finally settled by a Terry Conroy goal. Stoke were in a Wembley final for the first time. The seven hours of play had been stretched over four games and

49 days. Stoke had played 11 matches en route to the final, but they were there.

In the meantime, the year had turned, and the FA Cup was now under way. Stoke managed to get past their first opponents, Chesterfield, with a 2-1 win, but needed a replay to overcome Tranmere Rovers. Then it was another meeting with Hull City, who had proved such doughty League Cup opponents a few months previously. The game at the Victoria Ground was a much more comfortable experience, Stoke running out 4-1 winners. The reward, for the second time that season, was another away tie at Manchester United. But before that, there was the showpiece Wembley final against Chelsea in the League Cup.

It was, and remains, the greatest day in the club's history, a victory that made instant heroes of the players and which is still celebrated half a century later as if it all happened last week. Stoke were the underdogs. Chelsea's team was packed with star players like Peter Bonetti, John Hollins, Ron Harris, Charlie Cooke, Peter Osgood and Alan Hudson. But Stoke felt history was on their side and took an early lead through a rare Conroy header from close range. Just before half-time, an opportunist goal from Osgood levelled the scores.

Stoke's winner came from the unlikeliest of sources – George Eastham, at 35 the oldest man on the pitch. He finished a classic Stoke City move. Conroy beat his man down the left and crossed from the byline, Ritchie headed down from the far post, and Greenhoff smashed one of his trademark volleys goalbound. The ball struck a crowd of legs but then fell for the veteran playmaker Eastham, who joyfully rammed home his only goal of the season from four yards. Stoke held on, despite a late scare when an ill-judged back pass from Bernard put through the onrushing Baldwin. Banks saw the danger early and managed to close him down.

There was wild rejoicing, and an open-topped bus tour of the Potteries for the manager and the players who had brought silverware to a club starved of success for so long. And the fans were also daring to ask themselves the question: could they go all the way in the FA Cup as well? No team had ever won both competitions in a single season, and although the substantial obstacle of Manchester United lay in the way, they would surely never have a greater chance of pulling off an extraordinary double.

Two weeks after the red-letter day at Wembley, it was back up the M6 to Manchester for the FA Cup quarter-final. Just as the League Cup tie between the two had ended 1-1 at the end of October, so too did this one, Stoke's goal coming from Greenhoff. The replay went to extra time, but once again Stoke edged it with a Conroy goal, and the dream of a Wembley double remained very much on. These two games were seen by more than 100,000 people, in a season when Stoke City and Manchester United played each other seven times.

Who should be waiting in the semis though but Arsenal, the team that had broken every heart in the Potteries exactly 12 months previously. Once again, the first encounter at Villa Park ended in a draw – 1-1 this time. Once again, Arsenal came through in the replay, 2-1. And once again, there was a late controversy that left the Stoke fans nursing a burning sense of grievance.

Stoke were a goal up when Arsenal were awarded a highly dubious penalty early in the second half. That levelled things up. With a quarter of an hour to go there was an incident that caused bewilderment and outrage at the time, and has been talked about in the Potteries ever since.

Arsenal forward Charlie George collected the ball in what to most of the 56,570 people in the crowd was clearly an offside position. But the linesman's flag stayed down, and George crossed for John Radford to head what turned out to be the winner. Stoke were incandescent, and were hardly mollified when the explanation for the calamitous officiating error was later revealed. Stoke were playing in their all-white strip. The linesman mistook a man walking down the touchline in a white coat for a Stoke player playing George onside. The mystery man in the white coat was variously described afterwards as a seller of programmes, ice cream or peanuts. It was farcical, and would have been funny if it had not cost Stoke a second trip to Wembley in a few weeks, and the chance to appear in the FA Cup Final for the first time. Denis Smith revealed in his autobiography that he had later questioned the hapless linesman, who confirmed that he had mistaken the man in the white coat for a Stoke player. 'I was so taken aback, I couldn't bite his head off,' said Smith. 'It was just too ridiculous to take in.'

It was no use complaining. It never is. The dream was gone, and after an amazing 20 cup matches, the glorious campaign was over. Stoke had won one cup and reached the semi-finals of the other: that had not been done before. League form had understandably faltered – they finished 17th – but what a glorious year it had been. Gordon Banks was named FWA Footballer of the Year. George Eastham came third in the poll.

It was always Tony Waddington's ambition to have his unfashionable provincial club talked about, and he certainly achieved it in that lengthy season, which included the short-lived Anglo-Scottish and Anglo-Italian Cups as well as the two lengthy domestic cup runs – a total of 70 games in all. In the days before big squads and player rotation, this took a heavy toll, and many players took to the field when far from fully fit. Jackie Marsh, incredibly, played in 69 of those 70 games and several others played more than 60.

Mike Pejic described for readers of his *Sentinel* column what it was like being in the team in those days – and how much of the steel in their performance derived from Gordon

Banks, marshalling affairs from the back, and requiring others to meet the standards he set for himself, 'Banksy was demanding. You had to hit a level every week with him behind you, and he never left us alone. He'd play the ball to you in a tight area and expect you to make the right decision. He made you work, made you play, made you think.

'His high standards spread through the team and we used to bite each other. Bluto, Alan Bloor, was a quiet assassin. When he spoke, you listened. You followed Smithy, Denis Smith, with his performance. In front of us, TC, Terry Conroy, was always moaning and groaning, and Jimmy G, Greenhoff, same as Bluto, would deliver pearls.

'Peter Dobing could look after himself and had high expectations, and big John Ritchie up front was a fierce competitor who made sure centre-backs knew they were in a game.'

Waddington was soon looking for ways to strengthen the team and fill the gaps left by retiring players such as Eastham, Burrows and Dobing. Mike Bernard's ill-judged back pass in the final moments of the League Cup Final seems to have convinced Waddington that in spite of almost 200 appearances as a combative midfielder, he did not have the temperament for the big occasion. John Mahoney, who had been a substitute at Wembley, was now more than capable of taking on the role, and in the close season Bernard was sold to Everton for £140,000 – a record for the club. Bernard played for another five years before a calf injury forced him to retire. His departure left Waddington with the funds for two new signings ahead of the new season. He needed to strengthen his squad ahead of Stoke's first campaign in Europe, courtesy of their Wembley win. More goalscoring potential was at the top of his shopping list.

Jimmy Robertson was an experienced winger who was one of the few players to feature for both of those implacable north London rivals, Arsenal and Tottenham Hotspur. He had scored the first goal in Tottenham's 2-1 victory over Chelsea in the 1967 FA Cup Final. For the previous two years he had been at Ipswich Town, and Waddington paid £80,000 to bring him to Stoke. Robertson gave Stoke extra options out wide, especially given the regular knee injuries suffered by their other specialist winger, the charismatic Terry Conroy. The Scot quickly became a regular in the team.

Waddington's other signing was yet another to demonstrate his flair for dramatic interventions in the transfer market. He spent a further £80,000 on bringing to Stoke a bona fide national hero. On 30 July 1966, Geoff Hurst had written his name in the record books and secured a special place in the heart of every English football follower by scoring a hat-trick in the World Cup Final as England defeated West Germany 4-2 after extra time. From that moment, Hurst's status as a national treasure was assured. Now, six years later, he had just won his 49th international cap in a 3-1 defeat to the same opposition in the quarter-finals of the European Championship. Hurst had been substituted after an hour and, although he did not know it at the time, his international career was over. He had scored 24 goals for England – one every two games. Two weeks later, although again he did not know it, he made his 499th and last appearance for West Ham United.

Hurst's national reputation was nothing compared to the esteem in which he was held by West Ham, where two other 1966 heroes, Bobby Moore and Martin Peters, were also long-serving players. But in the summer of 1972, Hurst's current contract was nearly up and although he had no wish to leave, it became clear that the club were willing to let him go. Now 30, he had joined the Hammers as a 15-year-old apprentice, and maintained over his long career there the same prolific record of a goal every other game – 248 of them in all. He was annoyed that after his years of service, they still wanted a transfer fee for him, and a substantial one for a player of his age. But Stoke were willing to pay, and West Ham were ready to release him.

When Hurst heard that Stoke were interested in him, his mind had immediately returned to the titanic four-game League Cup semi-final between the two clubs only a few months earlier, and, in particular, his penalty miss – or Banks's amazing save to keep it out. He was at one of the lowest points of his footballing life because of the end of both his club and international careers. 'The two great pillars of my career were collapsing under me,' he wrote. It did not take the silver-tongued Waddington long to persuade him to head north to the Potteries.

SIGNING FOR STOKE: GEOFF HURST

'Although I was at the end of the contract I had signed in 1966, I had no burning desire to leave Upton Park. So I was disappointed to learn that the club was willing to release me. When Manchester United had tried to sign me five years earlier, Ron Greenwood told me nothing about the deal. This time Ron came to me and said that Stoke City had asked whether I was available. When United wanted me, I wasn't told. When Stoke wanted me, I was told. It was quite obvious to me that the club didn't intend to offer me a new contract. In the circumstances I felt there was no point in staying at Upton Park. Perhaps rashly, I told myself, "If they don't want me, I don't want them."

'There was no question of pleading to stay at West Ham. My view has always been that as one door closes, another opens. I'm not an emotional person. I was not the sort to put my heart out to the newspapers.

'With hindsight, I shouldn't have jumped so quickly. I should have given it a bit more thought. Had I done that, I would probably have come to the conclusion that, although it was time to move from West Ham, it would be beneficial for the family to stay in the London area.

'What disappointed me as much as anything else was that having decided my time was up, the club insisted on asking for a transfer fee. I'd been in the first team for 13 years and felt they could at least have given me a free transfer after that kind of service. I'd cost them all of £20 – the signing-on fee all ground-staff boys received when they were offered their first contract as professionals. Now they wanted £80,000 for me. That wasn't a fortune, even in those days, but I felt it was mean. I shouldn't have allowed it to happen but I did, and Stoke were willing to pay the money. It was a wrench to leave the club I'd grown to love. I was proud of my achievements at Upton Park.

'What made an impression on me at the time was the acknowledgement by the vastly experienced Stoke City manager Tony Waddington that, in his opinion, I remained among the most prolific goalscorers in the First Division. Tony was a smashing guy, a manager of the old school, rather than one of the tracksuited academic types. European football presented Stoke with a fresh challenge, and Tony knew he would need to strengthen his squad. He particularly wanted an experienced striker to lead his attack.

'Perhaps he saw something in me during that series of matches against West Ham that convinced him that I was the striker he needed, because one morning that summer Ron told me that Stoke had made a bid matching West Ham's valuation. "We don't want to lose you, but we won't stand in your way if you want to go," he said. The message was clear enough to me. I packed my boots and, 16 years after walking into Upton Park as a kid, took the family north to view the Potteries.'

Taken from *1966 and All That,* Hurst's 2001 autobiography.

It was a classic Waddington coup, recalling some of those trademark signings of the 1960s. A player who was a household name, around 30 and no longer wanted by his club, but with plenty of goals still left in him. Waddington's conviction that

Hurst would remain a prolific scorer for a few more years persuaded the disaffected striker to sign up.

Hurst liked Waddington, as most of the players did. His move also put him in the same team as those who had proved such tough opponents in very recent memory. As Hurst observed when asked why he has signed for Stoke: 'Firstly, so I don't have to play against Denis Smith, and secondly so I don't have to take penalties against Gordon Banks.'

Unfortunately for him, it didn't mean that people would stop asking him *that* question, the one he had been asked every day since July 1966, 'Did it cross the line?' They didn't have to explain themselves further. It was a reference to Hurst's controversial second goal in the World Cup Final, when his shot hit the crossbar, bounced down on, over, or just short of the line and then away. Hurst's answer has always been the same: if the record books say it was a goal, it was a goal.

Once again, Waddington could not have been less interested in the revival of the time-worn jibes about his tendency to sign old crocks. As far as he was concerned, Hurst was quality. He had a good football brain, he had shown that he could score goals in any company, and he had vast knowledge to share with a team that was about to lose some of its older and more experienced heads.

The new signings pushed season ticket sales to record highs. With Robertson and Hurst in the starting line-up for a 2-0 home win against Crystal Palace on the first day of the new season, and a European adventure ahead, there was an air of optimism about the prospects. But as every football fan knows, as soon as you allow yourself to hope, disillusion and disappointment are never far away.

League form was patchy, aside from a sensational 5-1 thrashing of Manchester City, and 4-0 and 3-0 wins over great local rivals Derby County. Peter Dobing, Stoke's captain for the League Cup Final triumph, was forced to call it a day after breaking his leg. Home form was good – only two defeats all season – but the team had a dismal time on the road, losing 16 of their 21 games. The shadow of relegation hung over the club, and only a sudden late surge of six wins in the final eight games banished it, and lifted Stoke to 15th. The mighty cup exploits of the previous two years were not repeated. The team lost in the first round of the FA Cup, and got through two rounds of the League Cup before being dumped out of it by Notts County. Worse, the UEFA Cup experience was over almost before it had begun. A 3-1 win in the home leg of the first round against the West German team Kaiserslautern was followed by a 4-0 defeat away from home, and that was the end of that. It was all something of an anti-climax.

The gloom deepened when the great Gordon Banks was forced to call time on his illustrious career. He had not played since his car accident in October 1972, from which he had emerged with a badly damaged right eye and facial cuts that required 200 stitches. His long-term understudy John Farmer took over in goal and acquitted himself well. But the loss of the incomparable Banks, a commanding presence in defence for the last five years, had a demoralising effect on the team, and they struggled in his absence.

Banks himself slowly recovered. But his sight did not, although there were serious discussions about whether he might be able to continue playing even with this huge handicap. Such was his eminence that many thought a Banks with one good eye was preferable to any other goalkeeper with two. But in the summer of 1973, he had to admit defeat and accept that his 250th game for Stoke the previous October had been his last. It was also the end of an England career that had brought him 73 international caps – the last of them only five months before his accident. But it was not the end of the road altogether. In 1977, nearing 40, he went to America to play for Fort Lauderdale Strikers. They ended the season with the best defensive record in the North American Soccer League and Banks was named Goalkeeper of the Year. He returned to the United States the following season before finally hanging up his gloves.

Denis Smith says the back four loved the way Banks commanded the penalty area. 'You always knew exactly where he was because he would constantly tell you, and he would tell you where opposing forwards were if you were under pressure. He was a massive part of our success, and a massive influence in the dressing room with his positive winning attitude. He was great for young professionals to be involved with, and every time I stepped out on to the pitch with him between the sticks, I felt that the pressure was immediately on the opposition who must have been thinking, "Oh no, we've got to beat this defence AND bloody Gordon Banks today." It was a massive thing psychologically.'

Stoke fans who remember Banks each have their own fond memories of his unique combination of positional awareness, rapid reflexes, safe handling and calm control of his penalty area. The world remembers him as a World Cup hero of 1966 and even more for pulling off *that* save against Pelé and Brazil in the 1970 finals in Mexico. Pelé was acknowledged as the world's best player and Brazil were the best team in the tournament, which they went on to win. But England, fielding six World Cup winners from 1966, proved a tough proposition for them in the group stages. The match was goalless when the Brazilian winger Jairzinho sent over a cross to the far post. It was met by Pelé with a powerful downward header, and as soon as he made contact, he shouted 'goal!' (in Portuguese) and wheeled away in triumph. But Banks had flung himself to his right and somehow got enough contact on the ball as it bounced to divert it over the crossbar. No one could quite believe what they had seen, least of all Pelé.

Banks described the save for *Duck*, 'I got the top of my hand to it, and I honestly thought it was a goal, I really did. By now, my body was hitting the hard ground, and the momentum saw my head turn and I glimpsed that the ball had gone over the crossbar and behind the goal. I won't tell you what I called myself – it did include the word lucky though.'

As the teams organised themselves for the subsequent corner, Banks later recounted that the following exchange took place:

Pelé: 'I thought that was a goal.'

Banks: 'You and me both.'

Bobby Moore: 'You're getting old, Banksy, you used to hold on to those.'

Pelé was not alone in regarding it as the greatest save in the history of the game. Banks was resigned to having to talk about it for the rest of his days. 'They won't remember me for winning the World Cup,' he said. 'It'll be for that save. That's how big a thing it is. People just want to talk about that save.'

Those of a certain age and with long memories believe that England might have won that World Cup had Banks not succumbed to food poisoning the day before the quarter-final against West Germany – a rematch of 1966. England blew a two-goal lead to go down 3-2 with a mistake by Banks's replacement, Peter Bonetti, leading to the winning goal.

But for his accident, Banks would surely have had a starring role in this story of the 1974/75 season. He was 35 when he lost his eye, and might have enjoyed several more seasons as a top-flight goalkeeper. In retirement, Banks maintained his contacts with Stoke and became president of the club after the death of Sir Stanley Matthews. A statue of Banks holding the World Cup was unveiled by Pelé in 2008, and now stands on Gordon Banks Drive outside the Stoke City ground. He died in 2019 at the age of 81.

For once, Tony Waddington did not go straight out to seek a replacement of international class, as he had done repeatedly in the past. He was content to hand the gloves to John Farmer, for so long the understudy to Banks, and as a result restricted to fewer than 100 appearances over seven seasons. Farmer was a good solid keeper, but the great man's boots were perhaps too large for anyone to fill. Confirmation that Banks would not be returning, and a summer of inactivity in the transfer market, meant that the optimism of 12 months earlier had been replaced by a degree of apprehension about the prospects for the new season.

One ray of light was the emergence of another top-class defender – and like the rest of the back line, a homegrown one. Alan Dodd had made his debut the previous season. A versatile defender, he offered cover across the back line, making him a valuable asset given Denis Smith's tendency to break limbs with such frequency, and the long-term injury problems of Alan Bloor. Bloor's lengthy absence gave Dodd the chance for an extended run in the side, and he took it so well that Waddington continued to find a place for him even after Bloor returned. The following season, with Bloor again the victim of long-term injury, Dodd missed only three league games and cemented his growing reputation as a top-class defender. With an unruly mop of hair, he was strong, athletic, commanding in the air and good with both feet. His only shortcoming seemed to be a lack of personal ambition, and occasional lapses of concentration. In Simon Lowe's words in *101 Golden Greats*, 'His temperament was placid, and he lacked that extra swagger or self-belief to make it to the next level.' With typical self-deprecation, Dodd himself agrees with this verdict.

SIGNING FOR STOKE: ALAN DODD

'Cliff Birks [chief scout] saw me playing for Stoke Schoolboys and asked me to join as an apprentice. There were one or two other clubs I could have gone to, but I was a fanatical Stoke supporter. They're very persuasive these scouts. But I said to all of them, "I'm going to sign for Stoke."

'Arsenal wanted me to sign. Their scout said to me, "Just come down and have a look." So I went down to London. I was introduced to all the first-team players. At that time I was just a football supporter and an autograph hunter. I used to wait outside the Victoria Ground and try to get the opponents' autographs – and when I went down to Arsenal, they were all there in front of me! The club took me to the London Palladium. I also played in a practice match – I actually played against John Ritchie's brother.

'After the match they said, "Right, we'd like to sign you." And I said, "I don't want to waste your time. I'm going to sign for Stoke." The maximum wage then for an apprentice was £8 a week. They said, "We'll give you 30 quid a week." So I think they wanted me to sign! But I was determined to sign for Stoke.

'Leicester City were interested too. They invited me to the Cup Final. We had two great seats just below the Royal Box and when the winners paraded the FA Cup, I managed to touch it. That's the closest I ever got to the FA Cup!

'I signed on straight from school, at 16, as a full-time apprentice – or full-time labourer as it was in those days. They had us painting, and in the summer we had to repair the concrete steps at the ground. It was like being in the building trade. I enjoyed it actually.

'The season I made my debut, when we played Arsenal, I was walking down the corridor at the Victoria Ground and Bertie Mee [Arsenal manager] walked towards me. He shook my hand and said, "I'm glad you made it." That's something I haven't forgotten.'

This welcome addition to the ranks apart, the 1973/74 season got off to a start as indifferent as the one before. George Eastham retired at the age of 37. Stoke blooded a promising and industrious winger in Sean Haslegrave, but did not seem sure how to get the best out of him. Hurst, Greenhoff and Ritchie were still scoring most of the goals, but there were not many of them. The national mood was bleak with the country handling the effects of an oil crisis, power cuts and the three-day working week. Matches kicked off at 2pm in order to be finished before it was necessary to turn on the floodlights.

It took Stoke nine games to record their first win, and although there were flashes of hope with good victories over Birmingham City and Queens Park Rangers, the more regular fare was narrow defeats or dull draws. At the turn of the year, Stoke were 17th and facing another struggle to stay up in the second half of the season. Then, miraculously, at the stroke of a pen, everything changed.

7

1974: JANUARY TO APRIL

WHAT DROVE that transformation was yet another audacious flourish by Tony Waddington. He had pulled a good few rabbits out of the hat in his decade in charge, and now he planned to halt the team's slide with another headline-grabbing swoop for new blood. This time his target was not one established star, but two: the Chelsea duo of Peter Osgood and Alan Hudson. And he was ready to splash out the then eye-watering sum of half a million pounds to secure the pair of them.

When word got out that Stoke were pursuing Osgood and Hudson, the footballing world reacted with incredulity and amusement. Then, as now, Chelsea were one of the most fashionable clubs in the league, and few believed that two of their most prominent high rollers would be prepared to exchange the attractions of the King's Road for the questionable charms of the Five Towns. Beyond that, these were two players of the highest pedigree. They had won the FA Cup with Chelsea in 1970 after a titanic struggle with Leeds; the European Cup Winners' Cup a year later, taking down Real Madrid; and reached the League Cup Final of 1972 – where, as we know, they had tasted defeat at the hands of the Potters. It was a vintage period for the club. So why would Chelsea's golden boys want to trek north to play for struggling Stoke?

Osgood and Hudson were on the transfer list because of a terminal falling-out with manager Dave Sexton. Their very public split had been big news for weeks. It came to a head when Sexton dropped them both for a New Year's Day game at Old Trafford. A row followed and the two stars were suspended and put up for sale. Several clubs were linked to the players, but their reputations as unmanageable mavericks and ill-disciplined lovers of the high life went before them. Lots of managers thought they were simply not worth the risk. Waddington was not one of them. In fact, he was willing to double down on that risk, and take a chance on not just one of them, but both.

Osgood ummed and ahhed. He was ready to leave Chelsea but he could not convince himself of the benefits of a move to the Midlands, even for a fee of £260,000. He eventually plumped instead for Southampton – with whom he was promptly relegated.

But Hudson – Hudson came. To the amazement of everyone, possibly including the player himself, his move went ahead. The price on his head was a little smaller, though at £240,000 it was still a British transfer record (soon to be surpassed by Osgood's £275,000 transfer to the Saints). Yet even today it seems a curious move for a highly gifted 22-year-old who loved the pubs and bars and nightclubs of the King's Road, where he had been born and brought up. He would surely be a fish out of water when transplanted from his playboy haunts in the fleshpots of London to the well-disguised allurements of Stoke-on-Trent. Those who said he would never do it, now had to change tack. He had done it. Now they confidently predicted that the whole thing would end in tears.

Hudson must have shared those doubts. So why did he do it? The short answer is that, like so many other unsettled talents before him, he was talked into it by Tony Waddington. An extraordinary relationship was to develop between manager and player, one that went well beyond the cliché of Waddington as the steadying father figure to the wayward young talent. Hudson already had a father figure – his father. Whatever the nature of the bond with his manager, it was so strong that Hudson later wrote an entire book about it. *The Waddington Years* reads almost like a love letter to the man who gave him direction both on and off the pitch. Stoke were badly in need of a playmaker, a link man with the vision to make things happen, and Waddington persuaded Hudson that he was the man for the job. The shackles that Sexton had attached to him at Chelsea would be removed. His talents would have free rein, and there was a powerful fan base ready to take him to their hearts.

SIGNING FOR STOKE: ALAN HUDSON

Hudson is fond of telling the tale of his first fateful meeting with Waddington. And why not? It's a great story. He wrote about it both in his autobiography and *The Waddington Years*, and he recalled it for his biographer Jason Pettigrove in *Huddy*. Scene one, featuring Hudson and Osgood, took place in a restaurant in the King's Road. For scene two, the action moved to the Russell Hotel in Russell Square. Hudson says he didn't even know where the Russell Hotel was at the time, although he would soon learn that it was Tony Waddington's London base. This is how he described their encounter in an interview for this book:

'We were at my all-time favourite restaurant in the King's Road called Alexander. It was like a second home. Ossie and I were having lunch. We knew we were being kicked out of Chelsea and we were talking about where we wanted to go. We were throwing names around: Liverpool, Man U, Arsenal. But nobody wanted us!

There was a phone on the wall outside where they hung the coats. Christine Matthews who part-ran the club took a message for me. She said, "You've got a meeting tonight with Tony Waddington at the Russell Hotel." I was kind of stunned. I'd already had a meeting at QPR because I didn't really want to uproot, but that didn't come off. It seemed Tony Waddington might be the only one who wanted me. I went back to Os, and I made up a couple of stories that I was going to see Shankly or Busby.

'So I found my way to the Russell Hotel. As I walked up the steps, the doorman was there with his suit on and he didn't even look at me, he said, "The gentleman you're looking for is over in the park." So I go round the side – it's now dark, half past seven, eight o'clock – and I walk through the park and there's not a sign of anybody. And as I'm thinking it's a hoax, I walk past a red phone box and the door opened and he comes out. He was in the phone box pretending to make a call, but there was no one on the other end. He said, "Alan. Come and sit on the bench."

'He spoke for about 15-20 minutes and that was it. He told me about all the players he'd signed – McIlroy, Vernon, Viollet, Eastham, Greenhoff. He says, "That's all I can tell you about me: I just love a footballer. I want you to come and play for me." We never spoke about money; he said, "Don't worry about money, I'll look after you," and he was true to his word. For someone who never got on with managers all my life, I met this man when I was in the worst form of my life, and he took me to the top and we became very close.

'When I left Tony in Russell Square I said, "I've got one more thing to do. I've got to discuss it with my dad." I went home. My dad said, "Best thing you could do!" I swear Tony must have called my dad before I got back to see him. I wouldn't put it past him!'

Hudson also told Jason Pettigrove, 'I recall my dad standing next to the fridge in their tiny kitchen and after listening to me explain the situation – and being fully aware of all the speculation in the papers – he was, as always, straight to the point. "Sign for this man. He knows a footballer when he sees one, plus it will get you out of this place. The bright lights of London will be the death of you."'

What was it about Waddington that struck such a chord with him? 'I liked him immediately, he was a gentleman. A man of morals, who did things his way. I couldn't fail to be impressed, especially after putting up with someone like Sexton for all those years. Tony's style was immediately engaging, warm and sincere, and our deal was all done and dusted within minutes. I hadn't been used to that sincerity at Chelsea.'

Hudson also retold the story in *The Waddington Years*:

'We shook hands. I remember it being cold, and we sat down quickly on a freezing wooden park bench. I had agreed to become a Stoke player quicker than it took Dave Sexton to tell me to f*** off out of Chelsea Football Club. I cannot remember any talk of money, just that he wanted me to take over the role of George Eastham, who was then the playmaker, which was more important to me than the greenback. After he rattled off the names of previous inside-forwards, he had sold Stoke City to me.'

In his autobiography *The Working Man's Ballet* – the title itself a homage to Waddington – he wrote, 'I loved the man, and every memory of him is a fond one. Those were the days when managers signed you, not chairmen or agents. I was a restless soul, brimming with insecurities, needing to be reassured.'

And reassurance was precisely what he got. Waddington divined exactly what the young man needed and what he wanted to hear, acknowledging his talent and promising to give it free rein at Stoke.

Still, there were a few practical details to be settled. Waddington had got his man, but he was not blind to the dangers of Hudson's taste for fast living, and his liking for wine, women and song. To make matters worse, Hudson's marriage was on the rocks, and his wife did not at first follow him out of London. Further, Hudson was the first to admit that he didn't know all that much about the club to which he had just committed his future.

'I arrived on the Monday morning,' he says. 'I saw this yellow Mercedes outside and I thought the club had bought it for me! I walked inside, and Geoff Hurst was there. It was his! I said, "What are you doing here?" I didn't even know Geoff Hurst played for Stoke. That's how much I knew about Stoke City.

'I said to Tony, "Are you going to book me in a hotel?" He said, "You're not staying in a hotel – you're staying with him." "Him" was Hurst. Tony said to me, "Do you think I'm going to put you in a hotel and let you run round Stoke-on-Trent on your own? No chance. You need a family around you." My missus had left me, I'd come up on my own. I was totally out of form, I was having trouble with my wife, I'd come up to Stoke all on my own with just my bags. I thought I was going to be staying in the North Staffs Hotel, but he stuck me in with Geoff and Judith. So Geoff was my landlord. I must say it worked out for the best – Judith was fantastic, and it suited Geoff because he could get out more and use me as an excuse! So it all worked out well.'

Waddington knew this could be only a temporary arrangement, so remarkably, he took it upon himself to try to patch up the Hudson marriage – and even more remarkably, enlisted the help of his chairman in the process. Hudson said, 'About six weeks later, he came down to London to see my wife and pleaded with her to come back up to Stoke. He was the one who got us back together – him and Albert Henshall came down to London and met my wife. He was the one that got her back to Stoke. He said, "You've got to come back."'

We can only imagine what young Maureen Hudson made of her unexpected visit from two middle-aged men, one the manager and the other the chairman of a First Division football club, knocking at her door and proffering marriage guidance. It was hardly part of a football manager's job description. Whatever her feelings, she yielded to their entreaties. For all Hudson's adoration of Waddington, this was one service for which he did not feel any immediate gratitude. As Waddington had feared, he was already enjoying himself far too much as a single man in a new city, 'I didn't really want him to do it. I had found there were more pubs in Stoke than in London, and the nightlife was fantastic. But Tony saw that I needed someone in my life to keep me under control.'

Monday night was social night for at least half a dozen of the first-teamers, and on the day Hudson arrived, Hurst took him down to their regular haunt, a nightclub called The Place. He met his new team-mates over more than a few drinks. Some were friendly enough, but others were guarded. The arrival of a big-name player can upset the balance of a team, and put noses out of joint. After a sticky patch, the team was then unbeaten in five, and felt that things were getting better and didn't necessarily need interfering with. Like everyone else, they were suspicious of Hudson's motives in moving to Stoke, and didn't really understand why he had come.

Terry Conroy summed up their thoughts. He told me, 'We didn't know what to expect. We'd heard stories about Huddy's lifestyle and at 22, he's leaving Chelsea to come to Stoke for a massive fee. It was a culture shock for us too: what's he doing leaving London at 22, leaving one of the biggest clubs in Europe and coming to Stoke? From the point of view of some of our lads it seemed like a backward step. Chelsea were a much bigger club than Stoke, and Stoke as a city wouldn't inspire a lot of people! He's leaving the bright lights and his reputation was around his social life which overshadowed his footballing abilities. He was still only young and you thought – a lot of money; not that that bothered us, but it was just:

where's the ambition for a 22-year-old to be leaving a big club to come to Stoke? That was the concern initially. That was on the players' minds: will he be up for the challenge?'

Those doubts turned to a degree of hostility at Hudson's first training session, the start of preparations for the visit of Liverpool at the end of the week. But the ill feeling was not of Hudson's making, rather the fault of his manager.

Waddington was never one for complicated strategy, and his ideas for getting the best out of Hudson were straightforward in the extreme. 'My philosophy on playing methods was simple, perhaps stemming from my Old Trafford days, which was to build attacks through midfield,' he explained. 'In all my teams I always had at least one outstanding midfield player who could control the game.

'When I signed Alan Hudson, I gave him a bright yellow shirt in practice games. He was the only one to wear this colour, which enabled him to stand out.

'Every player on his team, including the goalkeeper, would be instructed to find him at every opportunity. I had him playing in a deep-lying role, so far back that opponents who had been told to mark him would not be so keen to get out of position.'

Not surprisingly, this ploy did little to endear Hudson to his new team-mates at that first training session. He later wrote, 'Tony Waddington really put me under the most intense pressure and had me in a situation that caused a little animosity among a few in the dressing room.

'In a full-scale match against the second team, he put a different coloured top on me and told our players not to pass to any other colour but mine.

'Straight away our left-back Micky Pejic was my number one enemy, and he would do the very opposite when in possession of the ball. I took it as a great compliment from my new boss, but did not thank him for it.

'The likes of John Ritchie, Jimmy Greenhoff and Jimmy Robertson were all experienced players and did not like being told to give the ball to a 22-year-old troublemaker from the Smoke.'

Hudson told me the stakes for him personally were too high for him to worry too much about getting off on the wrong foot in training, 'At the time I just cringed. I didn't give a damn what they thought about me. I was more worried about my career going down fast. There wasn't a lot of love in the dressing room for me.'

'It did me a bit of a favour because this was on the Thursday and we were playing Liverpool on the Saturday, my biggest game ever. If it had all gone wrong, Tony would have been in trouble and I would have been in trouble. I knew not to go short for the ball off Pejic on Saturday because I wasn't going to get it. So I had to change my game – I was playing against Liverpool *and* Micky Pejic.'

Awkward though he may have felt, Hudson saw the move as proof that Waddington meant what he had said about making Hudson his playmaker. In *The Waddington Years,* he wrote, 'He was making the point that we were going to play all our football through the midfield, and that meant me in particular. It was a great compliment and gave me the much-needed confidence that I had lost at Chelsea. So overall it was the beginning of my love affair with him as regards him giving me complete responsibility to go and play all over the field.'

In later years, in a chance conversation in a pub, this was neatly summarised in a sentence, 'Somebody said to me once in the pub, "When Waddington brought you to Stoke, he didn't bring Alan Hudson, he brought a young George Eastham." And that was it in a nutshell.'

Hudson went straight into the team for the game against Liverpool. His mate Peter Osgood came up for the match, arriving the day before to have a few glasses with his old drinking partner. So within his first four days in Stoke, Hudson had already been on a couple of serious benders. But it did not affect his form against Liverpool. The new boy proved more than equal to the responsibility being placed upon him. His impact was immediate and electrifying. His fellow players – along with the 32,789 packed into the Victoria Ground to see the new Messiah – were quickly won over.

It was a tough debut – Liverpool, the defending champions, were on their way to finishing second in the league. But Stoke were the more threatening team for most of the match, and took the lead just past the hour through Geoff Hurst. All of Hudson's extravagant skills were in evidence in what ex-Wolverhampton Wanderers player and manager Stan Cullis described in his radio commentary as the best debut performance he had seen. Only a mistake by goalkeeper John Farmer, allowing Liverpool a last-minute equaliser, spoiled the occasion. Hudson had arrived, and served a clear message that he had plenty to offer. No one who saw it was in any doubt that Stoke's season was kick-started that afternoon.

Alan Dodd was one of those who had had his doubts, but who was quickly won over by the virtuosity of his new team-mate, 'When he signed, we had a practice match and I was playing in midfield alongside him. I thought I'd try and impress him, because he wouldn't have known who I was. Huddy was just taking things easy and I thought, "He's not that special, why have they signed him?"

'I played really well in this practice, but come the game against Liverpool on Saturday I was worn out. I'd given too much in the practice match! But obviously Huddy was using his head and saving his legs for the match on Saturday. That was the best debut I've ever seen in my life. We couldn't believe how good he was.

'We went from a bad team to a good team overnight. That was all about Hudson.'

A potent symbol of Stoke City's early 1960s decline: sheep graze on the Victoria Ground pitch; the new stand is unfinished because the money has run out

The two men at the root of Stoke's revival: Tony Waddington with Stanley Matthews

Right: *Tony Waddington makes a rare appearance at the training ground*

Bottom: *Stoke City first team squad, 1974/75. Back row l to r: Kevin Lewis, Alan Dodd, Terry Conroy, Eric Skeels, Sean Haslegrave. Middle row: Mike Pejic, Denis Smith, John Farmer, Mike McDonald, Alan Bloor, John Mahoney, John Marsh. Front row: Jimmy Robertson, Alan Hudson, Geoff Hurst, Jimmy Greenhoff, John Ritchie, Geoff Salmons*

Gordon Banks' favourite picture: he saves Geoff Hurst's last-minute penalty during the epic four-game League Cup semi-final against West Ham in 1972

John Marsh. Part of the celebrated home-grown back four, a speedy overlapping full-back

Mike Pejic, snapped in training before heading back to work on his farm

Top: Mike
Pejic wins the
ball during the
League Cup
Final, March
1972

Right: Alan
Bloor. His
partnership with
Denis Smith was
at the heart of
the Stoke defence
throughout the
early 1970s

Denis Smith, supported as ever by Alan Bloor, wins a header against Tottenham

Denis Smith scores the winner in the famous 3-2 win over Leeds in 1974, that ended Leeds' 29-game unbeaten run. Smith frequently went upfield to score important goals

Tony Waddington caps a fruitful few days by adding the signing of John Mahoney to those of Gordon Banks and Terry Conroy

A fit-again Terry Conroy against West Ham, Easter 1975. All the famous features are on display – red hair, extravagant sideboards, skinny white legs.

Top: A trademark celebration from John Ritchie after giving Stoke the lead in the 1971 FA Cup semi-final against Arsenal

Left: Jimmy Greenhoff. His arrival kick-started Stoke's rise to the First Division elite; his departure signalled the start of their decline

Tony Waddington with Jimmy Greenhoff and John Ritchie. The signing of Greenhoff and the return of Ritchie created a potent partnership in attack

Eric Skeels. Skeels showed his versatility in 1974/75, filling defensive gaps across the back line as injuries and suspensions took their toll

Hudson looked back on the day with understandable fondness. A lot had been at stake for him, and he had felt under pressure to deliver. He wrote, 'This Saturday was one of the most exciting and rewarding of my career. It is still talked about to this day in terms of the best performance ever seen at a ground already famous for so many Matthews virtuoso displays.

'If I had failed that day, I would have been called a burned-out, overrated star from the Smoke who, in his first four days in town, had spent more hours in The Place than on the training ground. Well, the only way to do it is to take the bull by the horns, and on this occasion it worked out. My debut was spectacular, with everybody jumping on the bandwagon to sing my praises; the same people who had their knives all ready, fresh off the sharpener.

'My first couple of passes were into the front players' feet so that I could pace myself, always staying behind the ball, never having to chase back.

'The pitch was heavy, but it was my pitch, and I was starting to hear the buzz around the ground getting louder and louder. I knew this was going to be my day, the day I won them over. Waddo gave me the freedom of the Victoria Ground and always did, just letting me go wherever I wanted whenever I wanted. How could I fail?'

Watching in the stands was the still-undecided Peter Osgood. He havered for some weeks, and appeared to be on the brink of following his drinking buddy to Stoke. But then Southampton made their move, and eventually he decided that, in lifestyle terms, the south coast held more appeal than the Midlands. There are plenty of veteran Stoke watchers who believe that had he signed for Waddington, the club would have won the title the following season. Hudson thinks so, and says his pal would have been a revelation, and gone down as one of Stoke's greatest players.

One man who was probably privately pleased that the deal had fallen through was John Ritchie. Osgood's arrival would have put his own place in danger. And he had no love for Osgood personally because of a disparaging remark reportedly made about him by the Chelsea striker, to the effect that Ritchie had his limitations as a centre-forward – he could head the ball but not much more. When Osgood visited the Victoria Ground with his new team Southampton in March, Big John felt he had a point to prove. It was 1-1 at half-time, but Ritchie won it for Stoke with a second-half hat-trick. He completed his treble when a shot from Hurst hit the post and rebounded on to the line. Ritchie got to it first, stopped it on the line and then got down on all fours to head it in. Whether or not there was any conversation between him and Osgood is not recorded.

For his part, Hudson continued pulling up trees and taking giant strides towards himself achieving that status as one of the club's greats. From the start, he was a demanding and dominant presence in the midfield, calling for the ball himself or instructing others where to pass it. He was comfortable on the ball, and prepared to shake off the attentions of his markers by coming deep to receive it. Wherever he was on the pitch, he wanted the ball. He saw a pass early and struck up an instant understanding with his forwards, Greenhoff in particular. We have seen that there was plenty of talent and potential in the Stoke team, but Hudson was the catalyst that turned them from a goodish team performing indifferently to one that within weeks was being talked of as having title potential. It wasn't all about Hudson, but he was the spark. The confidence that flowed through him transmitted itself to the team, and they started to put a run of results together. The draw against Liverpool was followed by three more draws and a win. But then came the biggest test so far of the new Stoke: the visit, at the end of February, of Leeds United.

Under manager Don Revie, Leeds were the dominant footballing force in the land. Since winning the title in 1969, they had finished runners-up three times in a row and then third. In February 1974 they were on their way to the title once again, and on an unbeaten run that stretched back to the beginning of the season – 29 games in all. The record – which had stood for more than half a century – was 30. They were strongly fancied not only to surpass it, but also to become the first team to go through an entire season unbeaten. The game drew a bumper crowd of 40,000 – myself and my cousin among them.

Nothing that happened in the first half hour of their visit to Stoke suggested anything other than a routine day at the office for Leeds. After only seven minutes they were awarded a free kick on the edge of the Stoke penalty area. While the backs began thinking unhurriedly about organising a defensive wall, Leeds captain Billy Bremner took the free kick at once, and lobbed it gently into the net. The Stoke players were stunned, and furious, but the thrust of their objections to the referee amounted to little more than 'That's not fair! We weren't ready.' In truth, it was a typical piece of opportunism and quick-thinking by Bremner. It was claimed later that even he was surprised to get away with it. Ten minutes later, Allan Clarke slipped the defence and cracked home a second. Joe Jordan thought he had scored another, but was ruled offside. The champions in waiting were well on top. It looked as though by five o'clock they would have equalled the record.

Another piece of quick-thinking, this time by Hudson, brought Stoke back into the game. They won a free kick almost in the centre of the goal and about 25 yards out. Hudson tapped it to Mike Pejic who scored one of his rare goals with a tremendous left-footed drive. With the crowd behind them, Stoke started to shift the balance of the game. A Robertson cross and a Ritchie header caused chaos in the

almouth, and Hudson chose the perfect moment to
ome his first goal for the club at close range. It was
barely half an hour on the clock.

Now it was all Stoke, and midway through the second half
a third corner in quick succession was headed on by Ritchie
and into the Leeds net by a flying Denis Smith. It finished 3-2.
Although Leeds would go on to win the title by five points,
their great run was over, and Stoke's – now ten unbeaten –
was still intact. Like the 5-0 thrashing of Arsenal in 1970, the
game is now part of the folklore of the club. Stoke supporters
also like to claim – without much evidence – that the bitter
memory of defeat at Stoke remained with Revie when he left
Leeds at the end of the season to manage England. He was also
said to be smarting that his world-record bid for a defender
had failed to persuade Waddington to part with the mighty
Denis Smith. Whatever the reason, he steadfastly overlooked
the strong claims of several Stoke players for a place in the
national team. Of those players, only Pejic and Hudson got the
call, but won just six England caps between them.

Stoke's run continued right through to the end of the
season, which finished strongly with four wins and a draw.
Since losing to Wolves just before Hudson had arrived, there
had been only two further defeats in 23 league games. They
had climbed from a relegation-threatening 17th in the table to
a heady fifth – a distant 16 points behind Leeds United, but
having qualified for Europe. This was title-chasing form. In the
second half of the season they had accumulated 28 points: if
they could manage that ratio over a whole campaign, it would
more or less guarantee a top-three finish. In the following
season, as it turned out, 56 would have been enough to win
the title with something to spare.

Alan Hudson had proved to be the energising force needed
to galvanise and cohere a strong group of players who had been
less than the sum of their parts and performing at below their

potential. His influence was felt throughout the team. 'In the last nine games of the season, after he came, we conceded just two goals,' says Denis Smith. 'I think that was in large part due to the fact that when Huddy was playing we tended to keep the ball a lot. He did not like the other side to have possession at all, and he hated giving it away. Every player responded to this, and confidence bred throughout the squad. Huddy also knitted the disparate elements of our team together by providing the link between defence and attack. He picked the ball up deep, played one-twos through the midfield and then into the front men. And what's more he could keep that incredible work rate up for 90 minutes.'

The range of his abilities was striking, and baffled as discerning a judge as Trevor Brooking. 'He was blessed with an uncanny ability to pass with pinpoint accuracy,' said Brooking. 'Hudson seemed to skim across the muddy Victoria Ground pitch. He appeared to possess what I can only describe as a revolving kneecap, which allowed him to turn in the tightest of situations, keeping the ball in his right foot all the time. To be so one-footed would be considered a weakness by some, but he would jink past a defender on both sides, using either the inside or outside of his right foot.'

Hudson's generalship, vision and all-round ability had turned a mediocre season into a very good one – the club's highest finish since their near miss in 1947. It had turned a tired-looking lower mid-table side into one that had people talking about Stoke as probable contenders next time round. The despair of December had been transformed into the wild optimism of spring. Title challengers! The fans dared to indulge themselves in that most faithless of emotions – hope.

8

MAY, JUNE, JULY

THE ARCHITECT of the team now regarded as potential champions did not fit easily into any managerial stereotype. It was often said that Tony Waddington looked more like a bank manager than a football manager. In an age of dominant and autocratic managerial figures like Matt Busby, Bill Shankly and Don Revie, Waddington appeared understated and self-effacing. Nor did he in the least resemble the later generation of hands-on coaches screaming from the touchlines. None of his players can remember ever seeing him in a tracksuit. In fact, they don't remember seeing much of him at the training ground at all. He was not a great tactician or strategist, and for the most part he left his players pretty much to their own devices, off the field and on it. His own chairman described his organisation as poor.

Yet this is the man widely regarded as the greatest manager in the club's history. In 17 years at the helm, he hauled Stoke out of the doldrums and into the First Division. He got them as far as the FA Cup semi-finals for the first time since 1899 – and repeated the feat a year later. When he won the League Cup in 1972, he delivered the club's first, and still only, major trophy. He came within a couple of games of winning the

First Division title. And along the way he kept Stoke in the headlines with a series of astonishing swoops in the transfer market, as he built what was – again, in the estimation of most supporters – the best team the club ever sent out on to the muddy expanses of the Victoria Ground. A team that was not only successful but highly watchable as well, mud or no mud.

These achievements might seem paltry enough when set aside those of the biggest names in the English game – the Manchester Uniteds, Liverpools, Arsenals, Tottenhams, Chelseas and the rest. Stoke didn't need a trophy room: a cabinet was more than sufficient. But those are unfair comparisons. The club's record stands up well enough when compared to others of equivalent size, standing – and means. Waddington inherited a team floundering hopelessly in a Midlands backwater. He transformed it into one capable of challenging for the highest honours, and turned the club into something about which the city and its football fans could be excited and proud.

But how did he do it? If he wasn't a coach, or a tactician, or a disciplinarian, or a figurehead with a powerful support team around him, what was he? What was it that enabled him to perform this great conjuring trick?

We have seen the basic elements of his philosophy in play already. It was not complicated. It was based, first and foremost, on quality. Above all else, Waddington was an outstanding and shrewd judge of a player. He knew a footballer. He was fond of saying, 'I can tell a player by the way they walk.' If a player had quality, Waddington would be interested in signing him. These days, when an outstanding young talent emerges and people discuss how swiftly they should advance, old heads will nod sagely and say, 'If he's good enough, he's old enough.' Waddington's attitude, at least when he was out and about in the transfer market, was almost the opposite – which is why he was often pilloried in his early days for signing so many players who seemed to be past their peak. As far as he was concerned, it was a case of, 'If he's good enough, he's young enough.'

Waddington expounded this outlook in a conversation recalled by Denis Smith in his autobiography, 'When I got my first managerial job at York City, I spoke to Tony. He said, "You want to be a good manager? Then sign good players. But if you want to be a great manager, sign great players."'

As we have already seen, that was the approach Waddington had always taken himself. Smith noted, 'The game was very simple to Waddo. What he did was pick good players and play them in their correct positions, building enough rapport and cohesion to make a team. It sounds simple to say it, but he was of course absolutely right.

'What he did was to get good players people were having problems with, like Dennis Viollet, Jimmy McIlroy – some unbelievably talented lads he signed for the club. He signed the world's greatest goalkeeper in Gordon Banks. To Stoke! Geoff Hurst, who scored a hat-trick in a World Cup Final! George Eastham. George was outstanding in midfield. Waddo bought them and welded them together.'

That may have been the key plank of his managerial outlook, but as Smith implies, it was one thing to identify a class act and another to get them to hitch their star to the Potteries wagon. This was when he was required to deploy what Conroy calls his 'silver tongue'. He was persistent and persuasive: he had the knack of inspiring trust and confidence. We've seen repeatedly how quickly he persuaded reluctant or non-committal players to come to Stoke – Viollet, Banks, Hurst and the others. His ambition knew no bounds: he was to claim that he had tried at various times to sign both Johan Cruyff and George Best, two of the greatest talents of that or any era.

What often helped persuade players to sign up was Waddington's own self-evident passion and enthusiasm for Stoke City, and his determination to put the club back in the limelight. His great transfer coups were primarily rooted in a desire to land the player, but he was always mindful of the positive attention and publicity they would generate for the club. He was a master at exploiting the potential for this to its maximum effect, from the signing of Stanley Matthews onwards.

'Bringing Stan back was incredible,' says Smith. 'I was a supporter standing in the terraces with the 8,000 before he came back; and there with the 35,000 against Huddersfield when he did come back. That's genius – he signs a 47-year-old bloke and says, "This is going to change the fortunes of the club."'

Conroy agrees. 'In any walk of life he'd have been top class,' he says. 'He was a great salesman and a showman. He portrayed Stoke in the greatest light – he should have been made a Freeman of the City, even posthumously, because of all he did for Stoke. He really was smooth-talking, but not smarmy with it. He was very charming, and when you think of all those players – it's a list as long as your arm – it was Waddo who brought them in.

'He was always plotting to make Stoke City a better club, a bigger club and put them on the map, and for that he deserves enormous credit.'

A slightly more complex portrait of the outwardly urbane and self-confident Waddington comes to us not from a player, but someone with considerable inside knowledge of the club in the 1970s. That person was Dudley Kernick. Dudley who? It's a good question, as he himself acknowledged in the title of his autobiography: *Who the Hell was Dudley Kernick?*

There was no single answer to the question. Kernick hovered around the fringes of football for more than half a century, as a player (or 'failed player', as he himself put it – a single season at Torquay before the war); as a manager ('the most successful in the history of Nuneaton Borough'), and as a club secretary, coach, television scriptwriter and broadcaster. In 1970, he joined Stoke City as one of the new breed of commercial managers. Football clubs were slowly waking up to the fact that they were sitting on a commercial asset from which money could be made. Nothing like the sums around today – we are talking matchday sponsors and club lotteries, not lucrative kit deals and multinational franchises. The first Stoke game to feature matchday sponsorship would be the imminent opening fixture of the 1974/75 season. The trailblazers were Sandbach-based commercial vehicle manufacturer Fodens, who parted with around £1,000 for the privilege of extensive advertising at the ground and having their celebrated works band entertaining the crowd at half-time.

The amounts were small, but it wasn't long before Kernick and his counterparts started filling club coffers with very considerable sums by the standards of the day, running into hundreds of thousands, even millions of pounds. Most of them felt unappreciated and frustrated by directors who knew little about football and were suspicious of their commercial activities. But they had the satisfaction of taking a big share of their own success – Kernick was on commission, and claimed to have been comfortably the best-paid person at the club.

Kernick's 15 years at Stoke overlapped with the later and most successful period of the Waddington era. The two men do not seem to have got on particularly well. Kernick's memoirs give some insights into the internal workings of the club, but concentrate mostly on his commercial work and trademark gimmicks, one of which involved parading a camel round the ground at half-time during a game sponsored by a local travel agent. However, he did find the space for some thoughts about the manager.

Kernick gave Waddington due credit for the enormous successes he achieved at Stoke, and the relaxed and friendly atmosphere that permeated the club. 'The players didn't want to leave Stoke,' he wrote. 'Why should they have done? We had a good team, and training and coaching was a lot less demanding than they'd have found almost anywhere else. In a nutshell, Tony Waddington was a players' manager. That's why it was such a happy time at the club.'

But on a personal level, he found the manager difficult: defensive, insecure, secretive and occasionally small-minded. Waddington never included Kernick in requests for ticket allocations for away games, and he was only able to get a seat by asking the host club for one.

Surprisingly, in view of his long and successful career at Stoke, Kernick claims Waddington never felt that the people of the Potteries really took to him: 'Because Stoke fans had a reputation for disliking Manchester people, I reckon Waddo was suspicious of not being liked. Tony once actually told me he felt he was disliked in the Potteries. I tried to reassure him otherwise but it was a belief he seemed to cling to until the day he left the club. I'm sure, though, Tony was well liked at the Victoria Ground and that he merely had a chip on his shoulder.'

It must be said that Kernick's opinions of manager and players were strongly swayed by how willingly they supported his efforts to connect with the fans and raise money for the club through personal appearances. He had appreciative words in this regard for Gordon Banks, George Eastham, Terry Conroy and Denis Smith. He found it harder to coax the retiring Jimmy Greenhoff to support his efforts. And Waddington steered clear of them too. Kernick said, 'I don't ever recall him going out to knock over a pile of pennies or present a pennant to a club or society. No supporters' forums for him, and rarely did he appear to associate himself with the average fan. When he did, it was with individuals or small groups. He seemed afraid of big gatherings.'

Kernick was a larger-than-life character clearly not lacking in self-confidence, and put some of this coolness on Waddington's part down to jealousy: 'I once went five years without speaking to Waddington, at a time when we were both established employees of Stoke City Football Cub. I always felt he was very defensive towards me and resented me being the club's chief link with the fan in the street. Waddington was insecure among people he thought were a threat to his authority.'

A more multi-layered and complicated, even brooding personality emerges from the Kernick portrait, 'He seemed to spend hours on the phone in his office, often while a long queue formed out in the corridor. Junior players, pressmen, salesmen and even the tea lady would be waiting to see him.

'Despite the long hours he spent in his office, Waddington would very rarely conduct any transfer business or contract negotiations in there. That would be done, of all places, either on the track round the pitch or in the centre circle. No chance of being bugged there! Perhaps that had something to do with the ridiculous layout of the offices, whereby the manager's office overlooked the street outside. Passers-by could if they so wished crane their necks and eavesdrop what was being said in the corridors of power.'

The Waddington that is more usually described – relaxed, gregarious, sociable – does break through on occasion though, as in this extraordinary anecdote from Kernick, 'Waddo was the definitive laid-back gaffer, never more so than in the build-up to one of our biggest matches in the 1970s – the away leg of our UEFA Cup tie against European giants Ajax [of which more later].

'The tie being delicately poised persuaded several thousand of our fans to go Dutch for a day or two. There were some supporters, however, who had the knack of turning up at the players' hotel and making a nuisance of themselves. Whether it was London, Norwich, Newcastle or Southampton, they'd do their homework, find out where the team was staying, and breeze in among the players on the overnight trips. These well-heeled gents decided against going on any of the many excursions I'd helped organise, preferring to go under their own steam.

'True to form, they were in the reception of the team's plush Amsterdam hotel. They were told there were no rooms left, but after drinking that night with Waddington, they imposed on Tony's generosity. Come bedtime he said they could catch a few hours' sleep in his room if they could find a bit of space. What a sight they must have been! There were five or six gatecrashers and one of them apparently spent the night in the bath. An unusual way, you might think, for a manager to spend the night before such a big game.'

In other words, Waddington was like any other human being, flawed and vulnerable, but with many strong and attractive personal qualities. His methods may have been a little chaotic, and he didn't mind flying by the seat of his pants. It was Albert Henshall who had called him a poor organiser. But the chairman added that he was a superb improviser.

One thing that was never in doubt was his dedication to Stoke City and his determination to transform them into a top club. His shrewd judgement of a footballer also seems to have been universally acknowledged. And it was but a short step from there to the formulation of his core managerial strategy: find thoroughbreds, and persuade them to come to Stoke. Starting at the back, with the man between the sticks.

Waddington's obsession with goalkeepers has already been noted, and from O'Neill to Shilton he signed a dozen of them during his time at Stoke. Today, it's a truism that a good goalkeeper can be worth a hatful of goals a season, and spreads confidence and belief through the players in front of him. But that was not always the conventional thinking, as witness Leicester City's difficulty in finding anyone prepared to pay a relatively modest £50,000 for the services of their World Cup-winning goalkeeper Gordon Banks. The best keeper in the world, and no one bar Waddington thought he was worth the asking price. It sounds absurd to say it now, but in his preoccupation with goalkeepers and his willingness to pay top dollar for them, Waddington was both unusual and ahead of his time.

Next step in the building process was a solid defence. 'Waddington's Wall' was an early sign of the manager's recognition of the need for a strong and reliable back four, and as time went on he was blessed with a wealth of homegrown talent that saved him many a potentially costly foray into the transfer market. Tony Allen, Alan Bloor, Denis Smith, John Marsh, Mike Pejic and Alan Dodd all rolled off the Potteries production line and all gave many years of sterling service. Alan Hudson, who had played against Stoke several times before he joined the club, and probably had a few bruises to show for it, echoed the respect most First Division forwards felt for the Potters' defence. 'When I went to Stoke, that was as tough a back four as you'd find anywhere on earth,' he says.

Further up the pitch, Waddington wanted his teams to have a dominant midfield player to control the game and initiate attacks through midfield. None of this is original thinking of course: his genius lay in spotting the players who could do these jobs for him, persuading them to come, and then slotting them into a formation that would allow them to shine. The key figures in the midfield role during his managerial term were Jimmy McIlroy, George Eastham and Alan Hudson. In signing each of them, he chose exactly the right moment to pounce, when they were at a low ebb and only too ready to listen to the Waddington blandishments. Each became the creative hub of the team in which he played, picking up the ball from the back and distributing it intelligently and to maximum effect.

After this, the Waddington philosophy seems to lose some of its simplicity and coherence. Having secured the basics, he simply looked for quality players in the obvious positions who could do a job for him and would fit in with those parts of the jigsaw he had already assembled. His decisions were based more on the calibre of the player than filling conventional positions.

With the arrival of Hudson in January 1974, he had most of the pieces in place. But such was his reputation as an operator in the transfer market that Stoke found themselves linked to every big-name player who was reported to be ready to move on. So it was in the summer of 1974, with Kenny Dalglish, Joe Jordan and Martin Chivers among others. The rumours about Chivers were the most persistent, but there is nothing much to suggest that Waddington made any serious inquiries for any of them.

Peter Shilton, the Leicester City goalkeeper, may have been an exception. We have seen how Shilton's virtuosity as a young keeper had persuaded Leicester that they could dispense with the services of Gordon Banks in 1967 – and how Stoke City had benefited from that. Shilton had duly followed Banks into the England team, where he competed for the jersey with Ray Clemence of Liverpool. By the summer of 1974, Shilton was getting itchy feet. Clemence appeared to be England's first choice, although the two of them often played in alternate internationals. Shilton felt that he needed to move on if he was to win club trophies and establish himself above Clemence in the pecking order. The World Cup that was then taking place in West Germany offered no shop window for him: England had failed to qualify. So he put in a transfer request, and Leicester – who once again had a good young goalkeeper coming through, in the shape of Mark Wallington – accepted it.

Stoke were one of several clubs immediately linked to Shilton – unsurprising given Waddington's record for signing top goalkeepers. But the likely asking price of around £300,000 was considered beyond their means. That seems to have been the case for others too, and maybe that lingering reluctance to value goalkeepers as highly as outfield players played its part. Whatever the reason, several weeks went by with Shilton up for sale, but no one willing to meet the asking price.

In August 1974, the rumours linking Shilton with Stoke began again. In attempting to dampen them down, the Stoke chairman Albert Henshall inadvertently gave them fresh impetus. There was no possibility of Stoke finding £300,000 for Shilton, he said, and added, 'We have not got that kind of money any more.' But he fanned the speculation by hinting that a player exchange might be possible. Several other clubs were making what were described as 'routine inquiries' about Shilton. But none of them came to anything, and Shilton began the new season still wearing the colours of Leicester City.

One of the reasons Stoke did not have the money to move for Shilton even if they wanted to was that Waddington had already splashed out £160,000 on what would turn out to be his only signing of the summer. Added to the cost of buying Hudson, that pushed Stoke's spending in the first half of the year to a giddying £400,000. The player he brought in was intended to complete the jigsaw. As usual, the means by which the signature was obtained were highly unorthodox, with many of Waddington's qualities of persuasion and opportunism in evidence.

In June 1974, Stoke joined Sheffield United and many Scottish and continental teams in a friendly tournament in Cyprus. It offered Waddington the opportunity to get a closer look at a player who had always caused Stoke problems in games between the two teams. He enlisted the support of Hudson in the pursuit. Hudson called it 'one of the most bizarre transfer deals I have ever seen done'. He told the story in his own book, and recalled it again in an interview for this one.

SIGNING FOR STOKE: GEOFF SALMONS

Hudson explained, 'We were in Cyprus after the end of the season. Tony said to me, "I want you to come to a football match tonight. I want you to come and watch a player, because I think he'll improve our team. 'I said, "Tony we're going to this club tonight. I'm going nowhere." He said, "I'll tell you what I'll do: you come to the first half with me, and I'll come to the club with you." So we went to see Sheffield United, who were also in Cyprus, and he said, "Watch Geoff Salmons play."

'Geoff played in midfield that night. He was brilliant. I said, "Well, the way he's playing Tony, he's going to take my place." He said, "No, he's a left-sided player, he goes down the left."

'We went to the club and he signed Geoff Salmons – apart from the actual papers – in the nightclub there and then. In the early hours of the morning, Waddington had Sammy up against the hotel bar, telling him what a fantastic place Stoke-on-Trent was. But Sammy was sold not on the area, but on the manager – just like I was after our first meeting on the park bench in Russell Square. Waddo said, "I've got a ready-made room-mate for you" – pointing at me – "him".'

Salmons's own recollections of an evening that seems to have featured much drinking are, perhaps understandably, a little hazy. 'I was tapped up,' he says today. Was he on the transfer list at the time? He says not. So was this legal? 'No, it wouldn't be would it?'

'We were just having a drink at night before we went to bed,' says Salmons. 'Waddington came in and he put me an offer – £100 a week. I was on 65, so what do you do? Albert Henshall, the chairman, was there too. I knew I would be leaving, but in the papers they were talking about Tottenham or Arsenal. I didn't want to go down to London.'

A move across the Pennines therefore suited him. But, taking up the story again, Hudson says agreeing personal terms included a rather unusual caveat.

'Sammy had to sort out the most important part of his deal, and that was to explain that this tour was not a one-off for him, and that he drank like that all the time in Sheffield. He said to Tony, "I'm going to tell you now before you sign me – I don't want you to find out afterwards and then we fall out. Wherever I live, I go out on a Friday night and have six to eight pints." And Tony said, "Well if you can play like that for me, you can have as many as you want." Tony was not interested in what you did Monday to Friday, he was only interested in what you did on Saturday.

'Sammy became our outlet on the left side, the player with the magic left peg. And he did not disappoint anyone with it. His ability to cross the ball at full speed was in the Alan Hinton class, and that, I can tell you, is the best compliment I could pay my old drinking partner. We were inseparable really. He did a fantastic job for us. For someone who drank so much, he was a great athlete and he had a great left foot on the run.

'The funny thing about Sammy was that he never really wanted to be a footballer. He always wanted to be a publican. And he became a very successful publican, and a very wealthy publican. He didn't take the game as seriously as I did.'

Waddington took the same view, but like everyone else he had a soft spot for his new recruit. 'Salmons was a great character who never took the game quite seriously enough. I once made him captain when we played against his old club and instead of shaking hands with his opposite number Tony Currie, he kissed him.'

The dubious tactics employed by Waddington in persuading Salmons to come on board may explain why at least three weeks passed after the teams returned from Cyprus before the signing was announced. Waddington played it with a straight face when it came to speaking to reporters. 'I mooted a deal for Salmons in Cyprus when we were on tour with Sheffield,' he said. 'I was not turned down out of hand, and the suggestion was there that he might become available.'

Salmons had joined the Blades from school and had become a crowd favourite at Bramall Lane, though sometimes overshadowed by the brilliant Tony Currie. Sheffield United were prepared to sell him because they needed money for the redevelopment of the ground. But the sale went down badly with their fans, who extracted a small measure of revenge a month later by voting Salmons their Player of the Year.

Waddington was understandably delighted with his new capture. 'Salmons is a left-sided midfield player of the type we have not had on that flank, and will give extra support to Micky Pejic,' he said. 'He will give us an ideal balance in midfield, with Alan Hudson in the middle and Mahoney on the right.' And so it was to prove. The move also confirmed that Stoke planned to stick with a 4-3-3 formation that had served them well in the latter stages of the season just ended.

Apart from seeing him in action in the bar in Cyprus, the other players didn't know much about their new team-mate. But when he joined them for pre-season training, they soon came to appreciate what he had to offer. 'He had a good build on him – he was a big lad,' says Smith. 'But he covered the ground – he ate ground up. He skimmed across the top and his left foot was to die for. He was so graceful with his movement.'

With the arrival of Salmons, Waddington was happy with his line-up and confident about the season now approaching. But there was no talk around the club about their prospects of winning the league. It just doesn't seem to be something they ever talked about – even later, as the season advanced and it looked more and more possible. As Conroy says, 'I can't recall that we ever spoke about it. It was a very relaxed environment – there was never any undue pressure placed on the players. The expectations maybe weren't as great as with bigger clubs. Maybe that was a problem. If we did do something, it would be a bonus.'

In any case, no one was talking much at this stage about the prospects for the new season. All eyes were on the World Cup in West Germany, even in the absence of British teams, and there were other developments on the domestic scene to catch the eye. In July, the legendary Liverpool manager Bill Shankly announced his retirement. In his 15 years at Anfield he had taken Liverpool back into the First Division and delivered three league titles. Meanwhile, across the Pennines, another dynasty was coming to an end. The Leeds United manager Don Revie, scarcely less successful than Shankly, left Elland Road to take over as England manager. Leeds were about to set the football world buzzing by turning to one of Revie's fiercest critics to take over from him: the brash and outspoken Brian Clough.

So there were plenty of other things to talk about when the Stoke players assembled for pre-season training on 18 July 1974. Getting ready for the new season involved a lot of running, and Waddington drafted in some Olympic talent to knock his boys into shape. Conroy remembers Derek Ibbotson joining them for runs round Trentham. Ibbotson had once held the world record for the mile, and although he was now past 40, he was still more than a match for most of the squad. Conroy claims that only he and John Marsh could stand the pace as Ibbotson stepped it up over two or three-mile stretches. Mike Pejic also recalls the runs with Ibbotson, and others with Roy Fowler, the former European and Commonwealth 10,000m runner, who worked with the team and with Gordon Banks in particular, for many years. 'We were fit as fleas,' Pejic recalled. 'We did running by the canal, we did speed work on the track and stamina work on Trentham Hills.'

Waddington was not much in evidence on the practice ground during the week. Training was in the hands of former Stoke stalwart Frank Mountfield, and the one-time Liverpool player Alan A'Court. When Waddington did put in an appearance, his contributions were brief and to the point – as Dudley Kernick recalled, 'The Wadd wouldn't interfere with the training methods of his coach, Alan A'Court. He couldn't. He wasn't often there. Rarely did he arrive before 10am, but if there was a big game looming, he'd pop to the training ground in his everyday suit. Not once did I see him put on a pair of football boots while he was manager, let alone don a tracksuit. He'd ask Alan to try a few set pieces, or tell him to vary free kicks, mainly to impress any press or tv people who'd turned up. Training was an intrusion really, and nobody stayed long.'

Denis Smith confirmed this account, 'He never took the training sessions himself. The training ground was behind the main ground at that stage, so he'd be there and have a chat. While we were doing things, if say the coach was having me and Alan Bloor bringing the ball out from the back, Waddo would be going, "Don't want that. You get it, and you give it to him." It was basic. When you get to that level you shouldn't need coaching, you just tweak a little bit. You don't coach when you get to the top level. What you need is advice – "you're dropping off a little bit there, you're pushing on a little bit too far, when you get it, have a look for him". Fairly basic stuff.'

Eric Skeels agrees, 'The only time I really had much conversation with Waddo was in the dressing room before the game – he'd say, "You're facing so-and-so today, try and keep him quiet, make sure you mark him. Make sure he doesn't have a lot of the ball because their defenders will be looking for him."'

Skeels says the advice dispensed by those who were doing the coaching was scarcely more sophisticated. 'Frank

Mountford used to say to me, "Look, as soon as you can after the game starts, don't be dirty but don't be shy of going in and tackling hard. When you do that, you'll find they'll be looking over their shoulder for you and going further back. Hit them early." I was always tight on the player. I wasn't frightened of clattering them even if they were bigger than me and I always went in 100 per cent.'

'He'd have a clear idea of how he wanted things done and would say if the coaches weren't doing it his way,' says Denis Smith. 'But he relied on signing good players. If Tony Waddington said you could play, you could play. When you look at the standard of the players he signed, they were excellent. They were sometimes troubled players, players with different attitudes to life. But he was very good at handling those. He got the best out of them. His man-management was brilliant.'

Hudson agrees that the light touch was the most appropriate way of dealing with seasoned players, 'We wouldn't see Tony from one Saturday to the next. He did his work in his head. All Dave Sexton did was coach all week – well, we didn't need coaching. Good players don't need coaching. They need keeping fit.'

Team talks, even when the season was under way, were also simple, when they happened at all. When there was a meeting, the message was not always clear, not least because of Waddington's frequent inability to remember the names of key members of Saturday's opposition.

Terry Conroy said, 'I can never really recollect a team talk of any length – it might have been basic stuff if Leeds were coming to town or United – "you've got to watch him". But it was very short. And names escaped him: he would say, "You've got to watch miladdo". You wouldn't interrupt him during his team talk, but afterwards people would be saying, "Who's miladdo?" You had to read his mind to know what he was saying.'

The closest he came to focusing on the next opponents was in those Thursday morning sessions. 'Before we got to training he'd be talking to Frank Mountford and Alan A'Court,' says Eric Skeels. 'He'd just say, "We're playing Man United next week and they play like this, so let's do a bit of a trial thing with the reserves, see how we play against that." He would let us know what we were supposed to be doing but he wasn't dead strict – he would let you do your own thing.'

'You'd play first team against the reserves, and the reserves would copy how you would expect the opposition to play,' says Conroy. 'Tony would instruct Alan A'Court on what system we were playing and who was doing what. But it was very uncomplicated basically: trusting the players you had and saying, "I bought you to do a job, you know what you have to do, so go out and do it." It was that simple. He saw the art of man-management as knowing your players and having faith in them and trusting them.'

Alan Dodd agrees that the focus was always on the way Stoke wanted to play, 'He never really talked about the opposition. He wasn't really concerned about the opposition, he only talked about how we were going to play. He had so much confidence in the players he'd signed, and the players he'd selected on the day. Tactically we didn't really talk that much, as we had players like Alan Hudson – he just let them do their own thing.'

'Tony was not a great tactician,' says Smith. 'His genius lay in his ability to put a good jigsaw puzzle together. He'd be able to slot the pieces in the right place and the right starting 11 to go out there on the pitch. He was no rousing speechmaker. He would simply say, "Go out and be solid. Don't allow them too much room, and keep the ball."'

That was the Waddington way: put together a team of quality players and let them get on with it. No micro-management, no dossiers on opposition players, no working out of plays or positions on a board. The message was simply, 'Go out and do it.' He trusted them to sort things out on the pitch if need be.

Smith says this put a lot of the responsibility on the players. 'He might say to Eric Skeels, "They've got George Best or Bobby Charlton – your job Skeelsy is to stop him playing. You follow him to the loo, you go everywhere with him. Then when we get it, we do this – we give it to George Eastham or Peter Dobing or Alan Hudson." But players made a lot of decisions themselves – if things weren't happening we'd be going "oi, he needs picking up, he needs closing down" and you'd be doing it as you went along if people were giving you problems. Then we'd try to give them problems, and we had enough good players to do that.'

Today's managers would doubtless be appalled by the lack of sophistication in this seat-of-the-pants approach. It seemed to work well enough, but it did have its drawbacks. When Alan Bloor was fit to return to the team to partner Smith, Alan Dodd kept his place but was employed more as a utility player. In his time at Stoke he wore every outfield shirt other than nine. But this bred uncertainty, which the manager did little to clear up.

'I never knew where I was going to play,' he says. 'I saw my name on the team sheet and then Waddo would say a few words before the match. At times I was like a fish out of water playing in other positions. I always liked to face the game. In midfield I found it difficult – I'd get caught in possession because I'd always played as a defender.

'Sometimes he would say after the match, "You played really well," and I'd think to myself, "I thought I had a nightmare today!" But if he was happy, that was the most important thing.'

Just as he kept his distance in training, so Waddington never watched a match from the touchline, believing he had a better view of play from the directors' box above the halfway line. He installed a telephone line for relaying orders from there to Frank Mountford on the bench. This was an innovative step for the time, but Mountford was no early adopter. He soon became so sick of receiving instructions that he threw the receiver into a bucket of water. After that, Alan A'Court answered the calls. Conroy swears that on one occasion Waddington called down and demanded to speak to George Eastham, and was unabashed when reminded that Eastham was out playing on the pitch. 'Bring him to the phone,' was the order. At the next break in play, Eastham was summoned across to speak to his boss by phone on the touchline.

Another Waddington ploy was to bring in the fire brigade to water the pitch if it became too dry and hard. What others would call a quagmire, he regarded as the perfect going to bring out the best in his teams – especially if one of his stars had a dodgy knee (Matthews) or a dodgy ankle (Hudson). The fire teams, all of them presumably Stoke fans, would pump thousands of gallons of water from the adjoining River Trent on to the pitch, or the training pitch nearby, to keep the ground nice and soft.

On one occasion, this ploy nearly killed one of his star players. The waters of the River Trent are not at their purest as they pass through the Potteries. After one heavy dousing of the training pitch, the germ-laden water infected a gash in Denis Smith's leg. Within hours, the apparently indestructible Smith was on life support in intensive care as he fought off septicaemia. The doctors warned his wife that he might not pull through. Thankfully, he did. And very probably played the following Saturday.

If Waddington was thin on detail when it came to tactics, he was highly effective in keeping his players happy and extracting the best from them. Again, his philosophy was based on trust. If he treated them as adults and kept them on a relatively long leash, he expected them to repay him by behaving professionally and keeping themselves in good enough shape to give of their best on a Saturday afternoon. As long as they did that, he didn't care too much about what they did with their time. As a result, there was a strong social side – which he actively encouraged – and for some, a culture of regular and quite heavy drinking. Today, such behaviour would not be tolerated. In those days, it was not unusual or regarded as a particular problem – as long as the players kept their side of the bargain, and did not allow their off-field activities to jeopardise their fitness.

The centre of the social scene was The Place, a converted warehouse that had opened as a nightclub in 1962 just in time to catch the mood of the Swinging Sixties. It was the first of several such clubs that helped make Stoke something of a social hub. Plenty of future superstars appeared at The Place in the days before they became famous – including Rod Stewart, David Bowie, Eric Clapton and Elton John. It became a regular haunt for a group of the players on a Monday evening – a healthy distance away from the next match.

'I was always at The Place on a Monday night,' says Conroy, who at the time was teetotal. 'It didn't matter that I didn't drink. It was a gathering of the lads, it was a night out and no one wanted to miss it. It was bonding, a social bonding session. So you would invariably get maybe eight, ten players there on a Monday night, most Mondays. Not Pej. Pej wouldn't know where The Place was.'

Geoff Hurst took Alan Hudson to The Place on his first night in the Potteries, which happened to be a Monday. Soon Hudson was at the heart of any social gathering. 'Because he came from the King's Road and was glamorous, Huddy had a lot of hangers-on,' Conroy recalled. 'You'd never go into a pub or restaurant and see him on his own. At the time he was married to a model, Maureen. He was trendy and she was gorgeous. They'd be in the magazines, with photographers visiting their home to snap them as though they were the Potteries version of Posh and Becks.

'But never once did Huddy have a big head. He'd talk to anyone and drink with anyone. He was very popular in the dressing room because he was never nasty or bossy despite his incredible talent. He just liked to have a good time.'

Smith was an occasional visitor to The Place 'I would dip in and out. Huddy would be there, Jackie would be there, Mickey Bernard before he left – different characters. I didn't drink when I joined the club at 18 as a pro. Because I wanted to be a footballer, I didn't drink. They soon changed that. They wouldn't accept that in the dressing room. I didn't catch up, though I enjoyed a drink. I didn't mix much with the players – I was more interested in people outside football. My friends were people I'd known for a few years or my new neighbours. I didn't really socialise with the players that much.

'Dobby [Dobing] was champagne, Huddy whatever he could get his hands on. Sammy could drink unbelievable amounts and it didn't seem to affect him at all, which was incredible. He claimed he couldn't sleep without it. When George Eastham took over, he stopped that. We were down in London and he said, "Look there's no drinking tonight," and Sammy said, "But George! I can't sleep if I don't have a drink!" And George said, "How do you know? You've never tried!" But admittedly he did function well when he'd had a drink.'

Salmons, unsurprisingly, agrees. 'I can take my beer. I'm not aggressive and I know when I've had enough,' he says. 'They were all good lads. I got on great with them.' The culture suited him just fine. 'Waddington was a magic manager. I've got total respect for him. I thought he was a brilliant bloke and he looked after me. He would have a drink with you, and so would the chairman. He had the full respect of the players, so you didn't abuse it.'

One thing that surprised him when he arrived was to be offered help with sleeping on a Friday evening. 'They came out with sleeping tablets for the night before a game. I said, "What's that? I'm not taking bloody tablets! I'll have a couple of pints and go to bed." I'd have a pint. But not sleeping tablets.'

Waddington's approach was the opposite of Eastham's – to the extent that he actively encouraged drinking, on the grounds that it helped bring the players closer together. One of those who tended not to join in was young Alan Dodd. Waddington even tried to change that.

'I never went out,' says Dodd. 'The lads used to try and get me drunk. Waddo used to say to one or two of the lads, "See if you can get him drunk." He liked his players socialising, Waddo did.'

Hudson says, 'There's a story he told me: he got a phone call one day from a publican in Stoke saying that two or three of the boys had been in the pub until two o'clock in the morning. He thought that by telling Tony, Tony would go in the pub and thank him. But Tony didn't like that. Nothing ever came of it, he never went into the pub and he didn't thank him. He thought that was invading privacy. He didn't even want to know the names of the players.'

As well as the sessions in The Place – where he spent his very first night in Stoke-on-Trent – Hudson was in a separate drinking school, which usually involved Salmons with his hollow legs, John Marsh and Sean Haslegrave. The foursome – 'our little rat pack', Hudson called them – would go out round the pubs in Stoke a couple of nights a week.

Waddington himself was not averse to a drop, and the Potters Club in Federation House was his second office. It was just across the road from the station – perfect for him to hop on the train back home to Crewe at the end of the day. It was claimed that the driver of his regular service would sound his whistle as he entered Stoke station, to alert Waddington and give him time to step across the road and board the train. Conroy for one believes it to be true, 'The driver used to toot the whistle for Waddo as he was approaching Stoke station. Even presidents and kings wouldn't get that treatment would they?'

The only player with whom Waddington socialised was Alan Hudson. They would often have long lunches at Federation House, cementing the extraordinary relationship between the manager and his star player. 'I don't think there's ever been a player and manager who've been so close,' says Hudson. 'Other players didn't like it but I didn't care. We used to go out for lunch and dinner.'

The relationship between manager and player was surely unique – and all the more surprising since Hudson was known for kicking against authority. 'I never got on with coaches and managers. I argued with them all the time,' he says. 'I didn't believe in most things they did. Tony and me had a unique relationship – we were just great friends. We went to the Potters Club one day and he invited my mum and dad. My dad was a decorator and he only had one suit, and he wore this suit. We finished lunch and I saw Tony and my dad talking. My dad obviously appreciated everything Tony did for me. I saw him shake hands with Tony – he never shook hands with anyone, my dad, and I saw this as a kind of symbol that he was passing me over to him. "I've brought him this far, now you take him to the next level." That's the way I read it. I loved him so much, he was like my second father, my mentor.'

No doubt the other players were wary of this extraordinary bond – and suspicious that they were being discussed behind their backs during these long conversations. But Hudson says that was not the case. 'All the time I knew Tony, I never spoke about anything that went on in the dressing room, anything that happened on the field. We never spoke about anything like that – it was all music, life and anything else.

We liked to have a drink together, we loved each other's company.'

Manager and players would mingle more freely when they were away from Stoke, on one of the many short breaks and overseas tours he would organise. 'Waddo loved his trips, whether it be in the UK or abroad,' says Conroy. 'Every opportunity he got, he would take the players away. We'd even go to Buxton for a couple of days just to break the monotony. It was training, but it just got the players away from the daily routine. It was a way of getting the players together, getting to know each other, socialising.'

These friendly contacts extended to the supporters as well. The players would mix freely with them on the train home from away games or in the social club. 'We always came out before away games with any spare tickets for the fans,' Jimmy Greenhoff recalled. 'Waddo insisted on it and we were happy to do it. He especially made the point of doing so on your longer journeys, to the likes of Norwich, Ipswich and for London matches. It was a big thing to Waddo. We socialised a lot with the fans. We always had lunch as a team in the social club and fans would be in there, too. It was great. We'd still do it now, I think. John Ritchie had his own pint pot behind the bar of the social club. Imagine that now!'

All the players felt a strong bond with the support. 'Of all the clubs I went to, it was at Stoke that the players had the greatest bond with the fans,' said Greenhoff. 'We used to play for the fans. We loved the fans. When Alan Hudson came to Stoke, we'd speak before games and we just wanted to get out on that pitch and entertain the fans. The one-twos we did we loved doing, but we know we maybe did a few too many as we always wanted to entertain.'

Mike Pejic endorsed this view in one of his *Sentinel* columns, 'The fans were tremendous, absolutely tremendous. They were hard-working people who made the Victoria

Ground a cauldron of hostility for the opposition. They knew they were on to a good thing with this side, and together we felt like we had the world at our feet. I can't tell you how much fun it was to have them on your side. I'd be in there, we were supporters too. There was a bond and you never wanted to let them down.

'It was like a cauldron when the fans got shouting and the noise bounced and bubbled around. Supporters were right on top of you, it was so tight and compact, and in the Boothen End we had Zigger Zagger and his crew making a fantastic atmosphere that you'll never forget. I still remember parking at the school and walking across chatting with fans before kick-off. They loved it, we loved it. We were just like them.

'There were nerves even for us, mind. Marshy used to do all sorts of things to try to help, anything he could imagine, from rubbing himself in olive oil or thermo rub to washing himself down before he ran out. But we had players who could give the opposition a stare too, just to make sure they knew what they were going into.'

After a good home win, Conroy says everyone would be cock-a-hoop. 'You'd go up to the boardroom, and Waddington would bring down two bottles of champagne and open them for the lads. It was a great club, very generous in lots of ways Waddo was. On trips abroad he'd be spending money. You couldn't fault him in that respect. They were a good crowd of directors too, they'd socialise with the players when they could. We were a happy bunch you have to say, when you look back.'

Gordon Banks had stopped playing by this time, but he was still closely involved with Stoke. He was another who enjoyed the atmosphere and ambience around the place. 'I couldn't have picked a better club. I was delighted to come to Stoke,' he told *Duck*. 'Waddo was so charismatic – he really sold the club to me. I knew the fans were great from playing in front of them, but everyone at the club was great, from directors, to fans, to the manager. Different class.

'We loved socialising together. We played and trained hard, but we loved life. Is there another club in this country that does this? I don't know, but I do know that our friendship and camaraderie is lovely. It would be nice to think the players of this age would be doing the same in 20 years' time, but I doubt it.'

'There was a culture of boozing, as we were a very sociable club,' says Denis Smith. 'Tony Waddington didn't have rules as such. He thought the lads going out together and having a few drinks wasn't a problem and most of the time it wasn't. His attitude was, "As long as you turn up on Saturday and play, and play well what's the problem?" Roy Vernon once told me that the problem with the club was that there were no rules. Waddo's attitude left you a lot of leeway to hang yourself.'

Conroy says that for the most part, the players did not take advantage of the freedoms they were afforded by an indulgent management. 'I can't remember players misbehaving when we were out on a group evening or get-together, whether it was abroad or in the UK.'

Skeels says the players were aware that they were in the public eye, and couldn't afford to misbehave, 'If you're in the pub, people will see you and say, "There's Skeels in the pub at ten o'clock drinking." They'd ring the club and say, "I saw Eric Skeels in the pub last night." That's what it's like if you're in the limelight. You go into a pub and the people running it think, "Oh we've got footballers in that'll bring more people in," and come closing time they'll say, "If you want to stay behind for a drink you can stay behind", and some did. But not daft. I wasn't a big drinker. Some of them could drink all night but I couldn't do that.'

According to Skeels, the unwritten rule was that the drinking stopped in the middle of the week, ' We had a policy of no drinking after Wednesday. You could go dancing or to a nightclub and have a drink, but after Wednesday, that's it until after Saturday's game. Waddo wanted you to enjoy yourself but when it came to the business, he wanted you there. He didn't go wild, he didn't fine you or anything like that. But he would give you a rollicking if you were out of order. But imagine if you're out enjoying life and going out late at night, and then you're in the team on Saturday and you have a nightmare of a game, then he's going to come down on that and think, "Right, you're not playing next week," and that's part of your punishment.'

Hudson admits that there were a couple of times when, as he puts it, 'I let Waddo down.' Temptation for him was at its greatest when Stoke were playing in London. They would spend the Friday night in the Russell Hotel, their London base, tantalisingly close to Hudson's old haunts. On one occasion, ahead of a game against Arsenal, he checked in to the hotel and then set off for Chelsea with Geoff Salmons and Eric 'Alfie' Skeels in tow.

Skeels ducked out early, but the other two carried on drinking until the early hours and didn't get back to the hotel until three or four in the morning. When they woke up, they were drunk. When they got to the ground, they were still drunk.

'We were in the dressing room before the game,' says Hudson. 'I was in the shower room in the back throwing cold water on my face. Eric Skeels came running in – he wasn't playing. He said, "Huddy we've got a problem."

'"What's that?"

'"Sammy can't do his boots up."

'You can't believe it can you? That couldn't happen in a Sunday pub game!

'"Alfie, do me a favour. Use your head. Go in there. Make out you're giving his calves a rub and while you're doing it, tie his boots up for him."

161

'So he had to go in and tie his boots up for him. Sammy came out and he said, "Oh, Al." I said, "Just keep standing on Pat Rice [the Arsenal right-back]. Stop him making a run and keep breathing on him!"'

Denis Smith also remembers the incident. In his account, Salmons was not the only one having difficulty lacing his boots. Smith was livid with what he considered completely unprofessional behaviour. 'I went berserk,' he wrote in his autobiography. 'I hauled Alan up against the wall in the dressing room, yelling, "What's going on? This is my living, it's my livelihood you're playing with."'

Just before half-time, Salmons, his bootlaces firmly secured by Skeels, pressured Rice at an Arsenal throw-in – possibly by breathing alcohol fumes over him. Rice threw to Kidd who was heavily marked and so tried an over-ambitious back pass to his goalkeeper. Jimmy Greenhoff nipped in to intercept and back-head the ball into space. Hudson picked it up on the D, left Sammy Nelson flat on his back and powered the ball home. The two night owls had contrived to give Stoke the lead.

Hudson was irrepressible. According to Smith, he came straight up to him and said, 'Den, I've scored. Now it's your job to keep them out!' It was the only goal of the game.

Stoke didn't win too many times at Highbury, but not everyone was happy. They didn't like the way Waddington indulged his less-disciplined players. Smith found it amazing that he had not hauled Hudson and Salmons over the coals before the game, 'He hated confrontation, and simply told me to calm down.'

Waddington didn't say much after the game either, but what he did say seems to have got the message across. 'Tony came in afterwards,' says Hudson. 'He said, "A couple of you didn't look at your best today. We won, but I'm not happy with it." And he glared at me.'

To Hudson, that was good man-management, and in spite of the result, he still counts that as one of the rare occasions when he abused the trust his manager had placed in him, and let him down. He knew that he was in a privileged position, and he felt his failings badly.

'Sexton didn't know how to handle me. Tony Waddington had a fantastic way with me. A couple of times I let him down when I was out before a game. He never said anything, he just looked at me. And he'd come in the dressing room afterwards and say, "We need extra training, a couple of you looked like you need a bit extra," and he'd glare at me and he would let me know that way. For me, that's great management, letting someone know without causing a big fuss.

'Because I got on so well with him and he did all this I knew that I could never let him down on the Saturday. We had such trust in each other and I had to keep my standards up.'

The Arsenal episode was just the sort of behaviour that had got Hudson thrown out of Chelsea. It was an era in which the Football League was blessed with a golden generation of flair players, many of whom coupled their talents on the field with a lively social life off it. As a result, some playing careers finished prematurely. George Best was the prime example, and he and others were seen in retrospect as having failed to achieve their full potential. What that usually meant was that they had not won as many international caps as their talents deserved. Successive England managers, Don Revie in particular, didn't trust these 'mavericks' and were reluctant to accept the ill-discipline and unpredictability (or, as they saw it, unreliability) that would be the price of putting them in the national team. As a result, a whole generation of sublime English talent was shamefully neglected. Players like Hudson, Frank Worthington, Stan Bowles, Charlie George and Rodney Marsh lit up the First Division week after week with their extravagant crowd-pleasing skills. Their home crowds adored them, opposition supporters could not suppress a grudging admiration. But guess how many England caps those five won. A pathetic 25, that's how many. *Between* them. None of them reached double figures. Charlie George won a single cap, playing out of position against the Republic of Ireland and being subbed after an hour.

These players fared best when they were not over-managed, and their wilder excesses were, if not condoned, then tolerated. At a club level, managers were more willing to accept the trade-off required by players who were a joy to watch on the pitch and a nightmare to manage off it. The sager ones realised that you could not have the one without the other. That was certainly Smith's verdict on Hudson, 'I think Huddy was a fantastic footballer – but I would regularly be crying at the other things he did which infuriated me. He could have been a world figure. The fact he wasn't is down to the way he conducted himself off the field. It was just a part of him. You can't separate Huddy the player, with his vivacious and audacious skill, from Huddy the person. I think he wasted his talent; he doesn't. Huddy and I will have to agree to differ on that one.'

Hudson's lifestyle represented a sort of double life, in which he played hard for half the week and worked hard for the other half. If he had been overindulging, he would train ferociously to get back to his fighting weight by the Saturday. Conroy says that training on Tuesdays was always the toughest of the week, and Hudson would often arrive after a lengthy session at The Place the night before. But then it was straight down to business, 'Huddy was somebody that had a weight problem to a degree – he'd put on five or six pounds in the space of an evening session. He wasn't a big eater but it was the alcohol, the drinking. But the next day, I promise you he was at it all the time. He never shirked a training session, was always at the front. He'd have a black bin bag on and he'd weigh himself and he was back to his normal weight. This was the dedication. People accused him of things but to my mind he was fantastic.' As Hudson himself said, 'I know what I was. But I always produced the goods. People forget that.'

The Waddington method of giving his players plenty of rope and trusting them not to hang themselves certainly worked as far as Hudson was concerned. The manager also had a sound core of players who looked after themselves and were low maintenance. So he concentrated his efforts on extracting the best from the others.

Denis Smith was one of those who could be trusted to do the right thing and not give his manager any grief, and he was happy enough to be left alone, 'I had very few conversations with Mr Waddington. It was strange. He made me captain in the end, but as far as conversations went, they were very limited. He tended to spend his time with the ones who were giving him problems – and he had plenty of those. The ones who just got on with it he left alone until something erupted in the dressing room, or there was a difference of opinion, and then he would step in. He was a very good man manager.'

Conroy agrees, 'He did indulge players but that's the art of man-management – some needed different treatment from others. There were a lot he didn't have to bother about – he didn't have to bother about me or John Mahoney or Marshy or Smithy, most of the team. But there were two or three he would fuss over and give special treatment to. But that's part and parcel.'

One of those fussed over by Waddington was the skipper, Jimmy Greenhoff. His behaviour gave no cause for concern, and his abilities were beyond question. But Greenhoff was a confidence player – an introvert who could get very down on himself if things were not going well. Making him captain was one way in which the manager tried to boost his confidence and self-esteem.

'Waddo idolised Jimmy,' says Conroy. 'He was very close to Jimmy. They didn't socialise a lot but they would spend more time during the week talking to each other than the rest of the players would. Making him captain was a boost to Jimmy's confidence. Jimmy was quiet, but the captaincy didn't play such an important role in the running of the team as it does with some skippers. When Peter Dobing was captain, he was quiet as well. George Eastham was quiet. If we had boisterous players on the pitch it would be maybe Smithy, Pej, Mickey Bernard and John Ritchie to a degree. But the rest were introverted, quiet, just went about their own business.'

After Hudson arrived, however, it soon became clear to Waddington that his new star had much stronger claims on the captaincy than Greenhoff. He had a big personality, he had the respect of the other players and he was running the show on the pitch. But just as he had boosted Greenhoff's confidence by making him captain, and just as Greenhoff was now blossoming as a player thanks to his understanding with Hudson on the pitch, Waddington now feared destroying that confidence by taking the armband from him.

He confided in Hudson. 'One day he said, "I'm going to make you captain,"' Hudson recalled. 'I said, "I don't know whether that's a good idea. I feel like I am captain, but I don't want to upset anyone." It was playing on Tony's mind, but he didn't have it in him to tell Jimmy he was no longer captain. He thought he would lose him, and it would knock all the confidence out of him.

'We were in the gym before a League Cup match on a Wednesday night. I was warming up and I saw Tony and I thought, "What's he doing here?" Tony had never been in the gym! He was staring up at something on the ceiling, and he was half pissed. He couldn't handle it, telling Jimmy. He was looking up and I knew what was going through his mind. And he walked away, and as he walked away he just patted me on the backside and he went, "Not tonight." He was frightened to tell Jimmy. I've never told Jimmy that. Tony didn't want to knock Jimmy's confidence because it was so fragile.

'You could see when he ran out he was very proud to be captain and I think that it would have hit him badly. People don't understand that football isn't just all about the football, it's all about emotions and how to get the best out of people.'

Another player who suffered perennial self-doubt about his place in the game was Alan Dodd, one of the quiet men. He had grown up as a football-mad kid who was fanatical about Stoke City. As we have seen, he turned down much better terms with Arsenal among others to join his boyhood heroes while he was still in his teens. He was living the dream. But the dream wasn't delivering quite as much as he had hoped or expected.

'When I was at school, it was my ambition to play for Stoke and play for England,' he says. 'I don't know why, but I lost my ambition. I remember even when I was a young professional of 17, I went working for my dad and my two uncles in the summer holidays. Labouring on a building site. And when I went back for pre-season training, I said to Waddo, "I feel like packing in – I really enjoy labouring." I know it sounds stupid. He said, "I'll give you a rise." I said that wasn't why I was thinking of it.'

The same diffidence resurfaced when Waddington told Dodd he had been picked to make his first-team debut. He took him to one side and said, 'You're playing tomorrow.' Thinking Waddington was talking about the reserve team game, a puzzled Dodd replied, 'I know.' 'No,' said Waddington, 'you're playing in the first team.' 'Oh,' said Dodd. 'I'm not ready.' His manager was taking no more nonsense, 'I decide when you're ready, not you. You're playing in the first team.'

By 1974, while fast establishing himself as a first choice, Dodd had still not regained the hunger and ambition of his boyhood. He would have been more than happy turning out for the reserves, and lacked the competitive instincts of some those alongside him. 'That was a bit of a problem I had,' he says. 'I should have been more aggressive and more vocal. But it just wasn't in my nature.' He stunned Alan Hudson when they were training together soon after Hudson's arrival, just after the two titanic struggles against Liverpool and Leeds.

'On the Monday morning after the Leeds game, we went on the track to warm up,' says Hudson. 'And I said to Doddy, "Come on, get up the front with me." And we were running round and he went, "Alan, I'm thinking of packing the game in." He didn't want to be a footballer really. He preferred fixing roofs! I thought he was joking. And I said to him, "Do you realise that in the last three weeks you've marked probably the most dangerous man in the air – Joe Jordan of Leeds – and the quickest forward at Liverpool – Kevin Keegan – and you've not given them a header or a kick? That's how good you are." And he went, "No, no, no, no." He found the game too easy. That was the only time I ever told Tony about another player. I had to tell him about that. I said, "You know what Alan Dodd said to me – you'd better have a word with him because you're going to lose the best young centre-half I've ever seen."'

Dodd remembers the conversation, 'At the time I must have been a bit frustrated. I've never been in love with the game of football. I've always said I'd have been happy just playing in the reserves. I was content playing in the reserves where there was no pressure at all. I definitely felt pressure in the first team. The crowds didn't affect me, but when I didn't play well I always felt as though I'd let the team down, and it would get me down a bit. Still, I played all those matches, so I must have done something right! But if I made a mistake, it would be on my mind and that would affect my game. It shouldn't do, you should forget about your mistakes because at the end of the day you're playing in a team – it's not an individual sport.'

While some of the players need reassurance and regular confidence boosts, others were more bullish. Mike Pejic, ever the contrarian, was one of those who thought the regime should be stricter and the organisation more rigorous. He often felt the preparations for big games were inadequate, and was not shy about saying so. Conroy remembers that this was sometimes the source of tension 'He did feel frustrated as we started getting better. He felt we could be more professional in games. He was always saying we could do better. We'd had success and we were getting to the stage where we were getting to be a top side. But Pej's frustration was that he thought we could do better sooner than we did. This was his gripe with Waddo.

'He wanted to be more involved on that side – maybe he was already thinking of coaching even at that early age. He wanted more of an input into what was happening. It didn't bother the rest of us – we just trained, turned up on Saturday, played, and that was our way of life. Pej wanted something different. He never put the ball away – even when you were relaxing, the game was always on his mind and he was constantly talking about it. The game was always uppermost in his mind. In the end that led to conflicts with Waddo.'

The group dynamic that emerges is that of a typical football team of any level – or indeed any disparate group of human beings thrown together by circumstance. A mix of personalities, some inward-looking, some extrovert. Some full of confidence, others beset by doubt. Some fond of the social life, others quieter family men. Some happy to go with the flow, others impatient to make things happen. Cliques, friendships, alliances, small rivalries and jealousies. None of this is specific to footballers. We can all recognise the picture.

A little creative tension is not always a bad thing. And team spirit was good. The confidence engendered by the great run at the end of the previous season had been carried through the summer to the start of the next. The programme of pre-season friendlies had yielded encouraging results. A 2-0 away win against Monaco was the first test of fitness after all that running in the Trentham Hills. It was followed by a run-out against Third Division Blackburn, where Salmons scored in a 1-0 win. Then came a two-match tour of Belgium, where Stoke beat Second Division Turnhout 5-0 with a Ritchie hat-trick, but lost the second game at First Division Mechelen by the only goal.

Spirits were high. The only worry was an injury to Alan Bloor, who had slipped and fallen awkwardly in the Turnhout game, and had a swollen knee. It soon became clear that the injury was more serious than first thought – a torn tendon that would sideline Bloor for some time. In fact, it was to rule him out for virtually the entire season.

Although they could ill afford to lose one of the pillars of their defence, the team as a whole was clearly getting better. Hudson had made a big difference, but others had responded and raised their game, and in Geoff Salmons they now had the effective left-sided attacker they had been lacking before. The team was 20/1 for the title. There was a palpable air of optimism around the Victoria Ground and among the fan base, so much so that manager Waddington felt the need to caution players and fans that success was far from guaranteed.

'Last season was the toughest First Division I have known,' he told the *Sentinel*. 'It will be harder this time. There must be no complacency. What we want to do this season is to merit the things that have been said about us. But although we obviously want to be at the top, it is going to be very hard.

'One or two people might think with the squad we have now, we just have to go out there and start winning. No one gave us anything last season and it is going to be just the same this time. Clubs have spent a lot of money this summer strengthening their teams, and we are going to find this another hard campaign.'

Still, everything seemed to be in place for a strong showing. Just as well: first up were the reigning champions, the still-mighty Leeds United. It was a tough opening fixture – but a good test of whether the wave of optimism running through the club would be justified when the referee blew his whistle at three o'clock on Saturday, 17 August 1974.

9

AUGUST

THE LEEDS United team that came to Stoke for the season opener was a very different proposition from the one that had taken part in that epic encounter almost exactly six months earlier. That first game had seen Stoke put an end to the great 29-match unbeaten run of Don Revie's men, but it had proved only a hiccup in their serene march to the title. They won it by five points from Liverpool and 14 from third-placed Derby County – large margins at a time when a win was worth only two points.

But just six weeks before the start of the new season, the Revie era had come to an end. After 13 years he had left the club to manage the England team, and Leeds had stunned everyone by installing Brian Clough in his stead. Clough had already mirrored some of Revie's achievements while he was at Derby, hauling them out of the Second Division and propelling them to the First Division title in 1972. In the process he had transformed himself from a young, brash, ambitious but little-known newcomer into a top-ranked manager whose motormouth had given him a reputation for straight talking and attracting controversy. He was also, very evidently, a winner. After a long-running battle with the Derby board, Clough and his partner Peter Taylor had left the club in October 1973, but were soon back in business at Brighton and Hove Albion. They were still bedding in there when Leeds came calling.

It was hard to understand why Clough would be at the top of the Leeds shopping list after the departure of Revie. Nor was it easy to grasp why Clough would want to join a club he had so frequently disparaged and indeed insulted. No one had been more critical than him of the way Leeds played, and of Revie personally. He had accused Leeds of cheating and foul play. He had called them the dirtiest and most cynical team in the country. He had publicly advocated demoting them to the Second Division because of their disciplinary record. He had accused Revie of encouraging unsporting behaviour. And besides, he was only a few months into his contract with Brighton.

But Leeds were determined to have him, and, whatever his motives, he was ready to accept – although Taylor elected to stay on the south coast. The deal was done amid much acrimony, with Brighton claiming that Leeds had reneged on a gentleman's agreement to compensate them for the loss of their manager. When he arrived at Elland Road, Clough found a group of players unprepared to forgive and forget his persistent criticisms of them. He walked into a dressing room seething with what he later described as 'dislike and resentment, if not downright hatred'. Typically, he did not moderate his views or seek to make his peace with his new charges. During an early training session, he told the players they could throw all their medals in the bin because they had not been won fairly. It was not an approach calculated to win over such decorated and battle-hardened veterans as Billy Bremner and Johnny Giles.

Both Bremner and Giles were in the line-up at Stoke for Clough's opening match as Leeds manager. Bremner had yet to begin a three-match suspension imposed after the Charity

Shield match at Wembley, when both he and Kevin Keegan had been sent off for fighting. But suspensions had robbed Leeds of two other key players in Norman Hunter and Allan Clarke. In Clarke's place they fielded Duncan McKenzie, signed by Clough from Nottingham Forest for £250,000 within three weeks of his arrival.

There was plenty of hype attached to the game beyond the usual excitement surrounding the opening fixture of the season. Everyone was eager to see what Clough's Leeds would look like. And there was some residual needle between the two teams from several muscular previous encounters, culminating in the game in February that had finished with a good deal of ill temper on either side.

In spite of Clough's repudiation of the allegedly dirty tactics of the past, Stoke had no illusions about what to expect. 'There was always a lot of friction against Leeds,' says Alan Dodd. 'Cloughie said they were a dirty side, and that stemmed from Don Revie. They were instructed to play that way. Brian Clough said to Johnny Giles, "You've been gifted with a fantastic left foot, why do you have to use it to kick the shit out of your opponents?" And yet he was such a nice bloke off the pitch.'

Giles was not your typical enforcer. He was short of stature and a creative midfield strategist. But Mike Pejic also picked him out as a sly and destructive opponent, rather than fingering the usual suspects like Norman Hunter. As we saw in Chapter 2, Pejic reckoned Giles was among the more ruthless and cynical players in the league. Conroy confirms that his fellow Republic of Ireland international was affable enough off the pitch, but a tough proposition on it. But he also says Giles told him that Leeds never relished coming to Stoke. They knew they would get a hard game and no quarter would be given. Denis Smith agrees, 'When you were playing a team like Leeds, who were physical, then there was always a little bit of needle. And you would expect it. We'd got a lot of lads in our side who weren't going to be intimidated – and so had they. But they could play as well – that's what people forget about that great Leeds side: they could play, as well as sort people out.'

The scene was set, the television cameras were there, and as was customary for the first game of the season, even in Stoke-on-Trent, the teams kicked off in bright sunshine. Stoke fielded their usual back five, gave Salmons his first league start in midfield with Hudson and Mahoney, and had Haslegrave, Ritchie and Greenhoff up front.

First Division: Stoke City v Leeds United

In the circumstances, it is not surprising that the start is tense and cagey. Stoke get into their rhythm the quicker and force corners, one after a run by Haslegrave that takes him past three defenders. The better chances then fall to Leeds: Giles spots Farmer off his line at a free kick, but the keeper gets back to tip his lob over the bar. Then Lorimer dispossesses Hudson, and one of his trademark drives whistles just past the post. There is no one to meet a fizzing cross from Hudson at the other end, and when the playmaker puts Mahoney through, the Welshman mis-kicks. Leeds are playing with more confidence now, with Giles pulling the strings, and Stoke are fortunate to keep their goal intact. Farmer twice smothers close-range efforts by Madeley, and Salmons heads a cross out for a corner. The best chance of the half, though, falls to Stoke. Marsh finds Greenhoff in space, but Reaney gets back to clear his shot off the line.

The pattern changes five minutes into the second half. Hudson collects the ball deep and carries it well into the Leeds half, looking for options. He plays it into the feet of Ritchie, who lays it off first time to Mahoney. Bremner tries to close him down, but Mahoney emerges from their collision with the ball at his feet. From the edge of the box, he sends a powerful, left-footed drive past Harvey from all of 20 yards. The goalkeeper barely moves – it looks as though he thinks the shot is going wide. Instead, it flies into the top corner. It is the first goal of the season, and it is a corker.

The champions storm back, with Farmer punching clear, then tipping over a Madeley shot. McQueen is only just wide from the corner. Leeds are now operating at full throttle, and a stretched Stoke defence looks shaken by the ferocity of the counter-attack. McKenzie is played in by Lorimer only five yards out, but the ball gets stuck in his feet and Farmer collects. Gradually they weather the pressure, and Salmons starts moves that threaten at the other end. He shoots just over. A long punt by Farmer is nodded on by Ritchie to Greenhoff who returns the ball as Ritchie continues his run. Harvey advances and Ritchie tries to chip him, but the goalkeeper makes just enough contact to send it over the bar.

Now it is Stoke who are looking the sharper, but they still have only a slender lead when, in the final few minutes, the match swings decisively in their favour. Some interplay in midfield ends with Pejic playing the ball forward to the edge of the penalty area. Haslegrave knocks it across into the path of Greenhoff, who steadies himself and shoots. Harvey shapes to dive to his right, but the ball takes a big deflection off Trevor Cherry and nestles in the opposite corner of the net.

With Leeds now chasing the game, Hudson picks the pocket of Madeley in the Stoke half and advances at speed towards the Leeds goal. Ritchie goes with him and Hudson slips the ball to him on the edge of the box. The pass is a tad short, but Ritchie adjusts, takes one touch, and riding Cherry's tackle, slips the ball under Harvey. Cue Big John's trademark double-fisted goal salute to put the icing on a highly satisfactory first performance.

Second-half highlights can still be viewed online, followed by an interview with Brian Clough. He is characteristically bullish, even after a 3-0 defeat. We missed a lot of goals, he says. We dominated 80 per cent of the game. We could have been 3-0 up at half-time. We had a spell in the second half when Stoke didn't touch it for ten minutes. Then, he acknowledges, 'We fell apart a little bit. We got whacked.' He reports that his players' heads are down on the floor, but he has reassured them that all is well. 'I said, "If you play like that, you'll not only win the league, you'll walk it."'

Stoke have the more reason to be pleased. They are not three goals better, but an emphatic victory against the reigning champions in front of a big home crowd is a good way to get your season up and running. Hudson says it gave them all a real boost, 'Leeds were not the same team – Bremner and Giles were getting on a bit. But that was the game when we realised we were going to have a good season. We outplayed them.'

The supporters are buzzing too, as well they might be. Their team seems to have started the season with confidence and self-belief, rather than discovering it only halfway through when it is too late to mount a challenge. Salmons comes through his debut in credit, starting quietly but coming into the game more as time passes. He has shown himself willing to do defensive donkey work, and his in-swinging corners from the right carry real menace. There are plaudits for most of the team – Haslegrave for his speed, Hudson for his probing, Greenhoff for his trademark darting runs, Dodd for his cool handling of new boy McKenzie. Mahoney's cracking goal has set them on their way. But Waddington is not to be carried away. 'We have to prove that we can put it together away from home,' he says. It will be only three days before they get the chance to try, in a tough away fixture at Everton.

Excellent though it is, Stoke's win is not the best of the day – Manchester City put four past West Ham at Maine Road.

Nor is it the most eye-catching: in their first-ever game in the top division, Carlisle United make the long journey home from London celebrating a 2-0 win at Chelsea. Carlisle's odds of winning the title are slashed from 200/1 to 33/1. Stoke's narrow too, to 8/1, making them fourth favourites behind Liverpool, who open with a win at Luton Town.

Stoke City 3 (Mahoney 50; Greenhoff 85; Ritchie 87)
Leeds United 0
Attendance: 33,534
Highlights available online

UNSUNG HERO: MY TEAM-MATE JOHN MAHONEY

TERRY CONROY: 'For a couple of years, Josh was the best midfield player in the country without a shadow of a doubt. His energy levels were colossal. Right foot, left foot – he would just do the simple things, but the main thing was this terrier-like aggression and ball winning. He could run all day, and he was an unsung hero. Others would take the plaudits, but everybody knew that John was the engine of the side, he was colossal.'

ERIC SKEELS: 'Very good worker, a grafter a bit like me. He was robust, a very good player to have in your team, a good ball-winner. He was two-footed as I found when I played against him in training! He could go either way.'

DENIS SMITH: 'Josh had a great shot in either foot and often scored from the edge of the box. I remember him for his hard work and defensive qualities. He could run for fun – but sensible running, an intelligent player.'

ALAN HUDSON: 'John "Josh" Mahoney is one of the strangest individuals I have come across on my travels, if only for his outlook on the game on a day-to-day basis. If you were to watch him in training, you'd wonder how he became a professional footballer. It seemed there was always a problem with one thing or another. Then you'd start a running exercise and he looked like he could hardly lift a leg. He was useless all week, in training, he wasn't interested. He was the worst player in training, the worst player in all the five-a-sides and you'd think he'd never played the game until Saturday came. But come Saturday afternoon, this complete stranger became your best friend as he dug into the opposition like a Welsh terrier. John Mahoney was fantastic for me. He was a tremendous ally and I think Tony kind of pieced that together. I'm a lover of the unsung heroes, and John Mahoney never got the credit he deserved. He played to his strengths, never trying anything elaborate, always putting the team first.'

ALAN DODD: 'A perfect partner for Huddy. He'd run all day and make sliding tackles all over the pitch – they were the ideal combination. He was a right joker and everybody's mate. Always taking the mickey, never too serious.'

The fixture list now paired Stoke and Everton for home and away games within eight days of each other, the first meeting being at Goodison Park. Everton were a tough proposition, though no longer the force they had been four years earlier when they had swept to the league title by a whopping nine points. Of their great midfield engine room, nicknamed the 'Holy Trinity', only Colin Harvey survived. Alan Ball had been sold to Arsenal in 1971 and Howard Kendall to Birmingham City in early 1974 as part of a deal that brought striker Bob Latchford to Everton. His £350,000 fee was a new record. Their form had slumped in the three seasons after winning the title, but in 1973/74 they had shown signs of recovery and finished seventh. The addition of Latchford suggested they might do better still in the new season, although their campaign had started with a goalless draw at home to Derby.

First Division: Everton v Stoke City

Stoke have Geoff Hurst in for John Ritchie, who is struggling with a thigh strain after the Leeds game. With the twin targets of Latchford and Joe Royle to aim at, Everton begin with an aerial attack that Farmer and Smith do well to repel. Stoke counter, with Dodd just failing to score a rare goal when heading narrowly wide from a corner, and Hurst taking the ball away from Lawson in the Everton goal only to send his lob just past the post. With just over a quarter of an hour on the clock, Greenhoff finds Haslegrave, and his first-time cross is flicked across goal by Hurst. Salmons charges up to head his first goal for the club.

Stoke seem to have the game well under control until the first of two self-inflicted wounds, after half an hour. An Everton corner causes chaos in the box with first Smith, then Dodd and finally Hudson all trying to hoof the ball to safety. When the dust settles, the referee is pointing to the penalty spot. It isn't entirely clear why, although it appears the offender is Hudson, who is adjudged to have pushed Steve Seargeant. Up steps Joe Royle to send Farmer the wrong way from the spot, and the game is level.

The goal seems to disrupt Stoke's fluency, and they are never able to exert the same kind of control again. Smith is involved in chances at both ends, first seeing a header well saved and then clearing off his own line. Perhaps the best opening falls to Conroy, on as a substitute for Greenhoff. He combines with Hurst to create a good opportunity with Lawson stranded, but can only send his lob straight into the goalkeeper's grasp.

A few minutes later, another self-destructive moment gifts Everton the winner. Pejic tries to chest the ball back to Farmer, but he misjudges the pace and distance, and the ball falls short. Royle is quick to pounce, sending a shot goalwards. As Smith struggles to clear it off the line, Royle follows through to knock it home.

Sent upfield for the last quarter of an hour, Smith twice comes close to securing an equaliser, a fierce half-volley just clearing the bar from close range and then a header drawing a top-class save from Lawson. But there are to be no more goals. It is a bitterly disappointing end to a game that began so promisingly for Stoke, the manner of the goals particularly galling. The Potters come away from Goodison with a strong sense of one point dropped, if not two, an opportunity missed, and a determination to make amends in the reverse fixture a week hence.

Everton 2 (Royle 30 pen, 73) Stoke City 1 (Salmons 17)
Attendance: 35,817

Sandwiched in between those games was a visit to Queens Park Rangers on the Saturday. Rangers had got off to a good start with three points from two away matches. They drew with Sheffield United and then inflicted a second successive defeat on Brian Clough, with a 1-0 win over Leeds. It was only QPR's second season in the First Division after promotion in 1973, the first having seen them finish in a very respectable eighth place. With the likes of Dave Thomas, Terry Venables, Gerry Francis and Stan Bowles in their ranks, they were already promising to perform strongly again.

Bowles was back from suspension for the Stoke game, although Venables was injured. For Stoke, Ritchie played in the reserves while working back to full fitness, and Hurst kept his place in an unchanged line-up. Denis Smith was making his 200th league start.

First Division: Queens Park Rangers v Stoke City

QPR are quickest out of the blocks when Givens leaves Dodd in his wake and unleashes a powerful left-foot drive that Farmer does well to tip over. The goalkeeper is then wrong-footed by a deflection, but the ball drifts past the post. Thomas crosses from the right and Bowles gets above Smith at the far post but heads wide.

When Stoke begin to counter, Mancini has a lucky break when heading a Salmons cross over his own bar without much idea of where the ball is. A succession of corners follows. It is the wingers who are causing most of the trouble – QPR's Thomas and Stoke's Haslegrave, who nearly scores with a fierce shot on the turn that is deflected just over the bar. By half-time it is still Rangers doing most of the attacking, and they pick up where they left off in the second period: Francis and Thomas combining to force a corner, and then Francis putting in Bowles, who hits the post. Gillard has two good efforts blocked. A rare Stoke foray upfield sees Salmons feed Pejic, but the full-back's shot hits the side netting. There is another brief respite when Rangers are stretched by a crossfield move. Marsh finds Hurst at the far post and he heads down for Salmons, whose shot hits Mancini and goes for a corner.

As the pace begins to slow, a draw seems the most likely result. Stoke certainly seem to have settled for that when, with less than five minutes remaining, the ball is moved out of defence to Salmons on the left. If you watch this move online, where it is still available to view, you get a sense of what players mean when they talk about Salmons's ability to skim across the turf with the ball at his feet and cross it without any diminution of pace. This time his near-post cross is met with perfect timing by Hurst, who finishes with a cushioned volley from close range. It is a classic piece of Hurst poaching, showing all his experience and his instinct for ending up in the right place at exactly the right time.

A second goal almost follows at once with Hurst again involved, back-heading to Greenhoff who shoots straight at Parkes. Dodd and Salmons then need to weigh in with a couple of late clearances as Stoke see the game out.

Hudson remembers the winning goal, and he too sees it as the result of Hurst's long experience, 'Sammy was a great outlet as a midfield player because he'd run anybody. He just ran it down the left and put a great cross in for Hurst to score. Great finish. That was his experience. Another player would have gone to the far post. Hurst knew exactly where Sammy was going to sling it and Sammy knew that Hurst was making his way.'

After repelling so many home attacks and then nicking the game with a late goal, Stoke find themselves coming in for criticism for negative and dull play – not an accusation that was often levelled against them in this period. There has been a hint of Waddington's Wall in the way they mounted a defensive siege to repel QPR's eager strike force – perhaps a reaction to the Everton experience. The cover is well organised, first-time clearances snuffing out danger. They do not even allow themselves to be distracted by the fact that QPR field two number nines in the first half, Givens and Beck both wearing the same number on their shirts. But they have probably played better in defeat at Everton than they have in winning here. QPR boss Gordon Jago reports, 'We are a very sick camp.'

Hudson, who sports a new close-cropped hairstyle for the game, acknowledges that it wasn't pretty, 'That was a very tough game. I don't think we deserved to win – we were on the back foot. But the way we won that game was pleasing.' Indeed it was. An away win against spirited opposition, if somewhat dourly achieved, is some compensation for having subsided against Everton, and it puts the show back on the road. And Salmons is continuing to catch the eye, with new England manager Don Revie saying he is watching him, and would have tried to sign him had he stayed on at Leeds.

Across London, Everton warm up for the return fixture at Stoke with a 3-2 win at West Ham. Liverpool also win again, the appointment of Bob Paisley to replace the legendary Bill Shankly seemingly doing little to disrupt their momentum. Brian Clough finally gets off the mark at Leeds with a 1-0 home win over Birmingham. And Carlisle steal the show once again: having won at Middlesbrough in midweek, they see off Spurs at home 1-0 and have now won all three of their first games in the First Division to sit atop the table.

QPR 0 Stoke City 1 (Hurst 86)
Attendance: 21,117
Highlights available online

ROLE MODEL: MY TEAM-MATE GEOFF HURST

ALAN HUDSON: 'Geoff Hurst was a master of his trade. He never stopped working on all the things that got him that hat-trick at Wembley on that monumental day. He never changed a thing in his game, because he knew that they were the things that made him famous. He would show for you, and you couldn't help but pick him out, but if it wasn't possible, he would dip and off he'd go making it as difficult as possible for his marker.'

TONY WADDINGTON: 'He had a supreme natural temperament. He was fully in control of his mental pressures. He never allowed a missed pass or goal to affect his approach. He was able to keep his standards on a level plane, and consistency was his strength.'

ALAN DODD: 'I can't believe we signed him really – a World Cup winner who'd scored three goals in the final. Hurst was a class player, and when he was younger he was one of the best players in the world.'

DENIS SMITH: 'Top pro. His standards – you realised when you worked with him why he got to the top, the way everything was done in the right manner. A total professional. He was a gentleman as well. He did everything right – a good example round the dressing room. You couldn't criticise anything – he turned up on time, did his job, worked – if you want to look at an example of how to conduct yourself – look at Geoff.

'He could score – perhaps he was just past his best by the time he came to us, but he was still good. He could hold it up. He attacked the near post – that was his thing, especially at West Ham. He would pull away and then come back across you at the front. He said the only reason he signed for Stoke was so he wouldn't get kicked by me any more.

'The one time I got attacked by a supporter was at West Ham: coming off at half-time a woman hit me over the head with an umbrella saying, "Leave my Geoffrey alone!"

'His movement was excellent. He was always trying to get out of line of sight so he could then move – pull away from you or come across you. You were forever checking your shoulder when Geoff was about. You didn't want him on your shoulder. You wanted him in front of you.'

TERRY CONROY: 'Stoke was a change for him because he'd had this understanding with Martin Peters at West Ham for many years and he came to a different system where maybe he would have been required to get more involved in the build-up. At West Ham he was the target man. It was a different role, but he did well at Stoke and his goal tally was a good return. A lot of people looked up to him because of his record. Geoff was modest and there was never a time when he sat down and said "this is how to do it" – like Banksy as well, they were modest people who just got on with doing what they were good at. There was a happy blend within the squad.'

GEOFF SALMONS: 'Great goalscoring touch, both feet. And head. I put a few on his head. When Geoff had his pub, me and Val used to go and work there one day a week – and I went on from that into the pub trade.'

ERIC SKEELS: 'He had probably lost a yard or two but he was still a fabulous player. I got to know him well – we'd go out together with our wives. John Ritchie was robust, Hursty was more clever. They were different types of player. He had to get used to playing with a new team [after so long at West Ham]. Sometimes I might play a ball in a gap and he'd gone the other way. But he always wanted to score goals. He read the game very well. A good influence in the dressing room. The younger players would watch him, to see how he behaved. He was older than a lot of the team – we had some youngsters coming through and they looked up to him. I did too. I used to knock about with him, but I still admired him.'

John Ritchie had proved his fitness by scoring four for the reserves, and he came back into the team for the resumption of hostilities with Everton. But Waddington sent shockwaves running through the fans by recalling him at the expense of Greenhoff. Partnering Ritchie and Hurst up front was seen as a sign that Waddington expected another tight and difficult game in which strength and power would be needed. But it was the first time he had dropped Greenhoff in the striker's five years at the club, and it set tongues wagging at a furious pace. It was the only change for either side from the first encounter. Everton had followed up the purchase of Latchford with a further sign of their ambition, spending another £300,000 on Burnley midfielder Martin Dobson. But the paperwork was not completed in time for Dobson to feature in the game.

First Division: Stoke City v Everton

Don Revie is in the crowd, and Hudson surely impresses him with another display of control, awareness and probing passing. The England manager also sees Pejic and Smith perform strongly. Stoke have the more flair in midfield, but Everton more than match them in most other departments – hard running, hard tackling and good organisation at the back.

Salmons is again involved in some strong bursts down the left, with Ritchie heading one of his crosses just wide, not long after Hudson has powered a 25-yarder only a few inches the wrong side of the post. Latchford comes close for Everton before Hudson twice puts in Ritchie, but his first shot is deflected and Lawson saves the other. It's an entertaining, high-octane contest, but at the interval the crowd is still waiting for the first goal.

It comes early in the second half, and it is Everton who go ahead. Latchford muscles past Dodd to bury a powerful header from a free kick. Farmer gets a hand to it but cannot keep it out. Latchford nearly repeats the trick later, but this time Farmer makes a great save, pushing another tremendous header over the bar.

John Mahoney is not best known for his goalscoring, but with 15 minutes left he is on target for the second time in four games. It is another header, the Welshman diving to head Haslegrave's cross from the right past Lawson. Stoke finish the stronger, with Haslegrave and Conroy both missing good chances. Once again though, the Everton defence holds firm and their impressive start to the season continues as they return to Merseyside with a point. The Hurst-Ritchie combination, showing a preference for power over the subtlety and precision offered by Greenhoff, does not really come off.

Stoke City 1 (Mahoney 75) Everton 1 (Latchford 53)
Attendance: 27,594

If Stoke had found the Everton defence difficult to break down across 180 minutes, they could expect little respite when Middlesbrough came to town. Boro were in the hands of World Cup winner Jack Charlton, who had moved straight into management on his retirement as a player with Leeds United, after more than 20 years and 600 games. The terms of his deal, agreed on his 38th birthday, gave some indication of his character and interests, and pointed to a hinterland lacking in so many men of football. He refused a contract and took a salary that was much lower than he might have commanded, but stipulated that there must be no interference from the board in team selection, and that he would have three days a week off for his hobbies of fishing and shooting. He later chose a fishing rod as his luxury when appearing on *Desert Island Discs*.

It was not an orthodox approach but it seemed to work. In his first season at Ayresome Park, Middlesbrough cantered to the Second Division title by 15 points. Charlton became the first manager outside the First Division to be named Manager of the Year.

Four games into the new season, Boro had already shown signs that they were well capable of handling life in the top tier, with two wins – both of them away from home – a draw and a single defeat behind them. Charlton had put together a physically imposing side in his own image, with bite and drive offered in midfield by a young Graeme Souness. Speaking ahead of the game, Charlton relished the prospect of the midfield contest between Souness and Hudson. 'If I had had the money at the time, I would have gone for Alan Hudson,' he said. 'It is going to be interesting to see how Hudson fares against Souness, who is no slouch these days. This match is going to be a real test for us, they are a very fine side.' It was clear that he meant to neutralise the Stoke threat with some robust defensive play.

Tony Waddington had meanwhile been dealing with the fall-out of his decision to drop the fans' favourite Jimmy Greenhoff for the previous game. 'There is no question of Greenhoff not having a future here,' he insisted. 'Certain games demand different combinations, and players have to appreciate that they have got to do well to keep their place.' He was not the first manager to have peddled such an argument, and he certainly wouldn't be the last. In an implicit admission that the combination of Hurst and Ritchie had not paid off though, he restored Greenhoff to the starting line-up – the only change from midweek.

First Division: Stoke City v Middlesbrough

The early exchanges are muscular but largely uneventful, although Hudson is again an influential presence and Salmons continues to impress more with every outing. But there are few chances until Stoke are awarded a penalty after 17 minutes. At first sight (and you can judge for yourself by watching it online), the decision looks a bit harsh. Hudson plays the ball forward from midfield and then sets off for the right of the penalty area. Mahoney picks him out and Hudson seems to head the ball on to the arm of Stuart Boam. But the camera angle from behind the goal tells a different story: Boam clearly puts out his hand to stop the ball as Hudson threatens to pass him. The referee is in no doubt, and points immediately to the spot. Ritchie goes down the middle as Jim Platt dives to his right.

But the lead lasts no more than a couple of minutes as Boro counter. The ball falls to Souness 20 yards out and he hits a powerful drive with the outside of his right foot. Farmer gets a hand to it but can't stop it. Souness limps off as half-time approaches, with both sides having reasonable chances to score again.

The second half is equally tight with a dearth of clear chances. Just as against Everton, Stoke are finding it hard to break down a determined and well-organised defence, and are stifled by Middlesbrough's determination to limit Hudson's ability to find space. Another penalty appeal for handball is turned down, and strong runs from Hudson and Salmons come to nothing. There are chances for Foggon and Mills of Boro, and Salmons is only just wide with a good shot. But the story is again one of a frustrated Stoke attack battling ineffectually against Middlesbrough's imposing defence. A couple of times they are in danger of being caught on the break, but their despair is obvious, and the game ends in a draw.

Charlton is characteristically frank afterwards, 'We came to stop Stoke playing football. We had no option, otherwise they would have torn us apart.' The plan worked. Waddington admits as much, and feels his team gave up too soon. 'The trouble was, their equaliser came straight after our goal, otherwise the game might have been more open,' he says. 'I don't blame Middlesbrough. They could not hope to take us on at football, and it was up to us to find a way through. But our players were so frustrated that there was a period when they might have gained both points if they had put in enough pressure, but they were satisfied with the one point.'

Of Hudson's difficulties in escaping the close attentions of defenders intent on stopping him from playing, he is equally philosophical, 'Alan has the skill to sort this thing out. He wants the ball, so he has to retreat into our own penalty area to get it.'

Stoke City 1 (Ritchie 17 pen) Middlesbrough 1 (Souness 20)
Attendance: 23,484
Highlights available online

It has been a frantic start to the season, with all the clubs playing five matches in the space of just 15 days. Liverpool are the early pacesetters, their emphatic 3-0 win at Stamford Bridge leaving them with four wins and a draw. Their neighbours Everton, who beat Arsenal, are the only other unbeaten team. Another defeat for Leeds confirms that all is not well under the Clough regime. After their sensational start, Carlisle are showing signs of faltering. But they still lie handily in fifth, a point ahead of their next opponents: Stoke City.

	AUGUST 1974	*P*	*W*	*D*	*L*	*Pts*
1	Liverpool	5	4	1	0	9
2	Ipswich Town	5	4	0	1	8
3	Everton	5	3	2	0	8
4	Manchester City	5	4	0	1	8
5	Carlisle United	5	3	1	1	7
6	**Stoke City**	**5**	**2**	**2**	**1**	**6**
7	Middlesbrough	5	2	2	1	6
8	Wolverhampton Wanderers	5	2	2	1	6
9	Sheffield United	5	2	2	1	6
10	Derby County	5	1	3	1	5
11	Queens Park Rangers	5	1	3	1	5
12	Newcastle United	5	2	1	2	5
13	Chelsea	5	2	1	2	5
14	Arsenal	5	2	0	3	4
15	Leicester City	5	1	2	2	4
16	Burnley	5	1	1	3	3
17	West Ham United	5	1	1	3	3
18	Luton Town	5	0	3	2	3
19	Leeds United	5	1	1	3	3
20	Tottenham Hotspur	5	1	0	4	2
21	Birmingham City	5	0	2	3	2
22	Coventry City	5	0	2	3	2

SEPTEMBER

NO LESS a judge than Bill Shankly reportedly described Carlisle United's ascent from the lower reaches of the league to the First Division as 'the greatest feat in the history of the game'. The man responsible was Alan Ashman, a former player with the club who, on retirement in 1958, had gone off to run a poultry farm. Five years later, when Carlisle were facing relegation from the Third Division and were short of a manager, they persuaded Ashman to abandon his chickens and take on the job.

Carlisle were duly relegated, but Ashman brought them back up the following year. Twelve months later they were Third Division champions. Twelve months after that, they narrowly missed promotion to the First Division, having led the table for much of the season. Ashman went off to manage West Bromwich Albion, but he was back at Brunton Park in 1972, and this time he did get them into the top division.

There remained something appealingly amateurish and Corinthian about one of football's remoter outposts. Carlisle fans were used to the jokes about 'hicks from the sticks', and kick-offs being arranged to suit the demands of milking time.

They were now having the last laugh, and the city had a serious dose of First Division fever. No wonder. For the first few weeks they had been living in dreamland, opening with a win at Chelsea, and following it up with another, even more impressive victory at Middlesbrough. When they beat Spurs in their first home game, they were yet to concede a goal and stood at the pinnacle of English football. A home defeat in the return fixture against Middlesbrough had been followed with a point away at Leicester, and though they no longer topped the table by the time Stoke came to town, optimism and fervour were still running high.

Stoke, in common with most other teams in the division, were not sure what to expect after Carlisle's dynamic start. Even arriving at the ground was a new experience, as Alan Dodd recalls: 'Most the grounds we played were in the middle of cities, surrounded by terraced houses. We got there and it was surrounded by fields and cows. I couldn't believe it. It was surreal, like being on another planet.'

First Division: Carlisle United v Stoke City

When the game starts, it is Stoke who are soon producing the football that is out of this world. They put on an inspired show, prompted by what Alan Hudson will come to regard as one of his best performances. Hudson opens the scoring himself as early as the fifth minute after a sweeping crossfield move involving Salmons, Greenhoff, Haslegrave and Ritchie. It ends with Hudson holding off a challenge to slip the ball past the goalkeeper.

Stoke continue to make light of the wet and windy conditions, and Carlisle cannot cope with the midfield combination of Hudson, Salmons and Mahoney, with even Dodd venturing forward into attack. A second goal does not arrive until almost an hour of play, with Hudson again at the heart of it. He finds Greenhoff, who eludes his defender as he traps the ball and gets off a fierce shot. Goalkeeper Ross can only parry it, and Ritchie follows up to volley it home almost on the line. Ross then has to make good saves from Ritchie and Pejic. Further chances follow with Carlisle subsiding long before the end.

It is a clinical all-round display, the best of the season to date. Alan Ashman is impressed. 'I thought we were playing 14 men,' he says ruefully. 'Stoke were brilliant, the best side we have met this season and a good bet for the championship.' He reportedly tells Tony Waddington that Hudson's showing is the best 90 minutes he has seen from any player.

With a raft of tough fixtures coming up, no one is getting carried away. If there is a worry, it is about whether Stoke are sufficiently ruthless when they are in control of a game. In spite of their dominance, it has taken them an hour to get the important second goal, and their performance probably merits several more. A goal in each half is a poor return for their domination.

Still, spirits must have been high on the train home. When it reached Crewe, Hudson and Hurst stopped off for a meal with the manager before continuing their journey home to Stoke in Hudson's car. After dropping his team-mate off, Hudson swerved to avoid something running across the road and crashed into a hedge. He wasn't seriously hurt, but his hand was in a bad way, and he needed ten stitches in his forehead. He was ruled out of the next game, a League Cup tie with Halifax. More worrying still, he had to be considered doubtful for the prestige UEFA Cup meeting against all-conquering Ajax, now only ten days away.

Carlisle United 0 Stoke City 2 (Hudson 5; Ritchie 58)
Attendance: 14,507

Hudson's misfortune was Terry Conroy's opportunity for a place in the starting team after a couple of appearances as substitute. Conroy's career was dogged by knee injuries that kept him out for long periods, and eventually took the edge off the lightning speed that was one of his main attributes. Now he was ready to make his first senior start in almost a year. Hudson's injury was relatively minor, but Waddington was reluctant to risk him, 'The main problem is his cracked knuckle. He might fall on it during a game. This type of injury can take time to heal.'

Waddington also made a like-for-like tactical substitution, bringing Hurst in for Ritchie. Having been sent off during Stoke's previous European adventure two years earlier, Ritchie was ineligible for the forthcoming Ajax game. Waddington wanted to give Hurst a run of matches by way of preparation for Ajax.

League Cup: Stoke City v Halifax Town

In the meantime, George Eastham has been to watch Halifax, and warns that they will be no pushover. And it does indeed take Stoke almost until half-time to penetrate a determined defence. After many attacks, and one or two minor scares at the other end, it is Conroy who opens the scoring on his return, heading home a Haslegrave corner.

In the second half it is one-way traffic, and the same Haslegrave/Conroy combination leads to a second. Haslegrave's cross is headed upwards by a defender and Conroy gets in first to nod it home off the underside of the bar.

Four minutes later the Irishman is running on to a through ball from Salmons when he is brought down from behind. He takes the penalty himself to complete his first hat-trick for Stoke.

In a frantic last period in which Stoke are hunting more goals, Greenhoff almost bags a hat-trick himself. He scores from a Conroy pass, but Hurst is offside. Then he shoots straight at the keeper and finally hits the post.

Stoke City 3 (Conroy 42, 67, 71 pen) Halifax Town 0
Attendance: 17,805

Conroy's sensational return was elbowed out of the headlines by equally sensational news from Elland Road, as after a turbulent 44 days in charge, Brian Clough was sacked as Leeds United manager. In his six league matches, Leeds had won only once and were 19th in the table.

For a buoyant Stoke City though, it was the visit of Coventry City that required their immediate attention. It looked like a very winnable fixture. Coventry had spent the previous three seasons hovering around the relegation zone, and were now propping up the table with a return of only three draws from their first six outings. If Stoke were to mount a serious challenge for the title, this was the sort of game they should be winning comfortably – even given that everyone's thoughts were already jumping ahead to the big match against Ajax, now less than a week away.

First Division: Stoke City v Coventry City

For Coventry, Hudson is back, though clearly protecting his injured hand, and hat-trick maestro Terry Conroy returns to the bench. Having promised Geoff Hurst a run of games before Ajax, Waddington changes his mind and brings back Ritchie. Stoke seem to have absorbed the lessons of Everton and Middlesbrough, when they had sent too many speculative crosses into a wall of dominant defenders. This is more like the Carlisle showing, with a series of darting attacks and a good deal of patience as they wait for the Coventry defence to crack.

That patience is eventually rewarded on the hour, when the in-form Haslegrave rides a robust attempted tackle and carries the ball from one penalty area to the other. He finds Greenhoff, who draws the goalkeeper before squaring for Mahoney to tap in.

A second, 20 minutes later, is a special entry in the John Ritchie goals catalogue as the big centre-forward is first to a dipping ball from Greenhoff. He meets it cleanly on the volley and leaves the goalkeeper sprawling from 20 yards. A cracker. The defence is never under much threat, and although Coventry offer more tenacious and cannier defence than Carlisle, the result is the same. Conroy replaces a limping Salmons for the final 20 minutes.

This is a convincing performance and completes three wins in eight days with no goals conceded. The disappointing home draws against Everton and Middlesbrough are forgotten, and the team seems to be tuning up nicely for European action. Tony Waddington is pleased with the approach of his players, 'Last season we would have rushed at Coventry, looking for two or three goals and possibly left ourselves open at the back. Now the lads are keeping it tight at the back and refusing to panic, confident that eventually they will slot in the chances. This is what happened today.'

Elsewhere, Liverpool suffer their first defeat of the season at the hands of Manchester City, Everton draw again, but Ipswich make progress with a 4-1 win at Luton Town.

Stoke City 2 (Mahoney 59; Ritchie 84) Coventry City 0
Attendance: 22,482

With the Coventry game over, all attention could finally turn to the match against Ajax the following Wednesday. After the disappointment of Stoke's first foray into Europe, hopes were high of a better showing this time. But their opponents, Ajax of the Netherlands, were the aristocrats of European football. They had won the European Cup three times in a row from 1971, although they had since lost two of their best players in Johan Cruyff and Johan Neeskens, both sold to Barcelona. Against Stoke they were still able to field three of the players who had appeared in the World Cup Final against West Germany only three months earlier. Both Ajax and the Dutch national team typified 'Total Football' in which all outfield players could play with almost equal facility in any position.

Alan A'Court and George Eastham had been sent to watch them, and came back impressed after seeing them win a league game 3-1. Eastham had been particularly taken with Ruud Geels, 'He looks like an elderly professor, but he cracked in all three goals and is a tremendous striker.'

Eastham's report to Waddington was clear: 'They are going to make things difficult for us. They get men back in depth and run well off the ball. It is teamwork basically, and every man is skilful, and they are all prepared to work for each other. I am sure they can be beaten, for there were signs of a suspect defence. Their opponents could not put on the sort of pressure to confirm this, but Stoke on form could make things hot for them. It all boils down to the fact that we have to play at our best.'

In the same way, Ajax had been running the rule over Stoke. Their manager Hans Kraay admitted that a win would be a very good result for them. He had liked what he had seen of Salmons, Greenhoff, Smith and Hudson, who had been passed fit to play. Kraay had only been in the job for three months, and was already frustrated by fans who expected him to find instant replacements for their departed superstars. 'People back home expect us to produce another Cruyff, but that is not possible,' he said. 'There is only one Cruyff.' With an admirable grasp of Potteries cultural references, he added, 'To find another would be like looking for another Stanley Matthews.'

For the newspapers, the most impressive aspect of the Ajax preparations appeared to be that they had brought their own chef with them. In those days, this was seen as taking a professional approach to extreme, even ridiculous, lengths.

While not enjoying the culinary delights the chef prepared for them, the Dutch players relaxed by playing golf and taking a tour of the Wedgwood pottery factory.

The *Sentinel* saw the tie as a watershed moment, 'For Stoke it will be a match that will show just how close they are to being recognised as a major power in the game after their convincing start to the season. The players knitting into a successful squad have had their confidence boosted by three wins in a row.'

UEFA Cup: Stoke City v Ajax

The evening of Wednesday, 18 September 1974 was a cold and foggy one. There was a crowd of more than 37,000 packed into the Victoria Ground. I was one of them, a prey to pre-match excitement, a knot of nerves, and a fear that I was about to witness a footballing masterclass, and not in a good way as far as my team was concerned.

The two-legged tie against Ajax was chosen by Denis Smith as his 'Match of My Life' for Simon Lowe's book of that name. Here is Smith's account of that first encounter:

'Ajax might not have been able to field Cruyff or Neeskens in their line-up, but they certainly had a fair side. Ruud Krol and Arie Haan were wonderful midfielders and they also had the Muhren brothers as well. Arnold Muhren became more well known over here with his skills and superb left foot during spells at Ipswich Town and Manchester United. Up front, Johnny Rep was the golden boy of Dutch football. In goal they had international keeper Piet Schrijvers, so it was a top-quality side.

'Waddington was a magnificent publicist. In the build-up to the game, he revealed publicly that he'd had the opportunity to sign Johan Cruyff when he was just 19. The story ran that a pilot friend of his had seen Cruyff play while on a rest day having flown to Holland. Waddo had put a bid in, but then had realised that the work permit in existence at the time meant Cruyff could not join a British club. What a signing that would have been – though it could well have been another of Waddo's famous tall tales!

'We really wanted a two-goal lead to take to Amsterdam if possible, but we knew it would be very tough. The problem was we couldn't get the ball off Ajax. They were in charge for the vast majority of the first leg, and gave us a bit of a lesson in controlling an away game in Europe. They were clinical, played keep-ball and they got to the crowd. In attack, they played neat patterns and kept the ball away from us, looking to simply steal a single away goal, while in defence they used the most annoying spoiling tactic there is: the offside trap. Our crowd had rarely seen a team play like that, and they didn't particularly like it. Neither did we, but we were finding it difficult to do anything about it.

'Ajax moved forward with such pace and eventually, almost inevitably I suppose, a quick one-two between Rep and Krol saw some space open up and Krol hit this fantastic shot which zipped into the net past John Farmer.

'Huddy now claims we'd have beaten Ajax if he hadn't had that car smash, but they were so good that night, so much in control, that I'm not sure even a fully fit and firing Hudson would have made that much difference. He was much quieter than usual going forward, although we didn't create much as a team in the first hour to be honest. Dusvaba hardly left Greenhoff's side and kept Jimmy as quiet as anyone I ever saw.

'Finally with 15 minutes to go, we managed to get a foothold in the game. From a free kick, Mike Pejic hit a left-foot shot but it was touched against the post by Schrijvers. I'd been in the penalty area in case the ball was crossed and had followed in after the ball, so I lunged in to prod it over the line leaving my marker sprawled on the ground in the process.

'We did put them under some pressure after that with some early crosses into the box and plenty more set pieces, and they were looking to hang on to the draw. I should have had a hat-trick with the crosses we put in to be honest. Ajax didn't like that approach to the game, and we unsettled them a bit. But essentially they were in control that night, although we felt we now knew enough about them to give them a good game over in Holland.

'I was fairly battered and bruised after that match and had to have three stitches in a cut just below my eye which I'd done lunging in to score the goal. But I had loved the competitive nature of the game and the cut and thrust of European competition. It was football at the highest level.'

Tony Waddington was pleased at the way his team had turned the game around after being given the run-around for an hour. 'We were not making a game of it in the first half,' he said. 'Then we pushed up on them and we might have won in the end. They will have to come out at us now, and this game is far from over.' Jimmy Greenhoff agreed, 'Ajax think they are going to find it easy there, but if we can score an early goal, we could go on to win.'

'There' will be the Amsterdam Olympic Stadium. The venue for the return leg had been switched because the ground's capacity was double that of the Ajax stadium.

Stoke City 1 (Smith 76) Ajax 1 (Krol 38)
Attendance: 37,398

There was little time to sit and chew over the lessons of the Dutch experience. Two more severe league tests loomed, with away games against fellow pacesetters Liverpool and Ipswich. Only two points separated the three of them at the top of the table. Liverpool had also been in midweek European action, but had a much easier night than Stoke, strolling to an 11-0 win over the Norwegian amateurs Strømsgodset. Stoke had not won at Anfield since the two sides returned to the First Division, but their form was good and they had scored in every game so far.

First Division: Liverpool v Stoke City

In truth, Stoke never look much like turning round their dismal record at Anfield. They spend most of the first half under siege, only occasionally breaking out to offer sporadic threats of their own. The match is emphatically settled either side of half-time with three unanswered Liverpool goals.

The first has a touch of fortune about it as three players go up to try to get their heads to a Liverpool corner, only for the ball to hit Ritchie and drop gently into his own net. Farmer then has to make a good save before, on the stroke of the interval, Phil Boersma embarks on a speedy run that takes him past three defenders before he prods the ball home.

Stoke fare better in the second half, but the match is over as a contest once Steve Heighway has cut in from the left and powered a shot past Farmer. It is a sobering experience for the team after a run of wins and a strong showing against Ajax. But they can have no complaints. Ipswich win again, so Stoke lose valuable ground on both of their two principal rivals.

**Liverpool 3 (Ritchie og 42; Boersma 45; Heighway 55)
Stoke City 0**
Attendance: 51,423

The visit to Ipswich was only three days later, and Waddington took the team to Clacton-on-Sea to prepare. It was overcast and windy on the east coast, but he hoped the sea air would do them good. 'I am hoping the change of environment will benefit the lads,' he said. 'This is a game we need to do well in.'

Ipswich promised to be opponents just as doughty as Liverpool. They had won seven of their first eight, and gone six games without conceding a goal. As things turned out, it was not the ideal game for a Stoke bounce back.

First Division: Ipswich Town v Stoke City

At first, all goes well. Salmons has the Ipswich full-back George Burley on toast and inspires some good attacks, while the defence looks calm and well organised. A lot of refereeing decisions seem to be going against them, but they look set fair to get something from the game.

All that changes after 55 minutes, when Ritchie challenges for the ball with the powerful young Ipswich defender Kevin Beattie. Ritchie at once falls to the ground clutching his left leg below the knee and crying, 'It's broken.' The referee waves play on, but when Farmer is eventually able to boot the ball into touch, the trainers come on and Ritchie's suspicions are confirmed. He is stretchered off, and Jimmy Robertson comes on against his former club.

As Stoke attempt to regroup, Ipswich are quick to capitalise on the situation. When Pejic fails fully to clear a cross, Colin Viljoen marks his 300th appearance for Ipswich by picking it up and shooting home off a post.

The atmosphere is now turning ugly as Stoke, upset at the injury to Ritchie and incensed that some dubious challenges are still going unpunished, begin to lose their heads. Smith goes up for a corner leaving Dodd to cover for him. But Dodd is caught out by a massive clearance kick that seems likely to fall into the path of the Ipswich striker David Johnson. Dodd instinctively reaches up and handles the ball. He has already been booked, but it is probably a straight red anyway. He is sent off, Stoke are a man down, a goal down, have a badly injured team-mate and a burning sense of injustice.

It is not a good combination and Stoke's woes continue when Hamilton taps in after 70 minutes in spite of their appeals for offside. Five minutes later it is Whymark shooting home, with Stoke again complaining that he was standing in an offside position. Stoke have the last word, Salmons powering home a shot at the death – the first goal Ipswich have conceded at home all season. But the final whistle can hardly come soon enough.

Waddington is livid and threatens to report the referee for his handling of the match, 'There would seem reasonable grounds for feeling that we did not get a fair deal in this game. We are not blaming the defender for Ritchie's fracture, but a great many furious tackles were allowed to go unchecked and the game appeared to be heading on a collision course.'

The news on Ritchie himself is not good. The injury is a double fracture, worse than at first thought. He has had an operation to set a broken fibula and tibia. 'The injury is severe,' says Waddington. 'There are other complications that needed the surgeon's attention. It is very upsetting to everyone.'

Ritchie is in the same hospital that treated Peter Dobing, who had broken his leg at Portman Road four years earlier. He is visited by team-mates and said to be 'quite comfortable'. Kevin Beattie pleads his innocence, 'It was a 50-50 ball, but at the moment of impact the ball seemed to wedge between my leg and Ritchie's leg.'

Denis Smith is not so sure. 'It's a bad tackle to be honest. To say John was unhappy was an understatement. He came straight through him. Good player Beattie, but it was a bad tackle.' He admits that Stoke couldn't cope in the period that followed as they attempted to reshuffle.

Ipswich manager Bobby Robson is emollient, 'I am very sorry for Ritchie. It had been a great game up until that point, a real cat-and-mouse affair.'

The dismissed Alan Dodd recalls the whole episode with a degree of bemusement. 'I never kicked anyone in my life, and I got sent off!' he says. 'The first one, I pulled somebody's shirt and then the second one, I caught the ball like a goalkeeper. I was the last man in defence and if I hadn't caught the ball it would have gone to their centre-forward.

'We all went to see Ritchie in hospital the following day and the first thing he said to me was, "Who's been a naughty boy?"'

Ipswich Town 3 (Viljoen 59; Hamilton 70; Whymark 75)
Stoke City 1 (Salmons 90)
Attendance: 24,470

TARGET MAN: MY TEAM-MATE JOHN RITCHIE

ALAN HUDSON: 'A great target man. The header in the League Cup Final [that led to the winner] just about summed John Ritchie up. Conroy went down the left, he crossed the ball to the far post and Ritchie just stood back and let it hit his head right into Jimmy's path. That's great centre-forward play. He was the perfect foil for Jimmy and a big strong powerful front man in his own right.

'Ritchie and I didn't get on. He looked down on me. He didn't like me, I didn't like him, but it never affected us on the field. He didn't talk to me but that didn't bother me. He was a good player though he suffered with injury. He was strong, no one knocked him off the ball, he was great in the air. There is no doubt that John Ritchie will go down as one of the most popular all-time Stoke City forwards and I can only say he earned that. He had a good touch for a big man and was very deceiving on the floor. He was a right handful for any opposing centre-half.'

ERIC SKEELS: 'All he ever said to us was, "Get the ball to the line and get it into the middle and I'll be there waiting for it," and he generally was. He wasn't as skilful as Jimmy with the ball at his feet but he was a good centre-forward – he could play today. He wasn't frightened of going for the ball, he'd just say, "Put it in the middle and I'll be there." He and Jimmy had the knack of each knowing what the other would do – a great couple they were. When he broke his leg, we didn't really have anyone as good as that to fill the gap.'

TERRY CONROY: 'As John got older, he got better. He became more adept, his control got better, his positioning got better. I always said that he was at his peak by the time he had to finish because of the leg break. Up to then he was always a presence, but he had become a more all-round player.'

MIKE PEJIC: 'It seems strange that even a prolific striker could be underrated but that's definitely the case here. A great leader of the line, strong and awkward to handle. He got hold of the ball well with his back to play and was powerful, hard and brave enough to look after himself at a time when centre-backs could pretty much do whatever they wanted to strikers. In and around the area he'd be knocking defenders out of the way with his elbows and knees. His heading ability was superb and with that he drew opponents. He could either make space for himself or for others – and for a man who ended with a goal record of about one in two, he was really unselfish.'

ALAN DODD: 'He was one of my heroes when I was a Stoke supporter. He used to win everything in the air. In those days every ball was directed towards the centre-forward, and most of the time John would win the ball and he used to score some fantastic goals. After the League Cup Final he wasn't happy because he hadn't scored. You want your strikers to be a bit selfish, but I think that's going over the top!'

DENIS SMITH: 'Of players with that goalscorer's instinct, John was one of the best, if not the best, I ever came across. He was a big old-fashioned centre-forward. John could score every kind of goal. Left foot, right foot, head, on the run, tap-ins. Rockets from outside the box. He was the complete centre-forward. He was a right miserable bugger when he hadn't scored, and we always viewed that as a good thing. John was desperate to score, and he thrived on it. He needed goals, he wanted the headlines that came with them and we needed him to score them for us. We could win a game, but if he hadn't scored he wasn't happy – he was that obsessed with scoring. Totally single-minded. He wanted us to win and him to score. I could live with that. We missed him terribly when he had gone.'

TERRY CONROY: 'He was a miserable get, honest to God. Saturday night we all socialised – the lads, with wives and girlfriends, we'd meet up after the game probably six or eight couples having a drink together. You'd be in John's company and you'd had a great win that day and everybody would be happy and John would be sitting there with Shirley his wife, and he didn't take part in any of the celebrations because he hadn't scored. If he'd scored, he'd get the pipe out, talk to everybody, he'd be 100 per cent. But if he hadn't scored and someone made a comment to him he'd go "don't talk to me".'

JIMMY GREENHOFF: 'I was always glad when John scored on a Saturday. It meant that he would come into the dressing room on Monday with a cheery "good morning". If he didn't score, he'd never say anything. He could be a grumpy sod.'

Speculation immediately began as to whether Stoke would look for a striker to cover for Ritchie's absence. The name of Martin Chivers was inevitably mentioned. Tony Waddington made it clear he was in no hurry to make a move. 'We will see how things progress and take it from there,' he said. 'We are quite well off for forwards: we have experienced men in Geoff Hurst, Terry Conroy and Jimmy Robertson, and a promising youngster in Ian Moores.' Moores had come through the Stoke Schools and youth teams, and was close to a debut in the first team.

First Division: Stoke City v Derby County

Hurst returns to lead the line at home against Derby for his first league start in a month. He brings much-needed calm and experience to a team still angry and resentful about what had happened at Ipswich. The manager has told them to calm down. Dave Mackay's Derby arrive on the back of a 4-1 win over Chelsea, and having scored 20 goals in their last six games. Francis Lee – often courted by Tony Waddington – has proved a good buy, and so has Bruce Rioch, a £200,000 capture from Aston Villa. Lee, Kevin Hector and Roger Davies are scoring freely. Like Stoke, Derby have ten points. The Potters are unbeaten at home and are desperate to make up the ground they have lost to the leaders. They also want to recover their form and equilibrium ahead of the return leg against Ajax.

It makes for an entertaining game between two evenly matched sides, with plenty of enterprise and attack at both ends. Just before the half hour, Stoke take the lead when Pejic fires a free kick into the box and Hurst flicks it home. Stoke have the better of the exchanges thereafter, but Derby are never out of things. They get back on terms with 15 minutes left when Lee scrambles the ball home in a goalmouth melee. Stoke force a series of late corners and Pejic clips the bar, but a draw is a fair result in a free-flowing and entertaining game. Defeats for Liverpool and Ipswich mean that both sides are happy with a share of the points.

Stoke City 1 (Hurst 28) Derby County 1 (Lee 75)
Attendance: 23,589

	SEPTEMBER 1974	*P*	*W*	*D*	*L*	*Pts*
1	Ipswich Town	10	8	0	2	16
2	Manchester City	10	6	2	2	14
3	Liverpool	10	6	1	3	13
4	Everton	10	4	5	1	13
5	Sheffield United	10	5	3	2	13
6	Newcastle United	9	5	2	2	12
7	Middlesbrough	9	4	3	2	11
8	Derby County	10	3	5	2	11
9	**Stoke City**	**10**	**4**	**3**	**3**	**11**
10	Wolverhampton Wanderers	10	3	5	2	11
11	Carlisle United	10	4	2	4	10
12	West Ham United	10	4	1	5	9
13	Burnley	10	4	1	5	9
14	Birmingham City	10	3	2	5	8
15	Coventry City	10	2	4	4	8
16	Leicester City	9	2	3	4	7
17	Luton Town	10	1	5	4	7
18	Chelsea	10	2	3	5	7
19	Leeds United	9	2	2	5	6
20	Arsenal	9	2	2	5	6
21	Tottenham Hotspur	9	3	0	6	6
22	Queens Park Rangers	10	1	4	5	6

11

OCTOBER

FOUR DAYS after the Derby match came the biggest test of Stoke's European career to date. The team flew to Amsterdam on the last day of September accompanied by 1,500 fans – rather more than the 50 or so that Ajax had brought to the Victoria Ground. A surprise member of the party was Brian Clough, newly dismissed as manager of Leeds United. In a gesture of solidarity with his fellow manager, Tony Waddington had invited him along on the trip as his guest.

It was an act of generosity that Clough would not forget as his career subsequently rose from the ashes at Nottingham Forest, where he was to taste considerable European success himself.

The journey was not entirely uneventful. Hurst was nursing a bruised Achilles tendon and Smith, inevitably, had stitches in a cut on his face. But the main drama was provided by Geoff Salmons, who arrived at the airport without his passport. After some frantic calls to his home in Mexborough, the passport was put in a taxi and raced to Manchester Airport. It arrived too late to catch the flight, but Salmons had been given special dispensation to board and to enter the Netherlands at the other end. The passport arrived the following day.

Stoke made their base at a modern out-of-town hotel and passed the time before the game training at a sports complex nearby, going bowling and visiting the cinema. Waddington and George Eastham were busy talking up their chances. The manager expected the offside trap to be deployed once again by Ajax, but saw that as a moral victory for his team. 'It was a compliment to us that Ajax used these tactics, and of course the Dutch national side employed similar tactics in the World Cup.' Stoke were the underdogs, but Eastham believed that on the basis of the first leg they were more than capable of a surprise. 'I believe we have a fair chance of springing a shock result. Ajax were stretched at times and could easily have been beaten.' The Dutch press did not see it that way, regarding Ajax as unbeatable at home and the result as a foregone conclusion.

For the Stoke chairman, Albert Henshall, simply having progressed this far was its own reward. 'We have come a long way since I joined the board in those depressing Second Division days,' he says. 'We had no money, but a lot of hope. And here we are, playing the cream of Europe. Just to be playing here in Amsterdam is a great feeling and to beat Ajax would be another step forward. But the experience alone is worth it, whatever the result.'

Denis Smith takes up the story of the second leg, as recalled in *Match of My Life*: 'Waddo had sent Gordon Banks and George Eastham to watch Ajax in their intervening games so we knew exactly what to expect. Ajax had switched the game to the Olympic Stadium from their own Stadion De Meer, I think because they could accommodate more fans there. We felt it gave us more of a chance because it was effectively a neutral venue.

'Having been caught a bit at Stoke by their offside trap, we were now prepared for the way Ajax played, though we didn't expect them to rely so heavily on it at home. Waddo had taken it as a compliment that Ajax had chosen to play that way against us at Stoke as they were obviously worried at our attacking strength, so we felt they might be a bit overconfident at home and leave some gaps for us to exploit.

'The game got off to an explosive start when Pej and Van Santen were both booked after a squabble near the touchline. It was the usual Pej thing, he was always getting himself into trouble. He was very intense. Geoff Hurst got booked early on too, I think for protesting about having his shirt pulled. I was soon in the wars again. This time I needed two more stitches when I gashed my knee, but we soon settled down to play some good football.

'They always say you should aim to silence the home fans in away legs and that's exactly what we did. It was what Ajax had done to us. They had thought this game would be a walkover, but so far, we were the better side. The closest we came was when Josh Mahoney surged past three defenders, but had his run ended right on the edge of the area when he was about to shoot. He was stopped by a great tackle.

'After half-time, when they'd had a chance to regroup a bit, Ajax began to hit back. They were too good to be completely out of the game. Farmer made a flying save from Haan and saved point-blank from Mulder cutting in off the wing. But we were still giving as good as we got as the game got stretched a bit. Haslegrave brought a fine save from Schrijvers and then Jimmy Greenhoff swerved a 20-yarder just past the post.

'It was a really good game and Huddy, Sammy and Josh were getting the upper hand in midfield. They began to create panic in the Dutch defence as it became obvious that one goal would steal the game. But the best chances came late on. First Schrijvers had to scramble back on to his line to tip over a Greenhoff chip. Then after he had come on as a substitute, Terry Conroy got to the byline and curled a cross against the bar. We were so close, but nothing had quite dropped for us in their box.

'Then right at the death came the moment that so nearly won us the game. As we pressed forward and Ajax looked to defend their away-goal lead, the ball bobbled around their penalty area before falling to our other substitute, Jimmy Robertson. He was about six yards out and only had the keeper to beat. The ball fell really nicely to him on the half-volley, but he slipped slightly as he struck it and didn't get a full contact. His point-blank shot hit the flailing Schrijvers on the left boot and ricocheted to safety. We were inches from taking the lead. Only that outstretched boot saved them from defeat.

'Shortly after that, amid some last-minute scrambles in the penalty area, TC shot over from about eight yards with only the keeper to beat. It was agonising. We had so nearly got the goal that would have put us through and sent Ajax crashing to only their second-ever European home defeat. Their fans were whistling for the referee to blow for full time for about the last ten minutes, they were so worried.

'Afterwards I felt that we had done so well that although I was obviously disappointed that we had gone out of the competition on the away goal, we had proved a massive point that we could compete at the highest level. It was a shame that all most Stoke fans ever saw of the game was some very short TV highlights, which didn't do us justice at all as they showed just three or four missed chances rather than the domination of the game we'd had. I prefer to remember what Brian Clough said to us after the game, "It deserved to be the final. It was that good."

'Sometimes you don't know what you've done as a player, what you've achieved. You don't understand what it means to the fans, what they're feeling, whether it be good or bad. But that night we exceeded everybody's expectations and delighted ourselves and that fantastic band of travelling fans.'

Ajax 0 Stoke City 0
Aggregate 1-1; Ajax go through on away goals
Attendance: 29,000

Waddington was also full of praise for the travelling support, 'The fans were really tremendous. I was very proud of them all. I am only sorry we could not get the right result for them, although the lads tried hard enough.'

The first Ajax match had been followed by back-to-back league defeats, a broken leg and a sending-off. Tony Waddington was determined not to let that happen again after the disappointment of the second leg. The following Saturday's opponents would be Sheffield United, who had already beaten Liverpool and Ipswich and had made a strong start. The manager bemoaned the European exit but promised to bounce back, 'If Sheffield think our midweek match knocked the heart out of us, they will be disappointed. We played so well that the lads have been lifted.'

First Division: Stoke City v Sheffield United

Waddington makes Salmons captain for the day against his old club, and it is he who mounts the first serious threat on the Sheffield goal. There is plenty of action at both ends before Robertson makes a strong run into the box and is sent sprawling by Badger. It's a penalty, and as usual, Hurst lashes it as hard as he can. The goalkeeper makes a good save but can only watch as Hurst follows up to turn it home. After that it is end-to-end stuff again before Salmons floats a cross in to Hurst. He cannot quite control the ball but manages to touch it to Greenhoff, who stumbles but recovers to score.

The second half starts in much the same vein, with Hurst and Salmons both having good efforts. Just before the hour, Salmons swings in a corner from the right, Robertson's shot is blocked on the line and Smith thumps it home: 3-0. United keep trying, and Woodward brings a sensational save from Farmer, who catches the ball with a flying leap. Greenhoff and Hurst are both close again, but just as they seem to be comfortably in control, Sheffield United are awarded a penalty when Smith bundles over Woodward. Eddy knocks it in, and with ten minutes to go Stoke look anything but comfortable when Field rises above everyone to back-head a long free kick past Farmer and make it 3-2. Tempers boil over, and when Badger trips Pejic he is sent off. Stoke hold out for the win at the end of a bruising and breathless game.

The manager is happy enough with the points, less so at the way the game has deteriorated near the end. He tells his players they need to cool down, 'We became too involved in a situation that had been boiling up with a series of niggling incidents. The players were told before the start of the season to concentrate on football and not to get involved in any dissent. The way the game is going now, it is important they keep a cool head.'

Stoke City 3 (Hurst 15; Greenhoff 38; Smith 57) Sheffield United 2 (Eddy 65 pen, Field 79)
Attendance: 21,726

The next opportunity to display that coolness of temperament would be the midweek visit to Chelsea for a League Cup tie. Alan Hudson was looking forward to another encounter with his old club. In the two league games he had played against them since arriving at Stoke, he had finished on the winning side both times and scored the only goal in the second encounter. No doubt a source of further pleasure to him was the news that his old adversary Dave Sexton had been sacked as Chelsea's manager. Sexton had departed after three losses on the trot, and Chelsea were only a point from the bottom of the table. A new manager – and a good cup run – could be the tonic they needed.

The big public talking points of the week were not about Chelsea, however, but the second General Election of the year, to be held the day after the game.

215

League Cup: Chelsea v Stoke City

Stoke are quickly into their stride and are in front with only six minutes on the clock. A quickly taken Hudson free kick finds Greenhoff in space. His shot is parried by Phillips in the Chelsea goal, but only into the path of the advancing Jimmy Robertson, who gleefully bangs it in. The winger nearly has a second shortly afterwards, when he is on the end of a move involving Hudson and Salmons, but this time the goalkeeper makes the save.

After 22 minutes, Chelsea are controversially on level terms. Hutchinson tries a shot from fully 30 yards but the ball hits the underside of the bar, bounces down and is safely caught by Farmer. The linesman signals that the ball has crossed the line, and the goal is given. Farmer cannot believe it. 'There is a mark on the line where the ball dropped,' he insists afterwards. 'It would not have come back at the angle it did if it had been over the line first.'

After the break, Stoke make another quick strike when a cross from Greenhoff is met at the far post by Hurst, who chests it down and prods it home. But five minutes later Farmer and Hutchinson are again the protagonists as Chelsea equalise for a second time, again controversially. A Houseman free kick finds Chris Garland, whose back-header is palmed on to the post by Farmer. He tries to drop on the rebound but goalkeeper and ball are both bundled into the net by the flying Hutchinson. Farmer is kicked in the throat and knocked out. It is only when the teams kicked off again that he is sufficiently aware of events to realise that a goal has been scored.

Pejic certainly isn't happy about the manner of the goal, because he is immediately booked for a lunging tackle on Charlie Cooke. A reinvigorated Chelsea then have several good chances to take the lead – culminating in a point-blank shot from Houseman that the still-groggy Farmer does well to keep out. Marsh and Salmons come close for Stoke, but it is a draw, and an unwelcome replay for a side that has played a lot of games in a short space of time, and faces a long journey up to Tyneside the following day. Waddington thinks he sees signs of fatigue. 'Normally when we score twice away these days, we expect to win,' he says. 'The lads are feeling the effects of all the travelling lately.'

Chelsea 2 (Hutchinson 22, 52) Stoke City 2 (Robertson 6; Hurst 47)
Attendance: 19,953

If the players were tired, a tricky away trip to Newcastle was not the ideal prospect. The Magpies had just won 4-0 at QPR with Malcolm Macdonald bagging a hat-trick and warning Stoke that his team was hitting top form. The table bore him out: Newcastle had dropped only one point at home, had not failed to score in any game, and had not lost since the very start of the season. It was a fixture that would require Stoke to summon all their resilience and determination. Their chances were not helped by the debut of their ghastly new away strip of bright yellow shirts with a diagonal blue stripe, and sky-blue shorts. You can check it out online, and also see some of the goals from this game. Sunglasses are recommended.

First Division: Newcastle United v Stoke City

This time it is Newcastle who make the fast start, and they have already twice come close to scoring when the first goal arrives after only five minutes. Dodd concedes a corner and when it comes in, the in-form Macdonald heads against the bar. Cue an almighty goalmouth scramble that ends with Keeley scrambling the ball home.

The pounding of the Stoke goal only intensifies, with a rampant Macdonald being denied twice and thumping the bar with another effort from 30 yards. Farmer is constantly busy as Newcastle pour forward. But then, as so often happens, a goal comes from nowhere, completely against the run of play. Marsh floats a cross into the middle of the Newcastle box and Salmons guides a precise header past McFaul from 12 yards.

Salmons remembers this goal, and says Newcastle would not have been expecting an aerial threat from him. His friend John Tudor is playing on the opposing side. 'Tudor would have told them not to worry about me,' he says. 'He'd have told them, "He can't head the ball, Sammy." And I probably had my eyes shut.' I remind him that he had already scored with his head earlier in the season, a diving effort against Everton. 'Never! Did I? I bet my eyes were shut then, too.' He did actually have trouble heading. 'I couldn't head it. I was the worst in the world at heading the ball. I had a problem. It used to give me double vision if I headed it too much. They sent me to see a specialist.'

The reprieve his goal brings is a short one as the Newcastle siege resumes, with Macdonald again the chief threat. A powerful shot on the run is tipped round by Farmer, but when the corner comes in, Tudor is there to head home powerfully. Half an hour gone and the hosts are ahead again.

The pace does not relent in the second period, with Stoke gradually establishing a foothold, during which Hurst misses from close range after being set up by Hudson. Mahoney has already forced McFaul into a full-length save with one powerful, left-footed shot, and with half an hour to go he lets fly with another that beats the goalkeeper and goes in off the post. Although the pace never lets up, there is no more scoring and Stoke can feel well pleased with a hard-earned point.

Elsewhere, there are wins for Liverpool and Derby, and Chelsea notch up a morale-boosting victory against Spurs as they prepare for the League Cup replay at Stoke.

Newcastle United 2 (Keeley 5; Tudor 31) Stoke City 2 (Salmons 25; Mahoney 63)
Attendance: 38,228
Highlights available online

HAPPY-GO-LUCKY: MY TEAM-MATE GEOFF SALMONS

DENIS SMITH: 'He'd pick the ball up on the run and he'd go past people, he'd get balls in and they'd be quality balls. Sammy was very, very good and doesn't get a lot of mentions because he wasn't at Stoke that long.'

TERRY CONROY: 'Left-footed, scored a few goals and a great crosser of the ball. He was supposed to be the final piece in the puzzle to get us the title. That was the ambition. Sammy was very laid-back. If you had a team talk you didn't need to involve Sammy. Just give him the ball wide and let him go past the full-back and get it in. He had an educated left foot, a fantastic left foot. He wasn't serious about the game, he was just a happy-go-lucky individual. His ambitions lay elsewhere.'

ERIC SKEELS: 'He would run at you, knock the ball past you and he was off, spinning away. He'd be getting the ball across and he scored a few goals too. Although he was a left-winger it didn't mean he had to stay on the left-hand side all the time: if the ball was coming down the right he might be in the inside-left channel or moving into the box. For his size, he was quick over the first five or ten yards – like Stan. Before you realised it, he was gone past you. He was a strong lad – you couldn't knock him about. Incredible left foot. I don't think I ever saw him kick the ball with his right foot!'

ALAN HUDSON: 'This really was one of Waddington's shrewdest buys, a player of immense ability down the left-hand side, one you could give the ball to and let him get on with it. Sometimes he didn't think about the game enough, but if he had, he would not have done the things he did for the team. He had this wonderful self-belief in his ability to run at defenders, go past them and put in the perfect cross. A snip from Sheffield United and the player that Tony had been looking for to piece his jigsaw puzzle together.'

League Cup replay: Stoke City v Chelsea

The return against Chelsea is another barnstorming game, but this time Stoke have to fight hard to avoid going out. After Chelsea take a 21st-minute lead through the effervescent Britton, Stoke throw the kitchen sink at them, with virtually every outfield player having some sort of scoring attempt. With the minutes running out, Greenhoff pops up with a deft header from a Salmons cross to the far post and the tie goes to another replay. 'Pure, hard football,' is Waddington's enthusiastic reaction. 'What a fine advertisement for the game.' He wins the toss for the right to host the second replay a week later.

Stoke City 1 (Greenhoff 80) Chelsea 1 (Britton 21)
Attendance: 24,376

Saturday's game brought a welcome break from playing Chelsea. After the two League Cup encounters, the second replay was coming up and only a few days after that the two teams would meet in the league. A change of scene was offered by the home league fixture against Burnley, but once again, Stoke would need to lift themselves to face a team that was going well. Burnley had just had good wins against Manchester

City and Ipswich, and had nine victories from their last 11. That run had taken them a point above Stoke who had now dropped down to ninth, though still only three points behind the leaders.

First Division: Stoke City v Burnley

After a week of rain, the pitch is wet and heavy – just the sort Stoke like – and they almost go ahead in the opening minute when Greenhoff pounces on a loose ball. This is followed by efforts from Hudson, Hurst and Haslegrave, who is back in the team for the injured Robertson. The first goal, when it comes, is something of a collector's item, being scored by Jackie Marsh – his first in more than five years and only his second career goal for Stoke. What's more he scores it with his weaker left foot, finishing an intricate passing move involving Mahoney, Haslegrave, Hudson and finally Dodd, who finds Marsh. The full-back cuts inside a defender and drives the ball home.

After half an hour it is 2-0 when Hudson senses an opening from a free kick and takes it quickly to Hurst, who shoots home. After that Stoke are in full control of the game. Their energy levels seem to dip a little in the second half but they rally to finish strongly. Apart from a couple of sporadic forays, Burnley show little sign of their recent form and have nothing to offer by way of a sustained attacking threat. The crowd want more goals, but the heavy programme of fixtures is beginning to take its toll.

Stoke City 2 (Marsh 13; Hurst 30) Burnley 0
Attendance: 23,466

Next up was game number seven of this busy month and game number three of four against Chelsea. After two attempts their League Cup tie was still deadlocked, but it was about to be settled in the most emphatic fashion. The disquiet about

Stoke's inability to put games to bed when they were in control was banished, for the moment at least.

League Cup second replay: Stoke City v Chelsea

In the previous game it had taken Stoke 80 minutes to penetrate the Chelsea defence. Tonight it takes only two as a Pejic pass is flicked by Haslegrave into the path of Hurst who slots it home. Hurst is involved with the second only a few minutes later as he half hits a pass from Greenhoff and the ball falls to Smith who crashes it in with his left foot. Stoke are now rampant, with Salmons, Pejic and Hudson combining particularly effectively down the left. The pressure has to tell, and it does so as half-time approaches.

A Salmons free kick beats the goalkeeper and as the giant Micky Droy stoops to try to head it away for a corner, he succeeds only into planting it into his own net. There is almost a carbon copy a few minutes later when a Haslegrave cross causes further chaos, and this time it is Harris heading a second own goal.

The goal glut continues after the break as Salmons makes it 5-0 with a free kick that bends around the wall and is helped into the net by the hapless Phillips. Hurst makes it six when Haslegrave's shot is parried straight into his path. To Chelsea's credit, they keep coming forward and when Stoke take their foot off the pedal, there are late consolation goals for Hollins and Baldwin. But no one is complaining about a 6-2 scoreline, least of all the manager. 'This was the sort of match to send people away happy,' he says. 'Not just because Stoke won but because of what they had seen. It was a follow through from the football we have been playing lately. We must keep it going now.'

The win earns Stoke a fourth-round tie at Ipswich, and the chance to make amends for the disaster of their visit there the previous month.

Stoke City 6 (Hurst 2, 67; Smith 10; Droy og 37; Harris og 44; Salmons 62) Chelsea 2 (Hollins 80; Baldwin 84)
Attendance: 26,271

UNBELIEVABLE ATHLETE: MY TEAM-MATE ALAN DODD

TERRY CONROY: 'Doddy could have been the best centre-half in England if he'd wanted to be. It sounds strange – but he didn't want to be! He was quick – I know in training I was pretty quick, but I would never beat Doddy over a hundred yards, never. It was effortless to him – training was effortless, playing was effortless and if he had had that ambition, and his mindset had been, "I'm going to go for the top," he could have done. He had pace and skill – a good defender, good reader of the game. He was such a casual lad – a lovely lad. There was no one in the club would ever have a falling-out with Doddy. That was his nature. That precluded him from getting to the top, but he was happy doing what he did.

'He didn't believe in his own ability – that was something that held him back. There was no reason he shouldn't believe, because it was there for all to see. But he was just one of these lads who was a natural at doing what he did, and he probably didn't think it was anything special. So it was a confidence thing. If you sat down and talked to Doddy there would be two topics of conversation: building a wall or going to a pop concert. Not football. He could talk all day about people like Wishbone Ash and Peter Gabriel. Most of the lads wouldn't have known Wishbone Ash from Knotty Ash. But he never spoke about football. That was Doddy.'

DENIS SMITH: 'He was an unbelievable athlete. The problem with Doddy was that he didn't know how good he was. He had to be pushed and coerced into even thinking about it. He barely had any sense of desire to win. He was almost entirely opposite in personality to me. He was, however, a fabulously skilful player who read the game wonderfully well and played the ball out from the back superbly. He just didn't really believe in himself. It was a way of making a living for Doddy. It just so happened he was a very talented footballer. He would probably have been just as happy being a builder or plasterer.'

ALAN HUDSON: 'Doddy was one of the loveliest people you'll ever meet. A friend said to me, "Tell me the best four players who've never played for England," and I said, "The best player I ever saw that never played for England was Alan Dodd." If he'd have gone to Manchester United he'd have been in the England team every week. Not that he'd have wanted to be.

'When he came into the side, we were a different team. He was superb, absolutely superb. As good as any central defender I've ever seen anywhere. All he lacked was the belief in himself and to come forward with the ball. He had the ability to do that.'

ERIC SKEELS: 'He was a quiet bloke, didn't do a lot of talking. But he had a bit of Bobby Moore about him, good on the ball, read the game well, didn't do any shouting. I can't recall ever seeing him angry. Very calm – he looked the same when he came off the pitch as he had when he went on. He just seemed to be happy doing what he was doing. He looked as if he was in gear six or seven and wasn't interested in going up to nine or ten.'

Hudson's sparkling form was at last recognised by Don Revie, who called him into his squad for England's friendly against Czechoslovakia – one of six uncapped players. Perhaps Revie had been reading the views of Brian Clough, who had made a guest appearance at Jollees Cabaret Club in Stoke to help raise money for the Eric Skeels testimonial fund. Clough had lavished praise on the team and some of its stars. Of Hudson he said, 'I have never known a player work so hard as he did when he came to Stoke. He put his life in order, worked at his game and grafted like hell.' If Clough had his way, Denis Smith would be joining Hudson in the England squad. 'He is a superb player,' Clough told the audience, who were probably wondering when they were going to see the female impersonator Dick Emery, who was topping the bill. 'He is full of guts and honesty. If you took a consensus of opinion among managers in the game, Smith would be in the top three centre-halves. Revie once tried to buy him when he was manager of Leeds. So now let him have the courage to pick him for England.'

Sipping beer and champagne during his hour-long turn, Clough also had nothing but praise for Tony Waddington, the man who had extended the hand of friendship to him after his dismissal at Leeds. He thought Waddington's efforts should be rewarded with bigger crowds at the Victoria Ground. 'He is doing a superb job at Stoke,' said Clough. 'I don't know how he carries on with the numbers that turn up. Get along there and support them! They have so many talented players. They are doing something good for football.'

By now, Stoke City and Chelsea players must have been sick of the sight of each other, as they prepared to do battle once again for the fourth time in less than three weeks. Stoke were on an understandable high after the midweek trouncing, which new Chelsea boss Ron Suart had told his team was 'just a freak result'. In terms of Stoke's bid for the title, it was to be a fateful meeting.

First Division: Chelsea v Stoke City
At first it looks as though Stoke are simply picking up where they left off in midweek. Their first goal is beautifully

contrived, from picking the ball up deep in defence to scoring a little over ten seconds later. Hudson collects a clearance and brings it out before slipping it forward to Mahoney. Mahoney drifts past Dempsey and sees Hurst making a forward run down the left and frantically signalling for the pass. Mahoney finds him but it's a little underhit. Hurst still manages to get a left-footed shot away, but it lacks power. It beats the keeper but is going wide until Greenhoff appears at the far post to tap it in.

Chelsea start applying some pressure and force Farmer into several good saves. Hutchinson is a thorn in the Stoke side all afternoon and it is one of his massive long throws that brings the equaliser. The giant Droy rises to meet it and heads in off the bar.

The action really hots up after the hour, when Stoke retake the lead with a simple goal: a Salmons corner glanced in by the unmarked Haslegrave. But only a minute later, another Hutchinson long throw causes more chaos and Chris Garland is able to fire in from a couple of yards.

Stoke go ahead for the third time with a messy goal of their own. Hudson sends a low cross into the box where a flick on first by Haslegrave and then by Smith leaves Robertson the simple task of tapping in at the far post.

There are only five minutes to go, but Stoke can't hold on as Chelsea counter-attack. A long Hutchinson throw results in a powerful volley from Steve Kember from outside the box which is headed off the line. Then yet another Hutchinson special from the other side is met by Droy and tipped over by Farmer. Right at the death, Britton sends in an innocuous-looking cross which Farmer should collect easily. But it bounces a little higher than he is expecting, and he can only spoon it up for Hutchinson to nod home. It is the final action of an entertaining 3-3 draw, but having led three times, Stoke are far from satisfied with their point.

After his two goals against Stoke in the first League Cup meeting, Hutchinson has been linked with a move to the Potteries. The defensive confusion he causes in this game with his long throws merely adds fuel to the rumours. But the manager's mind is elsewhere. Farmer's last-minute mistake, which gifts the Londoners a point, is a fateful moment. It seems to be the spark for Waddington to decide that Farmer is not good enough after all. It was a bad mistake, although Farmer's form is generally very sound. But the man who loves signing international goalkeepers finds his hands itching for the cheque book once again. His target is not Hutchinson, or Chivers, or any other goalscorer. The man who signed Gordon Banks has his mind set on another world-class goalkeeper.

Chelsea 3 (Droy 28; Garland 61; Hutchinson 90) Stoke City 3 (Greenhoff 13, Haslegrave 60, Robertson 85)
Attendance: 24,718
Highlights available online

Some small consolation for the dropped point is that little ground is lost. Of the top teams, only Liverpool and Middlesbrough win. At the end of an exhausting month comprising four cup ties and four league games, Stoke are unbeaten, and have inched their way back up the table to sixth – four points behind Liverpool, who are now back on top. It is still tight – nine clubs are within five points of the lead. It is turning into a dismal season for the London teams, with four of them in the bottom six, and Tottenham and Arsenal in the relegation zone.

Good news comes with the FA's decision not to ban Alan Dodd after his sending-off at Ipswich. The sending-off is upheld, but the FA take the view that his dismissal is punishment enough, given Dodd's previously exemplary record. No one is more surprised than Waddington, and

Dodd himself. They keep a straight face when they emerge. Waddington says, 'We had a marvellously fair hearing.' Dodd adds, 'It's a great weight off my mind.' He celebrates by making his debut for the England under-23 team.

	OCTOBER 1974	P	W	D	L	Pts
1	Liverpool	14	10	1	3	21
2	Manchester City	15	8	4	3	20
3	Ipswich Town	15	8	2	5	18
4	Everton	15	4	10	1	18
5	Middlesbrough	14	7	4	3	18
6	**Stoke City**	**14**	**6**	**5**	**3**	**17**
7	Derby County	15	5	6	4	16
8	Burnley	15	7	2	6	16
9	Sheffield United	15	6	4	5	16
10	Newcastle United	14	5	5	4	15
11	Birmingham City	15	6	2	7	14
12	West Ham United	15	5	4	6	14
13	Wolverhampton Wanderers	15	4	6	5	14
14	Coventry City	14	4	6	4	14
15	Carlisle United	15	5	3	7	13
16	Leicester City	13	4	4	5	12
17	Chelsea	14	3	6	5	12
18	Queens Park Rangers	14	3	5	6	11
19	Leeds United	14	4	3	7	11
20	Tottenham Hotspur	14	4	2	8	10
21	Arsenal	14	3	3	8	9
22	Luton Town	15	1	7	7	9

12

NOVEMBER

TONY WADDINGTON bided his time. He kept his poker face when the visit of Tottenham Hotspur gave rise to yet another burst of speculation that he was interested in signing Martin Chivers. He did nothing to dispel the rumours. On the face of it, Chivers looked like a classic Waddington target: approaching 30, international class, disaffected. The *Sentinel* went as far as to report that Stoke would buy if they could get him for less than £200,000.

The new Spurs manager, Terry Neill, thought Stoke were out of order making their interest known when Chivers was not even on the transfer list. Waddington was at his blithest in responding, with an air of injured innocence: 'Terry Neill was reported to have said he accepted he would have to sell the player. When a player of this quality comes on the market, you have to be interested. But that is as far as it has gone at the moment. Anything else is just speculation. We are very near winning something this season, and we have to strengthen our squad if at all possible.'

While he did not deny his interest, keen students of the Waddington way might have paid more attention to his further comments, 'Geoff Hurst has done a magnificent job for us after John Ritchie's injury, as indicated by the fact that we have gone ten games without defeat.' This was an indication of his true position. He did not feel he needed another striker. His focus lay elsewhere.

First Division: Stoke City v Tottenham Hotspur

For the first time in nearly two months Stoke have not had a midweek game, and for the visit of Spurs they name an unchanged team for the fourth match in succession: Farmer, Marsh, Pejic, Mahoney, Smith, Dodd, Haslegrave, Greenhoff, Hurst, Hudson, Salmons. They make what is becoming their customary fast start against a Spurs side showing signs of revival under Neill. There are only eight minutes on the clock when Salmons and Hudson combine, and Salmons sends a first-time shot zipping against the left-hand post and in. The great Pat Jennings in the Spurs goal seems to think it's going wide, because he makes no attempt to save it.

Spurs are fielding John Duncan, their new £150,000 signing from Dundee. He makes an immediate impact and shocks Stoke with two quick goals. His first is swept home when Steve Perryman wrong-foots the defence with a back-heel. Then Chivers and Martin Peters combine to get the ball to the Scot, and he curls the ball into the far corner.

Stoke have perhaps been guilty of complacency, but they rapidly restore order with an equaliser on 35 minutes. Salmons skins two defenders on the left and finds Hurst with a cross. Hurst traps it but cannot get his shot away. The ball is only half cleared, and Greenhoff scores with a swift left-footed shot on the turn.

The burst of scoring is followed by a quieter period, but in the second half both sides have plenty of chances. Stoke lack penetration, and Spurs are showing ample evidence of their improvement under Neill. The reaction of the supporters reflects the fact that it's a match Stoke would have hoped and perhaps expected to win. But 2-2 is how it ends, and at least their unbeaten run is intact.

Stoke's league position is helped by the fact that four of the five teams above them are playing each other. The blue half of Liverpool has double cause for celebration as Everton beat Manchester City and leaders Liverpool go down by the odd goal at Ipswich. But once again, no one is able to break clear of the pack.

Stoke City 2 (Salmons 8; Greenhoff 35) Tottenham Hotspur 2 (Duncan 25, 30)
Attendance: 24,668

So congested was it at the top of the table that every week seemed to bring a fixture against a top team. It was again the case after the Spurs game with a tough trip to Maine Road in prospect. Manchester City had just lost to Everton, but if other results went their way they could go top with a win over Stoke. For their part, if Stoke could pull off a rare victory in Manchester then they would be equal with City on points.

First Division: Manchester City v Stoke City

The game starts on a spectacular note when Alan Oakes comes close to celebrating his 500th Manchester City appearance with a goal when he unleashes a tremendous left-foot shot after a free kick. Thereafter the threat comes from the more established City strike force of Mike Summerbee, Rodney Marsh – with his socks rolled down to his ankles as usual – and Dennis Tueart, signed from Sunderland in March for £275,000.

It is Marsh who strikes after 20 minutes, benefitting from a horror show in the Stoke defence – which you can still watch in a nine-second clip online. At first Marsh cannot control a long ball forward. But the defenders make a hash of it too, and it comes back to Marsh. Mahoney is covering to make the tackle, but it falls again into the path of Marsh and this time he rifles it home from the penalty spot.

It is a poor goal to give away, and it heralds a period of intense City pressure that persuades Waddington to make a rare early substitution, throwing on Conroy for Haslegrave. The move helps stabilise matters, but it is still Manchester City who look the more threatening. That is the pattern for the rest of the game, with the home side showing more accuracy and precision. With Hudson well marshalled, Stoke threaten only occasionally, notably when Smith goes up to bolster the attack. In general though, it is a flat and disappointing performance that brings a tame end to a lengthy unbeaten run.

Tony Waddington admits that it is a substandard performance from his team, but denies that the problem lies with their tactics. 'It was not a case of changing to a defensive style,' he insists. 'We played just as we normally do, but too many players were below par. In fact at the end Manchester had only Marsh and Summerbee upfield, because they were growing afraid of us. If we had played up to form we would have had at least a point. I accept that Alan Hudson was restricted a little but I was not happy with our overall performance. Jimmy Greenhoff was operating on his own up front at times.'

Manchester City are not complaining – only Everton of the top group can manage even a point, as Ipswich go down at Wolves and struggling Arsenal shock Liverpool 3-1 at Anfield. It is the perfect combination of results for Manchester City, and they sit at the top of the table as the lead changes hands yet again.

Manchester City 1 (Marsh 20) Stoke City 0
Attendance: 36,966

Stoke did not have long to reflect on the end of their unbeaten run because the midweek matches were back, in the shape of a League Cup fourth-round tie at Ipswich Town. Memories were still raw of the league encounter six weeks before, when Stoke had imploded after what would turn out to be the career-ending injury to John Ritchie. There was a grim resolve in the camp to come away with a result this time, and to win it for Big John. Ipswich had lost a little ground in the league, but their home record was still formidable with only two goals conceded all season – one of them scored by Stoke in a losing cause in that ill-tempered earlier meeting.

League Cup: Ipswich Town v Stoke City

A rare absence of Jackie Marsh occasions some reshuffling, with Kevin Lewis being given only his second senior start, and the ever-willing Dodd switching to right-back. Robertson comes in against his former club to give Stoke more options on the right. The lanky Ian Moores is given a cup debut, and he chases and harries hard without making much of a dent in the characteristically obdurate defence. It is a game of many fouls – 38 in all – but the tie does not spill over into the open hostility of the league fixture. Once again, the match is closely contested for the first hour, with Stoke making light of all the changes and taking the game to Ipswich with a series of speedy attacks. Moores, Greenhoff and Smith all have good chances, and Greenhoff hits the post as they edge the first half.

Ipswich take the initiative after 59 minutes – the exact time of their opening goal in the previous game. Viljoen chips into the middle and Hamilton heads home unmarked – and in Stoke's opinion, from an offside position. Ipswich are quick to tighten their grip, fettering Salmons who has been the principal outlet for Stoke's attacking efforts. With 20 minutes left, a long ball finds Johnson and he holds off the defenders and beats Farmer. The timing of the second goal also mirrors that of the league game. Stoke are aggrieved and again claim the scorer was offside, and once again they protest in vain.

Parallels with the previous game are completed in the last minute when Robertson heads home an in-swinging corner, but there is no time to press for an equaliser, and Stoke are out of the League Cup.

Ipswich Town 2 (Hamilton 59; Johnson 72) Stoke City 1 (Robertson 90)
Attendance: 20,677

First Division: Stoke City v Luton Town

After a series of tough fixtures, it is something of a relief to return to Stoke for what looks like an easier game, against lowly Luton Town. Ian Moores is named as substitute after his midweek efforts and will come on to make his league debut. Stoke are four points off the top of the table but have a game in hand over most of their rivals, so the title race is as tight as ever.

They reprise their happy habit of scoring an early goal. Hudson has shrugged off a knock to be fit to play, but he is soon limping after forcing a corner from the first attack. When Salmons takes it, it is Hudson who controls the ball at the far post and cuts inside before shooting past Barber. Stoke now run the show with a series of attacks that could have extended their lead. Instead, they concede an equaliser when Anderson's shot after a long run hits Smith and goes in. The goal heralds a period of renewed Luton confidence and a series of scrappy Stoke errors, their early domination now a thing of the past.

Stoke need a goal but it is 15 minutes into the second half before they get one, with Robertson heading home for the second time in successive matches as he gets on to the end of a Salmons cross. Two minutes later, Salmons is again the provider, Greenhoff meeting his cross with a glancing header. Order is restored, and Greenhoff is soon there again to finish a move that begins with a short corner, and involves Hudson, Salmons and Robertson. The goal burst is completed by Luton with a close-range header, but after that things settle down and after a patchy performance, Stoke see out the game comfortably enough.

Manchester City's hold on the top spot is short-lived as they go down to a surprising 4-0 defeat at Birmingham. Ipswich win, but Derby lose and the Merseyside derby is a goalless draw, so Stoke are right back in the mix again.

Stoke City 4 (Hudson 3; Robertson 60; Greenhoff 62, 68)
Luton Town 2 (Anderson 30; Garner 73)
Attendance: 20,646

Tony Waddington was finally ready to show his hand and reveal what would prove to be his last great flourish in the transfer market. He was about to break the British transfer record for a goalkeeper by splashing out £325,000 for Peter Shilton of Leicester City and England.

The low rumbling of rumour about Shilton in the summer had never completely died away, although Albert Henshall's emphatic comments about not having the money for any other big signings temporarily put paid to it. Although it was well known that Shilton was available, the speculation revolved around other potential destinations, such as Arsenal, Everton, Coventry and Derby. Now it was revealed that talks between Stoke and Leicester, and with Shilton himself, were well advanced. They would continue in London where the England squad had assembled for a friendly. Once the deal was finalised, Stoke officials dashed off to FA headquarters in Lytham St Annes to register their new signing so that he could play against Wolves at the weekend.

No one who had followed Waddington's managerial career would have been surprised that he was prepared to spend so much money on a goalkeeper. He put more value on a reliable last line of defence than almost any manager before or since.

As he recalled in his later interviews with the *Sentinel*, to him it was a completely logical step, 'Peter Shilton was the obvious target for Stoke when we were looking to replace the quality goalkeeping of Gordon Banks. I believed Peter would give the defence that extra confidence to clinch the championship.' This airily skates over the fact that it was news to most people that Stoke *were* looking to replace the quality goalkeeping of Gordon Banks. John Farmer seemed to have been doing a perfectly competent job for the best part of two years. But the man who was selling Shilton, Leicester manager Jimmy Bloomfield, agreed with Waddington. Buying Shilton, he said, was 'the best ten-year investment any club could make'.

There was the pleasing symmetry with the Banks story – Stoke going back to Leicester to sign an England goalkeeper whose club place was being threatened by an up-and-coming newcomer. But there was little explanation about where the money had come from, or what had changed since Henshall's statement. Even with the increased success on the pitch, attendances had risen to an average of only around 25,000 – not enough to underwrite expenditure of this level. The fee of £325,000 took Stoke's spending in 1974 to around £750,000 – big money in those days. It was a heartening sign of the club's ambition, even if it meant going in hock to the bank. But they would surely need to win a cup or a title to justify the outlay.

The one thing that was not a matter of debate was Shilton's pedigree. He had represented England at every level from schoolboy onwards. At 25 he already had 20 senior international appearances behind him, and was determined to become the first choice after recently losing his place to Liverpool's Ray Clemence. He had also played in nearly 300 league games for Leicester, as well as an FA Cup Final. His dedication to his fitness and to his craft was legendary. After training with the first team at Leicester he often returned to work with the colts in the afternoon, and made weekly visits to a local army base to take part in a battle training course.

SIGNING FOR STOKE: PETER SHILTON

'Throughout the 1973/74 season I became increasingly convinced that, as a club, Leicester would never go the whole mile and bring in the one or two top-quality players who could bring major success to the club. I felt I was ready for another challenge.

'During the course of the season, a number of clubs had expressed an interest in signing me, including Arsenal and Manchester United. The fact that clubs of such stature were interested fuelled the notions in my head that now was the time to seek pastures new. When the club offered me a new contract, I said, "No thanks."

'Negotiations were still going on as the 1974/75 season got under way. Although I was still at the club, Mark Wallington took his place in the first team. In essence, Leicester were willing to sell me to the highest bidder. Offers were received from Arsenal, Manchester United, Derby County and Stoke City, at the time all top clubs. Surprisingly, given their financial clout, both Arsenal and Manchester United dropped out of the bidding, neither willing to match the offers made by Derby and Stoke, which were in excess of £300,000. Jon Holmes and Jeff Pointon [Shilton's agents] told me that the decision about which one to join was solely down to me. It was a tough choice.

'Both Derby and Stoke were among the pace-setters in the First Division and both stood a good chance of winning the title. Sometimes in life, people make a big decision on the strength of something small, even cosmetic. You and your partner may have decided to buy a house on the strength of the garden or the design of the units in the kitchen. I made a similar decision when opting for Stoke City rather than Derby County. In truth, there wasn't much to choose between the two clubs. The one thing that swung it for me was the pitch. Derby's Baseball Ground pitch was, if anything, worse than the one I had known at Filbert Street before it was relaid. In comparison, Stoke City's pitch at the Victoria Ground was a beauty.

'Stoke City were a club on the up. The team boasted players of real quality, and there was another attraction. One of the members of the Stoke City coaching staff was Gordon Banks. I was looking forward to seeing Gordon again, and had an inkling that he might have had something to do with my move, perhaps recommending me to the Stoke manager, Tony Waddington. The thought of linking up with Gordon at Stoke was very appealing to me, especially as I had now set my sights on becoming the best goalkeeper of my generation.

'Jon, Jeff and I met Tony Waddington and some members of the Stoke City board in a hotel just off the A45 near Northampton. I warmed to the directors straight away and was impressed by the great enthusiasm they displayed for me joining their club. The transfer fee had been set at £325,000 and all that needed to be sorted out were my personal terms. At the end of the meeting, the Stoke directors said they looked forward to hearing my decision soon, before asking Jon, Jeff and I if we would like something to eat while we discussed the possible move among ourselves. We said we would appreciate that very much, and one of the directors, Alex Humphreys, went to arrange some food for the three of us. We were expecting a plate of sandwiches and a pot of tea. What arrived was akin to Balthazar's feast. There were several bottles of champagne and enough food to have fed about 20 people.

'"Well Peter," said Jon. "Should you decide to sign for Stoke, I think we can safely assume you will be looked after up there."

'I did decide to sign for Stoke. I told Jon and Jeff that I had been impressed by Mr Humphreys and his colleagues and I didn't want to disappoint them.'

Taken from *Peter Shilton: The Autobiography*, Shilton's 2004 book.

We can perhaps surmise that the lure of working again with Gordon Banks was rather stronger than the desire to play on the Stoke pitch. Never before had anyone referred to the Victoria Ground surface as 'a beauty' while keeping a straight face. However, it was easy to see why it would win in a comparison with the Baseball Ground in Derby, widely acknowledged as the worst in the division.

Waddington's view that the signing of Shilton was 'an obvious step' for a club with title ambitions was not universally shared. Even his own players had their doubts about the wisdom of the move. They did not question Shilton's abilities. But given the loss of John Ritchie they wondered whether the money could have been better spent on bolstering the strike force. They were reinforced in this view by their confidence in Farmer – and their understandable loyalty to a team-mate. Many of them did not understand why Waddington had suddenly decided Farmer was no longer up to the job.

Terry Conroy's reaction was typical of many. 'Our defence had conceded just two goals in the final nine games of the 1973/74 season, which does make you wonder now quite why Waddo bought Shilton in for such a vast fee,' he wrote. 'Especially when you consider that John Ritchie has suffered a career-ending leg break only two months beforehand and so maybe a striker would have been a better addition. There was no better goalkeeper around. But was that what we needed at the time? I genuinely think that we wouldn't have been worse off having John Farmer in goal.'

Alan Hudson has always been prominent among the doubters, both at the time and subsequently. 'I truly believed we didn't need a new goalkeeper,' he says. 'I liked Farmer. I was a big Farmer fan. He made a big mistake in my debut, but he didn't make many mistakes.'

Alan Dodd agrees that the few mistakes Farmer did make tended to be highlighted, as is so often the case with goalkeepers. 'Farmer *was* good enough,' he says. 'But he made a couple of mistakes and they were spotlighted on television and that's when Waddo decided to go for Peter Shilton. We all make mistakes but if you're a goalkeeper it looks ten times bigger. But he was a great goalkeeper, Farmer. It was a shame it didn't work out.'

Denis Smith traces the decision back to the Chelsea game that had seemed to bring everything to a head, with Farmer's last-minute fumble gifting the Londoners a point. 'I remember John was having a bad time with crosses that day,' he wrote. 'Ian Hutchinson was slinging balls in for Chelsea's huge centre-half Micky Droy to come in and plough right into John, hurting him in the process. That eventually caused Farmer to stop coming for crosses or to drop some because he had half an eye on where Droy was, in case he got hurt again. Right at the death, John came for a cross and dropped it. Chelsea scored and Waddo, fuming at another in this series of errors by John, decided he had to act. That goal cost a vital point which would have seen us climb to third place. If we had true ambition to win the championship, we could not afford any more such incidents. It was a defining moment for John.'

Smith is one of those who admits that at the time he saw the capture of Shilton as a good move, 'It was a cruel but necessary choice in my opinion. Given the opportunity, any of us would swap a club goalkeeper for the one lauded as the best in the country, if not the world.'

Eric Skeels was another who felt that with Shilton between the posts, the quality of the team had definitely been enhanced. 'John Farmer was a good goalkeeper but he wasn't robust,' he says. 'Maybe Waddo wanted someone who was going to do a lot of talking and be bossy. Peter was a shouter: he'd yell "keeper's ball!" if he thought you were in his way. You want someone like that in goal, the last man – if he sees the ball coming, it's up to him to make all the noise and say, "get out of the way, I've got it!" John wasn't like that, he was a quiet bloke. You wouldn't see Johnny Farmer diving out at someone's feet when he might get kicked in the face.'

Smith also liked the message it sent out, 'The signing of Shilton convinced me that Stoke City were set to be a force to be reckoned with. Now Banks was gone, Shilton was simply the best in the business. We had sent a message to the football world. Stoke City meant business.' Conroy agrees, 'We could see that we were moving up the ladder.'

For Waddington and for Shilton, the best response to the doubters would come in the shape of what happened on the pitch. Shilton was brought straight into the team for the visit to Wolverhampton Wanderers. It was a big day too for teenager Ian 'Danny' Bowers, also making his first-team debut, though to rather less of a fanfare, playing in front of Shilton as a replacement for the suspended Pejic. A few days earlier, Shilton had been on England duty while Bowers had been playing for the reserves in the Central League. As the cameramen swarmed around Shilton before the game, Waddington took Bowers quietly to one side to help him prepare for his own big day.

First Division: Wolverhampton Wanderers v Stoke City

The match gets off to a breathless start with Stoke forcing three early corners and Shilton being relieved to see a Hibbitt volley fly over the bar. Shilton's long clearances are soon a feature of the game, and after only ten minutes, one of them results in a Stoke free kick 25 yards from goal. Salmons threads the ball through the defence and into the net.

As Wolves retaliate, Shilton begins to show his mettle, with a string of top-class saves. It takes a special half-volley from Powell to beat him after 30 minutes, and he leaves the field at the interval to sustained applause. Bowers, meanwhile, is also enjoying an assured start.

The second half is much the same, with Shilton equal to everything that is thrown at him before Stoke pinch the lead again, on the hour. Greenhoff breaks through and draws the goalkeeper before centring for Robertson to tap in.

At times it feels as though the action has been deliberately engineered to give Shilton the opportunity to demonstrate his virtuosity. He makes one save after another, with his team-mates showing their appreciation and Steve Kindon beating the ground in despair after being frustrated yet again.

In the end, though, Wolves get the point they deserve when Smith trips Richards in almost the last action of the match, and Shilton is beaten at last from the penalty spot.

But the England keeper has answered all of the questions and won over more than a few of the doubters. Even Hudson is impressed. 'He was absolutely brilliant,' he says. 'I was upstairs in the lounge after the game and Shilton walked in the bar. I was standing there with my dad. My dad never used to say much. I remember my dad shaking his hand, and my dad did that very rarely. I remember saying to my dad, "I think we've just won the league with this fella." He was that good. He was absolutely outstanding.'

Dodd was won over too, 'It was end-to-end football – it was a fantastic match for spectators and Shilton made two miraculous saves. One of his best games, his debut. I was very impressed.'

While all the attention was at Molineux, Manchester City were beating Leicester 4-1 and returning to the top of the table.

Wolverhampton Wanderers 2 (Powell 33; Hibbitt 90 pen)
Stoke City 2 (Salmons 10; Robertson 58)
Attendance: 28,216

Hudson remembers Tony Waddington 'looking mightily pleased' with his new signing. And why not? Shilton had put on a bravura display. If the capture of Salmons had been the last piece in the jigsaw, the arrival of Shilton simply reinforced the idea that Stoke were an ambitious and strong team that could challenge for major honours. Shilton went on to have a glittering career, becoming England's most-capped player and enjoying European triumphs with Nottingham Forest. He was one of the best goalkeepers the world has seen. So why, half a century later, is there still an animated debate about whether or not Waddington should have bought him?

The answer is twofold. One factor had nothing to do with Shilton personally. It revolved around the argument about what sort of reinforcements the team needed if there was money for new players. In retrospect, the feeling is that Waddington's enthusiasm for goalkeepers got the better of him, and he should have been trying to shore up his attack instead.

The second issue is more complicated, and stems from a feeling that Shilton was not at his very best when he was at Stoke, his many miraculous saves tempered by occasional lapses in concentration. Added to that is the view that his style of play somehow didn't fit, that a defence accustomed to playing in front of Gordon Banks for so long struggled to adapt to Shilton's different way of doing things.

Denis Smith, who, as he says, was 'one of the very few people who played for a sustained period directly in front of both men' explains, 'We just couldn't get an understanding at all. As a ball came over the top, I would be thinking, "Why is he back on his line?" Other times I'd think the ball would be mine, only to find Shilton had come out to collect and I'd be in danger of running into him. Shilton was more of a line keeper and a shot-stopper. He hated being beaten, even in training. He was great one-on-one, brilliant, the best I've ever seen, but as far as reading the game and all-round play Banksy was far better.'

The view that has hardened over the years is that Shilton was a superb keeper, but that if the money had been spent on a striker instead, the title would have been won. Like most football arguments, indeed all arguments conducted in hindsight, there is no way of knowing whether that is true or not.

And the fact that people are still talking about it suggests there is still plenty of substance on both sides. But the debate perhaps illustrates why, through little fault of his own, Shilton's time in the Potteries was not as successful as it might have been, perhaps as it deserved to be.

For now, though, he was looking like a great acquisition, up there with Waddington's best transfer coups. No one was complaining, and the home fans were eagerly looking forward to their first glimpse of the new star in their midst, which would come in the midweek fixture against Queens Park Rangers. QPR now had Dave Sexton at the helm after his dismissal at Chelsea and were on a good run of four wins out of five.

FITNESS FANATIC: MY TEAM-MATE PETER SHILTON

DENIS SMITH: 'Shilts was my room-mate and we would go out in the afternoon to do extra practising of through balls so we could try to get on the same wavelength – little things, but they're massive. He was fanatic – he'd be back in the afternoons and at times I'd have words with him and say, "You don't need to keep training so much – you'll be like a block of wood come Saturday because you've been putting it in." He trained and trained and trained to the extreme. At times I think he overtrained. He was a better shot-stopper than Banks, though in my opinion Banks was a better all-round keeper.'

ALAN HUDSON: 'Shilton would have been happy if we'd have gone through a season with every game 0-0. He'd be happy if he didn't let a goal in even if you finished halfway down the league. Gordon wouldn't give a monkey's if it was 3-2 as long as we won. Shilton's mentality was all about keeping clean sheets – well that's not football. If every game was 0-0 there'd be no spectators.'

TERRY CONROY: 'Shilts would always be last off the training pitch, caked in mud after doing extra sessions, particularly shot-stopping and catching crosses. He had this particular style for catching high balls, which saw him take the ball as it came down and then fall to the ground with it, curled up to protect it. Shilton was a keeper who looked after his own game and made great saves. He was phenomenal at that. His training routine was incredible. There is no questioning Shilton's ability as a keeper at all, but he didn't pull the strings for the back four like Banks had.'

First Division: Stoke City v Queens Park Rangers

The gate is only a modest 22,000, but the home support gives Shilton a rousing welcome, and he soon gives them something to shout about with some tidy saves. In the reverse fixture in London, Hurst had settled things with the only goal in the closing minutes. Here he is quickly on target, as a long clearance from Shilton is controlled by Hudson who advances to the edge of the box before deftly finding Hurst. A swift left-footed shot and Stoke are one up within ten minutes.

More goals seem likely as Stoke pour forward and Shilton has much less to do than in his frantic debut of a few days earlier. What there is he handles efficiently, but in spite of a dominant performance Stoke are unable to make further inroads. The win is enough to lift them to third though, just behind Manchester City and Liverpool, with the tantalising prospect that they might even go top if results on Saturday go their way.

Stoke City 1 (Hurst 9) QPR 0
Attendance: 22,403

Eric Skeels, who was recovering from a broken leg at the start of the season, made his first appearance against QPR, and would remain in the team from now on. As injuries and suspensions piled up, the versatility and reliability that 'Alfie' invariably displayed became ever more valuable. His nickname had come from the time a few years earlier when he had lived close to the ground and used to bring his dog to training with him. The dog's name was Alfie. 'It was a corgi,' says Skeels. 'I used to take it to training sometimes and someone in the office or at the ground would look after him, or I'd tie him up until I came back. They didn't seem to bother about it being there. I got my nickname from the dog!'

MR DEPENDABLE: MY TEAM-MATE ERIC SKEELS

DENIS SMITH: 'For long periods Alfie never seemed to be the first choice and yet he holds the record for playing more games for Stoke than anybody else. But that sums Alfie up. He could play anywhere across the back line or midfield and go do a decent job on the wing. You need someone to fill any position and Alfie could do the job. He was possibly the ultimate utility player and certainly a manager's dream. He trained well and was a strong character in his own quiet way, never wanting to be beaten. Much like "Bluto" Bloor, Alfie was a very unassuming chap. He was just 5ft 9in tall but could compete with forwards five or six inches taller. On the ball he was two-footed and played neat, simple passes. He so rarely made mistakes and became known as "Mr Dependable".'

These testimonials were published on the *Sentinel* website on the occasion of Skeels's 80th birthday:

TERRY CONROY: 'Reliability is the word to describe Alfie best of all. As a man marker, there was none better. I spoke to Johnny Giles about Eric recently and he said, "Oh, that little ****, he always used to kick me." Now coming from Johnny Giles, that's quite a compliment.'

JIMMY GREENHOFF: 'Thinking back on all the clubs I played for and all the players I played with, if I had to name one who could be relied on to do the job the team wanted, then that player would be Eric Skeels.'

HARRY BURROWS: 'When he was in his prime, he would be the first name on the team sheet for me. I played against him as an 18-year-old and he was marking me. I thought, "Who the hell is this?" because I just couldn't get rid of him.'

ERIC SKEELS ON HIMSELF: 'Every game was 100 per cent for me whether we were top or third or wherever. I'd still be playing as hard for 90 minutes – that was my approach. Maybe that's why Waddington kept me in the team, because he knew I would work for 90 minutes. I was lucky, nearly always fit. I wasn't a great footballer, but I was a good worker, and I could read the game.'

First Division: Stoke City v Leicester City
Saturday brings another home fixture and, in the way of these things, it pits Shilton against the club he had left only a week

earlier. Mark Wallington, the man who has replaced him in Leicester's goal, is injured, and 20-year-old Carl Jayes is given his first outing.

It looks as though Stoke have again scored early when Jayes can only parry a Smith header and Hurst knocks it in, but the goal is disallowed. Hudson and Salmons are in a dominant mood, but chances for Hurst, Moores and Greenhoff all go begging. Jayes is having a dream debut and dealing calmly with everything that is thrown at him, while his illustrious counterpart is only sporadically called into action at the other end. Shilton has plenty of leisure to reassess his view of the Victoria Ground pitch, which is cutting up badly after recent rain and looks anything but beautiful.

In the second half, Leicester often have ten men behind the ball and in spite of all the pressure from Stoke, no breakthrough is forthcoming. When an effort from Moores hits the post, Leicester start to believe they might escape with a point. But with only four minutes left on the clock, Moores knocks the ball forward for Smith who has decided to try his luck upfield, and he smacks an unstoppable shot past Jayes. It proves to be enough to secure a hard-fought win.

Then it is off the pitch and into the changing room to listen to the radio and see how the other results have gone. The news is good: leaders Manchester City have gone down 2-1 at Newcastle, and Liverpool have managed only a point at Coventry. For the first time in 37 years, Stoke City are leaders of the First Division.

Stoke City 1 (Smith 86) Leicester City 0
Attendance: 29,793

My cousin and I are among the nearly 30,000 who witness this historic moment, though we have to wait to get back to our car and turn on the radio for confirmation of the results.

When the famous title music of the BBC's *Sports Report* fades away, we hear the longed-for news: there is yet another new name at the top of the table in this topsy-turvy season, and it is that of Stoke City. I am so carried away I take my foot off the brake and run into the rear of the car in front. Luckily we are moving very slowly, there is no damage done, and the driver of the other car is just as excited as I am. Like every other Stoke fan, we are daring to dream.

	NOVEMBER 1974	*P*	*W*	*D*	*L*	*Pts*
1	**Stoke City**	**20**	**9**	**7**	**4**	**25**
2	Ipswich Town	20	11	2	7	24
3	Liverpool	19	10	4	5	24
4	Everton	19	6	12	1	24
5	Manchester City	20	10	4	6	24
6	West Ham United	20	9	5	6	23
7	Derby County	19	8	6	5	22
8	Newcastle United	19	8	6	5	22
9	Burnley	20	9	4	7	22
10	Sheffield United	19	8	5	6	21
11	Birmingham City	20	8	4	8	20
12	Middlesbrough	19	7	6	6	20
13	Leeds United	19	7	4	8	18
14	Wolverhampton Wanderers	19	5	8	6	18
15	Coventry City	20	5	8	7	18
16	Tottenham Hotspur	19	6	5	8	17
17	Queens Park Rangers	20	6	5	9	17
18	Arsenal	19	6	4	9	16
19	Leicester City	18	5	5	8	15
20	Chelsea	19	3	8	8	14
21	Carlisle United	20	5	3	12	13
22	Luton Town	19	1	7	11	9

DECEMBER

AS AN indication of Stoke's new status as the First Division pacesetters, the television cameras showed up at their training ground as they prepared for their first assignation as leaders – a visit to Birmingham City. Birmingham's recent form had been patchy to say the least. They had thrashed leaders Manchester City 4-0 and then lost 4-1 at Everton. Their manager Fred Goodwin said he expected Stoke to present a difficult challenge. The Potters' form had come as no surprise to him – other than that it was even better than he had expected. 'We know that Stoke are a talented side. I expected them to do well this season. I am a little surprised they are coming to us when at the top.' He was confident his team would make sure that their sojourn at the summit would be a brief one.

First Division: Birmingham City v Stoke City

John Mahoney is back after missing three games through injury, but a swollen elbow means that the reassuring presence of Denis Smith, the match-winner against Leicester, is missing from the heart of the defence. The ever-dependable Eric Skeels teams up with Alan Dodd at centre-back and Ian Moores continues his run in the first team at the expense of Geoff Hurst.

Once again, Stoke waste little time in asserting their dominance, and when they do it is through a sensational goal. Skeels plays the ball out of defence down the right-hand side, where Robertson back-heads to Greenhoff on the extreme corner of the box. In one movement, he chests it down, swivels and volleys it into the far corner. So swift and fluid is his movement, and so rapidly does the ball travel, that it is a moment before the crowd – and the television commentator – realise what has happened. By then Greenhoff is being mobbed by his excited team-mates.

Most of the players have difficulties today in remembering individual matches and goals from nearly 50 years ago. But they all remember this one. It is a special goal even by the standards of a player well known for his volleying prowess.

'It would be impossible to pick out the greatest goal in Greenhoff's collection of gems,' wrote Alan Hudson. 'I would watch Jimmy in training and purr at that wonderful touch of his. A touch like silk and an uncanny awareness. Jimmy was probably the best volleyer of a moving ball I have ever seen. His volley at Birmingham that year was, I think, Goal of the Season, but he would hit them like that all the time.'

A second is not long in coming, and Greenhoff is involved again as he wins a free kick in the centre circle. Hudson looks up, sees Moores moving forward, and takes it quickly. Moores takes a touch to give himself an angle then fires a low shot into the left-hand corner from 20 yards. It is his first goal for Stoke, and a memorable way to open his account.

Birmingham are now reeling, and after 36 minutes it is Greenhoff again on target to put Stoke out of sight. This time it is a simple training-ground move assisted by slack defence. Salmons sends in a low free kick from the left touchline and Greenhoff has made space for a glancing header.

Greenhoff is looking for a hat-trick when he rises with Joe Gallagher for a Robertson cross, but he comes off second best in the challenge. He is clearly dazed and is replaced by Hurst with half-time still five minutes away.

Birmingham rally in the second half and have a few decent chances without being able to dent Stoke's superiority. Stoke miss opportunities to extend the lead, but by the end they are playing possession football and seeing out an emphatic victory. Along with Greenhoff's goals there have been dazzling displays of footwork by Hudson, pace by Robertson, and coolness under pressure by Dodd. They stay top, although Manchester City, Middlesbrough and Everton also win, while Liverpool draw with Derby. So at the mid-point of the season in terms of matches played, it remains very tight.

Tony Waddington is happy with a performance that is worthy of potential champions. With his customary lack of detailed briefing, he has told the team to 'just go out there and express yourselves', and they have taken him at his word.

'The title race will be won away from home and we have enough skill and talent in the side for the lads to play as they want to on away grounds,' says the manager. 'I was even more pleased with our second-half performance, because we had a strong wind against us and Birmingham were obviously going to throw everything at us. We also had a couple of bonuses out of the game in Alan Dodd, tremendous at centre-half, and Ian Moores who had his best game and is almost there now.'

Moores is 20, and has been given his chance because of the absence of Ritchie. He was first spotted with Knutton Youth Club in the Sentinel Shield competition and had a season in Australian football before coming back to become leading scorer for the reserves. He is now rewarded for his breakthrough performances with a call-up to England's under-23 squad.

Greenhoff has broken his nose and will need an operation. But having helped defeat one of his old clubs in Birmingham, he says he hopes to be fit to face another, Leeds, in the next match. His injury completes an eventful 24 hours for the Stoke favourite. As well as recalling his superb volley, Alan Hudson also remembers some unorthodox preparation the night before the game in the hotel bar. Greenhoff was not really one of the team drinkers – he would often ask what haunts Hudson planned to patronise on a Saturday evening, so that he could be sure to avoid them. But on this occasion, he seems to have made an exception.

'The night before the game, we were booked into the hotel in Birmingham,' says Hudson. 'We had dinner and we went through to have a nightcap in the bar. This fella came through and there was a wedding. And Jimmy was with us. Me, Jimmy, Alan Bloor and Geoff Salmons. We started talking and we had a drink and he said, "Come and join us in the wedding." We went to the wedding reception. We walked out of the reception at about half past three in the morning and we were playing at three o'clock that afternoon.' Proof, says Hudson, that late nights and booze do not necessarily affect performance. 'We tortured Birmingham, so that's a fallacy!'

Birmingham City 0 Stoke City 3 (Greenhoff 14, 36; Moores 29)
Attendance: 33,999
Highlights available online

VELVET TOUCH: MY TEAM-MATE JIMMY GREENHOFF

ALAN HUDSON: 'When we were both on our game together – and we were quite a lot in those days – we were close to impossible to stop. We had an uncanny playing relationship. But we were never close off the field, and never really spoke much about the game to one another. But one day in the gym we were just playing, and we were, like, telepathic. That was something I have not known elsewhere. And we said, "Look, we've got to do this on Saturday." I could pick up the ball on the edge of our box and, like radar, get signals of where he was moving to and pinpoint balls into that space. Then without looking to see if he had the ball under control, I would take off and run wherever for a return pass. His technique was as good as any player I have ever played with, and some mornings on that bumpy old training pitch, I would be bewildered by the way he controlled and cushioned the ball with such ease. He was an all-round footballer. There was a lot to his game.

'I think Waddo saw me as the one to get the best out of Greenhoff by giving him the kind of service he needed. Tony saw me as the key to Jimmy G, and that was the thing that changed the team. We didn't get on well off the field – we do now, but we didn't then. He was a dull Yorkshireman! He really was.'

MIKE PEJIC: 'Jim was one of the highest technical ability players in the league. He was a banker.'

DENIS SMITH: 'He was always available for the ball into feet. He made your life easy as he was a super target man, and you could get it into him no matter what. He would really back into his marker, receive the ball and either play a quick pass to get us going forward, or win another free kick. It's sad that people never saw what he was capable of doing on the international stage. He was blessed with sublime skills and a wonderful ability to hit volleys cleanly. Less of an out-and-out striker, more of a link man. When Jim scored goals they were usually worth seeing because he struck the ball so sweetly. I would say he's the best volleyer I've ever seen.

'The problem with Jimmy was that as a person he was an extremely shy, nervous type of lad. He needed confidence to play, and when the fans shouted his name, you could see his chest puff out and he would lift his game. At those times he could be unplayable. Equally, sometimes when all wasn't going well, Jimmy would deflate. He was quite a complex character and a completely different animal to Ritchie. John had the inner belief that he was the top striker around. Jimmy wasn't sure. He would be a nervous wreck before each game, and it could get to him during a match too.

'He wasn't over keen on training, and he wasn't over keen on running if it wasn't necessary. He kept it to a minimum, but his brain was in gear all the time so he'd be going into the holes and spaces. Even then people would get obsessed by stats. Jimmy would do the sprints, no problems, but long running – no thank you. But as he said, "In games, I only sprint." He'd got a velvet touch. You could ping anything into him and it was dead. And he had awareness of what was around him. Technically he was perfect all round: his touch, both feet, volleying, heading – technically it was very difficult to find weaknesses.'

ALAN DODD: 'Class player. He'd enjoy the game today, Jimmy, the way it's played and the pitches. Greenhoff could spray the ball all over. He had great touch with both feet. He and Huddy played together like nobody I've ever seen. It was like a telepathic understanding. Huddy would just play the ball into space and Jimmy would be there, and that was how it was from the first match.'

TERRY CONROY: 'Phenomenal – right foot, left foot, ball control – instant, and he'd get it away quickly. Jimmy's skills were second to none. His skills were denied to England because of Don Revie: when Jimmy left Leeds, Revie wasn't enamoured of him leaving "the family". So there was maybe a bit of a grudge there from Revie's point of view. Jimmy was exceptional, he really should have been recognised and he wasn't.

'In tight areas where he was marked by a defender, he was great at shielding. He was strong enough, powerful legs and he wasn't knocked off the ball easily. Tremendous volleyer. In training he would practise volleying – after training, someone would cross for him and he perfected his skills that way. It came naturally to him, but he still practised.

'Hudson's understanding with Jimmy G – the two of them could have been blindfolded and they'd have found each other. That's how good they were. We'd play games where he'd play with Jimmy and they'd play these one-twos but it was never seriously worked upon – it was two bright and agile minds being able to read each other.'

ERIC SKEELS: 'Always looking for the ball. He wasn't a shouter, but he was skilful and he could really play. He could turn left or right and he scored some cracking goals. He's quiet – if there's four or five of you sitting round in the pub, he's not the one that's going to do all the talking. He's a good listener.'

Now managed by Jimmy Armfield, Leeds were making a slow but steady recovery from their disastrous start to the season under Brian Clough. Although narrowly beaten by West Ham last time out, they were looking for payback for the beating they had taken at Stoke on the opening day. Playmaker Johnny Giles was back from injury, and Duncan McKenzie had scored five times in his last five outings. It was a much more forceful and confident Leeds than the side that had begun the defence of their title back in August. Stoke by contrast had Smith back, but were without Greenhoff. They came into the game with Ian Moores the only recognised striker in front of a packed midfield.

First Division: Leeds United v Stoke City

Leeds are in all-out attack mode from the start and Stoke are already firmly on the back foot when they go behind after 20

John Farmer. He was obliged to make way as first choice keeper, first for Gordon Banks and later for Peter Shilton.

Jimmy Robertson. A canny and skilful winger whose contribution to the 1974/75 campaign was ended by a broken leg on Boxing Day

Sean Haslegrave. A combative midfielder, and ever-present for the first part of the 1974/75 season

Tony Waddington with Geoff Hurst – the England World Cup hero was yet another of his eye-catching signings.

Geoff Hurst shoots just wide in the 1-1 home draw against Derby County, September 1974

Alan Dodd. 1974/75 was his breakthrough season as he deputised for the absent Alan Bloor and was picked for the England Under-23 team. He would make more than 400 appearances for Stoke.

Right: Alan Hudson arrives at Stoke station after becoming Stoke City's record signing in January 1974

Bottom: Alan Hudson already calling the shots in his Stoke City debut against Liverpool

Greenhoff and Hudson celebrate Greenhoff's late equaliser in the League Cup tie with Chelsea in October 1974

Denis Smith, Geoff Salmons and John Farmer celebrate a win in the early part of the 1974/75 season

Geoff Salmons – 'the final piece in the jigsaw' – in action against Arsenal.

Peter Shilton making another save on his outstanding debut for Stoke against Wolves

Two of England's greatest goalkeepers: Peter Shilton and Gordon Banks in a publicity shot after Shilton's arrival at Stoke at the end of 1974

Terry Conroy maintains his hot scoring streak with both goals in the vital match against Liverpool on Easter Monday 1975

Top: The day the dream finally died in the mud of the Victoria Ground. Jimmy Greenhoff struggles to shoot in the 0-0 draw with Newcastle that finished Stoke's chances of taking the title

Right: Stoke directors view the damage caused to the Butler Street stand by the storm of January 1976, which led to a financial crisis and the break-up of Waddington's team.

minutes. A Bremner free kick is met with a dipping header by Gordon McQueen and the ball loops over Shilton. As the goalkeeper scrambles back, the ball hits the post and cannons in off his body. The record books credit McQueen with the goal and it ends a run of three clean sheets for Stoke. They begin to work their way back into the game but are fortunate not to go further behind when Terry Yorath heads against the post.

The reprieve is a short one, because five minutes into the second half Joe Jordan heads into the path of Peter Lorimer who gives Shilton no chance with one of his trademark thunderbolts. Stoke throw on Hurst to try to give the attack some substance, and he twice comes close. But it is Leeds who are calling the tune and they wrap things up with ten minutes left. It is an outstanding individual goal by Terry Yorath, who starts the move in his own half and then finishes it after an interchange with Bremner.

A goal for Stoke in the last minute is scant consolation, though a fitting reward for the wholehearted effort of Moores. Hudson sends Robertson away and his fierce snap shot is only parried by Harvey. Moores is there to score his second goal in successive matches. But Stoke, missing the subtlety and variety of Greenhoff, are well beaten by a display of positive and aggressive football by Leeds. And as all bar Derby of the chasing teams are victorious, it is the end of their brief reign at the top of the tree. They are displaced by Everton and slip back into a jostling pack that still numbers more than half a dozen teams.

Leeds United   3 (McQueen 21; Lorimer 50; Yorath 80)
Stoke City 1 (Moores 89)
Attendance: 34,685
Highlights available online

The day after the game, John Mahoney had a narrow escape when his car hit a kerb, crashed through a hedge and overturned in a field. He was only slightly hurt, although his passenger had a fractured pelvis and broken ribs. Mahoney was said to be suffering from shock and was expected to be a doubt for the visit of Arsenal. So was Hudson, as his perennial ankle problems had flared up again. Greenhoff was passed fit but his manager was worried about his ability to head the ball so soon after his operation.

The day before the game, Tony Waddington was named Manager of the Month for November. The award was a well-known poisoned chalice since it invariably heralded a slump in form. The Leeds result seemed to suggest that might happen in this case, although Arsenal were having a torrid time of it down at the bottom of the table and the expectation was that Stoke would see them off. They were only a point behind Ipswich and Everton, so a win could see them back in the top spot.

First Division: Stoke City v Arsenal

It is a more attacking line-up than in the previous game, with Hurst and Moores up front and Mahoney recovered from the effects of his car crash. Greenhoff is not risked. Once again there is an early goal, but this time it goes to the visitors. Brian Kidd races clear after only five minutes and although the advancing Shilton parries his shot, the ball rebounds to Kidd and he scores easily.

After that, the Arsenal goal is under siege for the best part of half an hour, as shots and headers rain in. But some heroics by goalkeeper Rimmer and characteristically bruising tackles from Storey and Simpson keep the Arsenal goal intact.

But Kidd again proves Stoke's undoing as half-time approaches. A harmless-looking cross from Alan Ball finds the defence motionless and Kidd takes advantage with a smart first-time volley. Kidd is best remembered for scoring for Manchester United in the 1968 European Cup Final on his 19th birthday. He has just joined Arsenal following United's relegation to Division Two, and will end a forgettable season for the Gunners comfortably their top scorer.

Alan Dodd has painful memories of marking Kidd when they were both only aspiring juniors. 'I remember playing against Brian soon after I'd signed for Stoke from school. He must have been at Man United for a few months. I played in the reserve team against Man U in the Central League and I did something I've only ever done once. I went out for a drink with the lads the night before the match and I got drunk. I was absolutely kale-eyed and I was still drunk the following day. I thought to sober up I'd walk to the ground. It was six miles! I had to mark Brian Kidd and he dragged me all over the place and he scored a hat-trick. I was still under the influence.'

Dodd's natural diffidence – the modesty that might have stopped him becoming a seasoned international – is illustrated in a small incident before the Arsenal game started. He was in the tunnel looking at the pitch, when he saw Alan Hudson and Arsenal's World Cup winner Alan Ball in conversation and heading towards him. 'Being a bit shy, I thought I'd go back into the dressing room and make myself scarce. There were two double doors behind me. I was wearing a unisex coat, but my wife had made some alterations to it and it was too tight and I couldn't get my hands out of the pockets to open the door.' He had no choice but to turn and face Hudson and Ball as they came off the pitch. Hudson at once made the introductions, 'Alan, this is Alan Dodd, he's one of our up-and-coming players.' Ball stuck out his hand. But Dodd's arms were still trapped in the folds of his coat and he couldn't free his hands. 'Eventually I managed to lift a flap and get my hand out. I was so embarrassed. The two of them just burst out laughing.'

Kidd's first-half double has Stoke reeling and Radford has a couple of chances to add further to their misery before the break. It is a measure of Stoke's dismay that Moores is taken off at the break, with Skeels coming on to bolster the defence as Denis Smith is pressed into service as centre-forward. It heralds another period of sustained pressure but the closest they come is when Hudson smacks a 20-yarder against the crossbar. Stoke press hard but it is one of those days when the run of the ball is against them, and in spite of a performance that is dominant at times, those two Kidd goals decide the outcome. Hudson remembers the game but still can't credit the result: 'We murdered them. I remember smashing the bar and thinking, "We're not going to score today." It was a very heavy pitch and we were terrific. How they escaped with that win I don't know.'

With the holiday only four days away, the Potters feel they have gifted Arsenal an early Christmas present. Consecutive defeats have seen them slip to seventh.

After their sensational start to life in the First Division, Carlisle have been on the slide, but still regularly produce a series of eye-catching and improbable results. On this day they visit leaders Everton and beat them 3-2. With Liverpool and Derby also going down, and none of the others in the leading pack managing a win, Stoke have missed the chance to return to the top. But they are only a point adrift and might return there if they can reverse the mini-slide with victory at Coventry City on Boxing Day. They hope to have Jimmy Greenhoff restored to the attack by then. Without his link play and subtle runs, Stoke have looked short of fluency and attacking ideas.

Stoke City 0 Arsenal 2 (Kidd 5, 38)
Attendance: 23,292

First Division: Coventry City v Stoke City

Hopes of getting the show back on the road at Coventry get off to the worst possible start. With only a minute on the clock,

Chris Cattlin goes in hard from behind on speedster Jimmy Robertson and for the second time this season, a Stoke City player is stretchered off with a broken leg.

It is a sickening blow for a team short on goals and confidence, and Coventry sense their opportunity. Stoke's usually slick passing game deserts them and Hurst is ploughing a lone furrow up front. The returning Greenhoff looks understandably tentative and the goal threat is limited. Coventry settle the match with two goals midway through the second half, when first Cross turns the ball in from close range, and then Shilton punches clear only for Hutchison to meet it on the volley and smash it into the roof of the net. It is another dispiriting result, morale further hit by the injury to Robertson.

The winger is not impressed with the tackle, 'It was a direct kick on the bone from behind. If I had made a tackle like that I would have expected to be booked. I felt the bone go, but thought it might have been a trapped nerve. It is the first time I have broken anything apart from a collarbone.' Note how in those days, when men were men, even the victim of a leg-breaking tackle from behind believes it warrants nothing worse than a booking.

Alan Dodd remembers Robertson being rather less tolerant of Cattlin in private after the game, 'I remember Jimmy Robertson on the treatment table in the dressing room. He was lying on the table and Chris Cattlin, the guy who broke his leg, came in to apologise. Jimmy told him to eff off. He didn't deliberately break his leg, but it was a bad tackle.'

In the continued absence of Conroy, the loss of Robertson further limits Stoke's options down the right. The Scot is a somewhat underrated player. 'He was a good player – a good crosser,' says Smith. 'Good balls into the box. He was quick and could look after himself. Wingers in those days needed to be able to look after themselves and Jimmy certainly could.'

The loss extends a dismal run to three defeats in a row, with the team groping for form. Waddington remains cautiously upbeat, 'We know where we are going wrong, and it is up to us now. It is mainly a question of confidence, although on yesterday's display the answers may not be found instantly.' They do not have much time to find them: West Ham at home is the next fixture, only two days later. But remarkably, Stoke remain only two points behind the leaders.

Coventry City 2 (Cross 65; Hutchison 73) Stoke City 0
Attendance: 22,345

After three losses, the West Ham fixture had taken on extra significance. Stoke could hardly afford to fail, but once again they were coming up against a team in top form. John Lyall had just begun what would be a lengthy period in the manager's chair, and West Ham were unbeaten in nine games under him. They were missing two of their legendary players for this game, Billy Bonds and Trevor Brooking, but that run had propelled them into the ever-growing crowd of teams near the top. They had been scoring freely too – beating Leicester 6-2, Burnley 5-3, Wolves 5-2 and Middlesbrough 3-0. All things considered, Stoke could have been forgiven for approaching the match with a degree of trepidation.

Stoke had spent part of the free day between games having a frank team talk lasting three hours in an effort to sort out what had been going wrong in recent weeks. They were boosted by the return of Terry Conroy for his first league start of the season. A big holiday crowd of more than 33,000 was there to welcome him, and the cameras were there too.

First Division: Stoke City v West Ham United
West Ham play with the confidence that their recent form has given them, but Stoke match them in an entertaining first half

in which there are chances at both ends. Hurst of Stoke Gould of West Ham both draw tremendous saves from goalkeepers from close range, and there is no score at the break.

That changes eight minutes into the second period when Pat Holland meets a perfectly flighted cross from Ayris and gives Shilton no chance with a fierce header. Although Stoke press hard to get back on level terms, with 20 minutes left it is beginning to look as though another depressing defeat is in prospect. But when Marsh swings in a long free kick, Denis Smith is obstructed and Stoke are given a penalty. Salmons steps up to take his first spot kick for Stoke. His strategy, he claims today, was 'close your eyes and belt it'. There are plenty of players who can't bear to watch their team take a penalty: their number does not usually include the taker himself. In any event, the Salmons plan works and the scores are level.

Six minutes later, Stoke are ahead thanks to the persistence of Mahoney and the nous of Hurst. Mahoney makes a surging run that breaks two tackles, either of which might have been given as fouls. The referee plays on, and Mahoney unleashes a cracking left-footed shot from almost exactly the same spot from where he had scored against Leeds on the opening day of the season. Mervyn Day in the West Ham goal does brilliantly to get a hand to it, but unfortunately for him he is able only to touch it against the bar. The wily old predator Geoff Hurst is the only player following up, and is able to score against his old club with a simple header from all of a yard.

West Ham are not done and Shilton has to be at his world-class best to tip over a Frank Lampard free kick from 20 yards. But they hold out for a win to steady the ship after the recent bad run. It will be a fortnight before the next league game, and they are able to enjoy the New Year celebrations rather more than the Christmas ones.

Even so, there is still considerable congestion at the top, with two points covering the top five and five points covering the top 13 – more than half the clubs in the table. Ipswich Town and Middlesbrough have their noses just in front as the old year comes to an end. It has been close from the start, and more than halfway through the campaign, any one of 15 or more clubs could emerge as champions if they are able to put a good run together.

Stoke City 2 (Salmons 70 pen; Hurst 76) West Ham United 1 (Holland 53)
Attendance: 33,498
Highlights available online

	DECEMBER 1974	P	W	D	L	Pts
1	Ipswich Town	25	14	2	9	30
2	Middlesbrough	25	11	8	6	30
3	Liverpool	23	12	5	6	29
4	Everton	24	8	13	3	29
5	**Stoke City**	**25**	**11**	**7**	**7**	**29**
6	West Ham United	25	10	8	7	28
7	Burnley	25	11	6	8	28
8	Manchester City	25	11	6	8	28
9	Derby County	24	10	7	7	27
10	Newcastle United	23	10	6	7	26
11	Leeds United	25	10	5	10	25
12	Wolverhampton Wanderers	24	8	9	7	25
13	Queens Park Rangers	25	10	5	10	25
14	Sheffield United	24	9	6	9	24
15	Coventry City	25	7	9	9	23
16	Birmingham City	25	9	4	12	22
17	Tottenham Hotspur	25	7	7	11	21
18	Chelsea	24	6	9	9	21
19	Arsenal	24	7	6	11	20
20	Carlisle United	25	7	3	15	17
21	Leicester City	24	5	6	13	16
22	Luton Town	24	4	7	13	15

1975: JANUARY

THE FIRST Saturday in January holds a special place in the affections of all lovers of English football. It is the day the teams in the top two divisions enter the FA Cup having been given a bye directly into the third round. The draw throws up many apparent mismatches, with the heavyweights of the top tier often pitched against the minnows of the lower divisions or non-league football – many of whom will already have come through several rounds to get to this point. Everyone loves a giant-killing – except the giants of course. Over the years the FA Cup has delivered many sensations, with Goliaths slain by Davids dozens of places below them in the footballing hierarchy.

The third-round draw in the 1974/75 competition was not kind to Stoke. True, they avoided the minnows and therefore the danger of a humiliating exit but instead they got perhaps the toughest task imaginable: an away trip to Anfield, the fortress of Liverpool Football Club. Liverpool were also the holders. As soon as the draw was made, Stoke fans were more or less writing off the cup that year, and consoling themselves with the thought that an early exit would allow them to concentrate on glory in the league. They had already been soundly beaten at Anfield earlier in the season, and had not won there since 1959. Liverpool were fresh from a 4-1 trouncing of Manchester City.

The players were not so defeatist, of course. Hudson thought Stoke could win the FA Cup *and* the First Division. 'We know we are good enough to win at Liverpool,' he said. 'If we get a good result, then we can go on to win the Double. No other team would stop us.'

I was working in Liverpool at the time and was able to get a ticket for the match, joining nearly 50,000 others in the cauldron of Anfield. I loved Hudson's optimism but I had a sinking feeling in my stomach. Like many fans, I also doubted whether we had the resources for both league and cup: in a small squad, two key players – Bloor and Conroy – had barely featured because of injury, and two more were out for the duration with broken legs. And there was still a long way to go.

FA Cup third round: Liverpool v Stoke City

It is a classic cup tie, end-to-end stuff with both sides taking the game to the opposition. Most of the pressure comes from the home team as they attack the Kop end, but Stoke's defence is strong and courageous.

Salmons might have hoped for some change from the inexperienced right-back Phil Neal – a new signing from Fourth Division Northampton Town. But the youngster shows the composure and skill that will make him a long-term fixture in the Liverpool defence. At the other end, Shilton is in imperious form – and he has to be, as Liverpool flood forward. Stoke give at least as good as they get with their confident midfield play but suffer from a lack of penetration up front.

It seems unlikely that such an engrossing and fast-paced match will end goalless, but there is no score with only 15 minutes to go when Liverpool finally unlock the stubborn Stoke defence. Hall and Cormack combine on the right, and

Shilton comes out to challenge Toshack for the cross. The goalkeeper gets there first but his punched clearance only reaches Steve Heighway, who promptly drives the ball home. It is worryingly similar to the goal conceded at Coventry on Boxing Day.

Stoke are hit on the counter-attack in the last minute as they press for an equaliser. Again it is Hall crossing from the right to present Kevin Keegan with a simple header. It brings an end to a brilliant and breathless encounter, with Stoke ruing the error that gave Liverpool the all-important first goal. 'Every time we make a mistake these days, we are punished for it,' says Shilton, who but for this one slip has been outstanding. 'I think it is the best we have played since I joined Stoke.'

So, as anticipated, no cup run. Back to the league, and a home game against Birmingham City that offers Stoke the chance to get back on terms with the pacesetters in this tightest of campaigns.

Liverpool 2 (Heighway 75; Keegan 89) Stoke City 0
Attendance: 48,723

Tony Waddington was looking for cover for Jimmy Robertson and Terry Conroy, who was now fit again, but serving a ban for being sent off in a reserve match. The manager asked Manchester City to release Mike Summerbee on a month's loan. Summerbee had been at Maine Road for nearly a decade and had enjoyed a great career, but at 32 he was in the reserves. Waddington insisted he was not looking for anything permanent, but Manchester City turned down the request anyway.

After the cup exit, it was back to league action and preparations for the visit of Birmingham. Blues manager Fred Goodwin said their 3-0 home defeat to Stoke only a month earlier still rankled, and they were keen to make amends. Denis Smith was ruled out with a strained calf muscle and an eye infection – it took at least two ailments to keep him from turning out.

First Division: Stoke City v Birmingham City

The *Match of the Day* cameras are at the Victoria Ground, but if they came expecting a hatful of goals they will be disappointed. The recalled Haslegrave is Stoke's main attacking threat in the early stages, although Hudson rattles the bar with a free kick and then almost scores directly from a corner. He later claims the ball crossed the line before Latchford scooped it out. Birmingham concede a string of free kicks as they are pushed backwards, but they defend with more resolution than they had shown at St Andrew's, and test Shilton with a couple of good efforts of their own before half-time.

The second half follows much the same pattern, with Hurst and Mahoney having attempts, and Hudson trying his luck with an overhead kick. Birmingham show their own goal threat when Howard Kendall fends off Skeels and hits the bar. Kenny Burns scores from the rebound but is ruled offside. Dodd has the ball in the net at the other end from a corner, but the referee orders it to be retaken, and Hurst heads over at very close range. Hurst has another good chance before making way for Moores, but Stoke cannot land the killer blow, and a goalless draw is a disappointing result. Stoke have not played badly, with Hudson's probing inspiring some fine flowing moves, but no one has been able to apply a finish.

But once again, so tight are things at the top that they do not lose touch with the leaders. Some of the other leading teams are playing each other: Derby beat Liverpool and Ipswich beat Middlesbrough, while Everton also win. After an indifferent series of results, with only one win in six and the goals having dried up, Stoke are still fourth and just two points off the top.

Stoke City 0 Birmingham City 0
Attendance: 26,157

GREAT CROSSES: MY TEAM-MATE JOHN MARSH

DENIS SMITH: 'Good player, Jack. He played midfield, played full-back – good on the ball. Not the best defender in the world, but going forward – extremely good. The same with Pej but you wouldn't fancy taking them on because they'd both got a nasty streak. Because you've got your Jimmy Greenhoffs, your Alan Hudsons, your Peter Dobings, your Gordon Banks – the superstars – other players like Alan Bloor and Jack Marsh get forgotten. You get taken for granted. But you don't play as many games as Bluto and Jack did without being good players at that level. Jackie was quiet in his own way but he'll have a couple of drinks then he'll start talking.

'Considering how well he struck a ball, you would think his goalscoring record would be better – especially as he and Pej were basically very attacking full-backs. In fact Jackie started as a midfield player, Pej as a left-winger and their job was getting forward and getting crosses in. Jackie was the best crosser in the club by far – better than the wide players.'

JIMMY GREENHOFF: 'Jackie was so skilful. I'm sure if he had played for Man United he would have played for England. He was a defender who played like a midfielder.'

ERIC SKEELS: 'Came through the ranks. Nippy. Not tall but he read the game quite well. You'd always get the odd winger that would give you a hard time but generally he was very good. If they were fast he was fine, but if they were tricky he had more problems. He wore contact lenses and sometimes they would drop out and he'd be looking for them while the game was still going on!'

ALAN DODD: 'He was a great full-back and a great player. Liked to get forward and swing crosses in. He used to strike a lovely ball.'

ALAN HUDSON: 'Jackie was a comedian. He was very, very fit. He could run like the wind. He was a good full-back. I used to say to him, "Why do you never pass to me?" He'd get the ball and whack it, get it up to John Ritchie. We would go out, me, him Geoff Salmons, Sean Haslegrave, we would go out twice a week round all the pubs in Stoke, that was our little rat pack. I said, "No matter how much I drink with you, you still won't pass to me on a Saturday afternoon!" We got on great. He was a good full-back, not many went by him. Good striker of a ball, good athlete, got up and down.

'Jackie was a player and a man who lacked inner confidence, but as nice a man as you'll ever meet. He was quick once in his stride, and that stride got him forward to join attacks at all times, something we relied on in this side. Because of our ability to slow the game down and then pick up the pace, we needed pace from the backs coming forward and both our full-backs would join in the play, in fact they loved it. He could hit a sweet ball and worked tremendously hard for the team, although he needed leading around at times. He was not always sure he was doing the right thing, that being the confidence thing.'

TERRY CONROY: 'If I was playing on the opposite team on the left wing and he was marking me, I wouldn't have got much change out of him. He was quick, attacking. All day he was up and down – his energy levels were phenomenal. To overlap and get the ball into the box was just a natural part of his play. A great crosser.

'I had a great understanding with Jackie because if I cut inside the full-back and took the full-back away, Jackie would be steaming behind to make space. I knew that I could use him to get in behind and whip in a dangerous cross. Very effective he was. The only time he ever worried about wingers was a couple of times a season. When he was playing against Steve Kindon [Wolves] he knew he would get a chasing, because of Kindon's pace. And the other one was Leighton James [Burnley] who was a tricky winger. He had great battles with Kindon and James particularly, and they were the only two he would say, "Today I could maybe get a bit of a chasing." He respected the skills of the wingers.'

Amazingly, as a tiring season approached its climax, Stoke were planning a series of friendly games. After heavy spending in the previous year, and their early FA Cup exit, they needed to find alternative revenue. The first of these fixtures was to be in Morocco and would guarantee the club a £5,000 payday. It was a friendly match in Casablanca against a team that were hoping to qualify for the Olympic Games. Now Stoke were out of the cup there was some spare time in the calendar, with only two league games in January. After Birmingham, the second of these was at Leicester, where Shilton would come up against his former team-mates – and supporters – at their home ground.

Alan Dodd, who had stepped so capably into Alan Bloor's shoes, had flu and was unfit for the trip to Leicester. Tony Waddington had never had much truck with players crying off with illness or injury, and frequently told them to lace up their boots on the grounds that 'you look all right to me'. In Dodd's case though, he was forced to give way.

'I had flu,' Dodd recalls. 'Waddo phoned me and I was in bed. I was really poorly. I thought I was dying. I'd missed training for a few days but Waddo took it for granted I would be fit enough to play without even seeing me. When I didn't turn up, he called me. "Where are you? We're going to

Leicester, the bus is outside." "I'm not fit enough." "Well come down, we'll have a look at you."

'I didn't get dressed. I just went down in my pyjamas and my slippers and I went into the dressing room. He couldn't believe it. He had the shock of his life. He looked me up and down and then he accepted it.'

First Division: Leicester City v Stoke City

Leicester are without a win in 11 games and are deep in relegation trouble, but they show real fighting spirit from the off. Shilton is roundly booed every time he touches the ball. After only five minutes, though, he shows his class when reacting to Alan Birchenall's diving header from only six yards out. The television commentator has already said 'that's a goal' when Shilton manages to parry it at full stretch, and is then back on his feet to block Frank Worthington following up. The early pressure is all from Leicester, but Stoke's confident passing game begins to reassert itself after the early offensive, with Greenhoff finally looking back to his best form after his broken nose.

Just before the hour, Stoke go in front. From a Shilton punt, Hurst wins a cheap free kick by backing into Munro. The two of them then take up positions in the box and Salmons floats the free kick in towards them. They both stick out a foot, but Hurst gets there first and flashes a cracking volley past Wallington.

For the rest of the game it is a struggle to retain that lead as Leicester show a spirit and skill that belies their position in the table. Three minutes from time their persistence is rewarded courtesy of some not very impressive defending. Worthington and Kember work a position on the right and Kember slings over a cross that evades everyone except Len Glover at the far post, and he scores with a simple downward header. Shilton has no chance. 'At last the great man is beaten,' says Hugh Johns on commentary.

It is another disappointing result, with an equaliser conceded in the dying minutes. Results elsewhere are not very helpful either. Carlisle confirm their reputation as the great disrupters, beating Ipswich at home, but there are wins for Manchester City, Derby and Everton, who now go top. Their season has been founded on a series of draws – 13 of them – but only three defeats. Burnley now creep into the leading group for the first time, as three points cover the top eight. Next week, the FA Cup takes over again, so Stoke end January with a meagre return of two points and elimination from the cup. They will need to do something special in the next game against Manchester City, who have the same number of points, and whose confidence will be high after a 5-1 demolition of Newcastle United.

Leicester City 1 (Glover 87) Stoke City 1 (Hurst 57)
Attendance: 21,734

	JANUARY 1975	P	W	D	L	Pts
1	Everton	26	10	13	3	33
2	Ipswich Town	27	15	2	10	32
3	Burnley	27	13	6	8	32
4	**Stoke City**	**27**	**11**	**9**	**7**	**31**
5	Liverpool	25	13	5	7	31
6	Middlesbrough	27	11	9	7	31
7	Derby County	26	12	7	7	31
8	Manchester City	27	12	7	8	31
9	West Ham United	27	10	9	8	29
10	Leeds United	27	12	5	10	29
11	Sheffield United	26	10	7	9	27
12	Newcastle United	25	10	6	9	26
13	Queens Park Rangers	27	10	6	11	26
14	Wolverhampton Wanderers	26	8	9	9	25
15	Coventry City	27	8	9	10	25
16	Tottenham Hotspur	27	8	7	12	23
17	Arsenal	26	8	7	11	23
18	Birmingham City	27	9	5	13	23
19	Chelsea	26	6	10	10	22
20	Carlisle United	27	8	3	16	19
21	Leicester City	26	5	7	14	17
22	Luton Town	26	4	8	14	16

15

FEBRUARY

A WEEK of rain had turned the Victoria Ground pitch into even more of a gluepot than usual for the visit of Manchester City. Realising that something needed to be done to reverse the recent lacklustre form, Tony Waddington made a rare strategic intervention. He was usually happy to pick his best 11 and trust the players to deliver the goods, but now he established a tactical 4-3-3 formation with Hurst and Moores partnered up front and Greenhoff in a wider role. Skeels came in for the still flu-ridden Dodd at the back. Manchester City were without Rodney Marsh, who had scored the only goal in the reverse fixture, but had a more than able replacement in Joe Royle, recently signed from Everton and already having scored two goals against Stoke earlier in the season. Mike Summerbee also returned to the City line-up to face the club who had wanted to sign him on loan a fortnight previously.

First Division: Stoke City v Manchester City

Summerbee and Royle combine to test Shilton but the early pressure is all from Stoke, with MacRae in the City goal only grabbing a typical long-range effort from Mahoney at the second attempt. When Manchester City come forward they are met with typically robust defence – Tueart is so incensed by one Pejic tackle that he tears off his shirt and throws it at the full-back. A booking for Smith means he has now accumulated enough points for an automatic suspension, which will put further strain on already stretched resources.

Stoke mount a series of attacks with all the forwards prominent, but the pitch is now cutting up badly. There is a nasty moment when the ball sticks in the mud as Skeels tries to clear, and has to be scrambled away for a corner. Shilton saves well from Summerbee when the ball comes in.

Stoke deserve to be in front, but it takes them until the stroke of half-time to take advantage of their territorial superiority. The goal is a classic example of how deep Hudson likes to come to collect the ball and then how much ground he covers. He picks it up just outside his own penalty area and advances before passing to Greenhoff who sends a cracking ball out to Mahoney on the right. By the time Mahoney has controlled and come inside, Hudson appears outside him on the right wing and is calling for the ball. He skins Asa Hartford before putting a cross right on the head of Ian Moores who scores from six yards.

The goal gives Stoke confidence, and their second-half domination is rewarded by another classic Hudson contribution after 68 minutes. He takes a throw-in about halfway inside the Manchester City half on the right, gets the ball back and then sets off on a mazy run across the penalty area. He plays a brilliant one-two with Moores that would have set him up for a left-foot shot – if he ever used his left foot for shooting that is. Instead he checks back inside. It looks as though the opportunity has gone, but from a standing position he threads the ball through the Victoria Ground mud and a mass of defenders into MacRae's right-hand corner. 'It did not seem possible,' says Hugh Johns on commentary.

Stoke are now in complete control and looking like title contenders again as Hudson outshines the England midfielder Colin Bell. The Hurst-Moores combination is working well and they now take over the scoring. A loose pass from Tueart sees Hudson again there to pick up just outside his own box. He punts it up to Salmons who has Hurst outside him on the left flank. Hurst cuts in and his low cross into the centre of the box is met by a diving Ian Moores for his second of the afternoon.

An overlapping Marsh then puts Moores through in masses of space. With a hat-trick beckoning, he completely mis-hits his shot. But then he turns provider. Receiving the ball with his back to goal in the middle of the box, he shifts it forward to Hurst who is galloping down the left and clips a left-footed shot past MacRae. The mud then comes to Stoke's aid as it frustrates Royle when he has only Shilton to beat, but at the other end Salmons narrowly fails to complete the rout with a lofted shot on to the crossbar. It is the last act in the team's best performance in weeks, and puts their title challenge right back on track. I was at the game, and it is one of the best performances I remember from all my time following Stoke. Hudson was completely dominant. With Liverpool losing at Arsenal, and Derby going down at QPR, it also consolidates their position in the table, moving them to third with only two points covering the top four.

After the game, Waddington singles out Hudson's display as one of the greatest individual performances he can remember. 'He has that special kind of skill that Stanley Matthews and Tom Finney had,' enthuses the manager. 'It's the ability to stand still with the ball and make defenders afraid to tackle. Critics talk about him needing to prove his character to gain an England cap, but he does not have to prove anything. He has been with us just over a year now and he has revitalised the team.'

Waddington is also delighted with the form of Moores, who has been involved in all four goals, and with the success of his tactical switch. 'It was a risk in a way, playing without a winger on the right and we could have been exposed by Tueart. But John Mahoney was given a wider role and did his job superbly.'

Stoke City 4 (Moores 44, 84; Hudson 68; Hurst 87)
Manchester City 0
Attendance: 32,007
Highlights available online

SUBLIME ABILITIES: MY TEAM-MATE ALAN HUDSON

TERRY CONROY: 'When you played alongside him you knew it was phenomenal what he could do. His energy levels too – when him and John Mahoney got together they were the best midfield duo in the country. Huddy was able to do what he could do only because of John's energy and John's commitment. Huddy was more than capable – 90 minutes, he could go, 180, and then he would go out on the pop for two or three days and then come back and produce the same that he had in the previous game. He was just an athlete, a natural, someone who loved the life he led, but knew that when he was called upon to produce on the field, he could do it. That's why Waddo indulged him. He wouldn't let Waddo down. Regardless of being out on the pop until maybe three o'clock on a Saturday morning, come three o'clock that afternoon it didn't bother him, it didn't go against him. That was what made him the player he was. His lifestyle maybe helped him to have this arrogant cocky approach on the pitch.

'Sometimes Smithy and Pej would want to push him further up the field as he was getting so deep. But that suited him. He had a fantastic first touch and it was like he glided over the ground. He skipped tackles easily and he'd play a five-yard pass and get it back, then a ten-yard pass and get it back, so he weaved these patterns throughout the pitch rather than in the last third, so he could build up to the stage where eventually he could play a killer ball. Sometimes the opposition didn't take him quite seriously because they felt he was a bit of a playboy, he wouldn't be up for the challenge. They gave him a few smacks. It didn't matter – he had this great ability to evade tackles.'

GEOFF HURST: 'Alan had far more ability than most of the other players during my time in the game. His passing, short and long, was sublime. Although predominantly right-footed, his vision, awareness and speed of thought allowed him to wriggle out of the tightest situations and set up attacking moves with the minimum of fuss. He also delivered the ball from corners and set pieces with unerring accuracy.'

JIMMY GREENHOFF: 'Alan always wanted the ball. Whether he was free, or had players surrounding him. In that sense he was like me. We both wanted it all the time.'

DENIS SMITH: 'Huddy was a truly great footballer who should have played 100 times for England. He had everything – incredible skill, vision, a change of pace, a drop of the shoulder to earn vital inches to play a pass, the light-footed ability to skim over the treacherous surface of the Victoria Ground, supreme fitness and athletic prowess despite his playboy aura, and the charisma to match that sublime blend of abilities. I first discovered this when he left me for dead in our first training session together. He turned me inside and then out, leaving me on my backside that first day, and I thought to myself, "If you can do that, son, you've got to be in my team."

'His whole rationale was to use every blade of grass on the pitch and every player in the team to keep the ball, work opponents out and then strike. He loaned you the ball, did Huddy. He gave it to you, saying, "You can have it, as long as you give it me back," and we were all, especially the likes of Jimmy Greenhoff, Terry Conroy and Josh Mahoney, soon on the same wavelength.

'People talk about his touch and his vision – very one-footed, which was incredible. His left foot was only for standing on, but what he could do with his right foot was incredible, and as an athlete he could outrun any of us. This is something people don't talk about, but he was an incredible athlete.'

GEOFF SALMONS: 'When I moved from Sheffield United to Stoke I had played with Tony Currie at Bramall Lane and they had me compare them. They were similar. Currie could knock a good long ball. Huddy could just dictate a game. One touch one-twos, back and forth. He was a great ball player. It was a pleasure to play with him.'

ERIC SKEELS: 'He'd say to me, "Alfie if you get in any trouble, just look round and give it to me, I'll be near you all the time." All you'd do was look and he was there, and he might be being marked but somehow he got away and you'd play it towards him and off he'd go. He was full of energy. He could go out and have a good night and the following day in a hard day of training he'd be there, running as if he'd not touched a drink. Full of fitness he was, and a cracking player. If he wasn't getting the ball he'd go looking for it because he wanted to be in the game 100 per cent for 90 minutes, and to be the star – and he was. He controlled the ball so easily, his skill was unbelievable and he could beat a man easily and lay the ball off. And he'd work for the whole 90 minutes.'

'Once when he was still at Chelsea I was marking him tightly. And after the game, I went towards the bar and Alan was already there. So I just leaned past him and he turned round and says, "F***ing hell, the game's over now Skeelsy – will you leave me alone! I've had nothing but you on me for 90 minutes and you're still here now. Go away!" Then he bought me a drink.'

TERRY CONROY: 'Alan worked harder on his fitness than any of us. He would often wear a couple of black bin bags, cutting arm and leg holes in them, to make himself sweat more to help him shed the extra pounds and the alcohol he'd taken on board after the game on a Saturday afternoon. Huddy was very focused in the sense that he knew he had to pay for having that good time, and he was prepared to do it. Combining the lifestyle with the way he played was, frankly, nothing short of miraculous!'

With four of the top pack playing each other in the next round of games, there was a further chance to make progress with the trip to Tottenham. Spurs had only one win in nine, but Stoke had never won at White Hart Lane. The main threat would again come from Martin Chivers, so often linked with a move to the Victoria Ground. But Smith was available to mark him before he started a two-match suspension.

Jackie Marsh, however, was out with a stomach bug, and Dodd was missing too. He had recovered from the flu that led to his pyjama-clad visit to the dressing room to prove his unfitness to play, but now he had back problems. He missed the trip to London but did nothing to improve his fitness while remaining in Stoke.

'I had a bad back,' he recalls. 'Then my dad phoned me up on the Saturday and said, "Can you come and help me move these concrete slabs?" I asked him how many there were and he said 20. I said, "I'm supposed to have a bad back, that's why I'm not playing today." He said, "You'll be all right." So I helped him. I didn't tell Waddo.'

First Division: Tottenham Hotspur v Stoke City

Waddington might have forgiven Dodd given how well the team manages even with its weakened defence. Spurs offer some spirited resistance early on but Stoke are the more incisive and score from a training-ground move after 23 minutes. Full-back Kevin Lewis, deputising for Marsh, sends over a cross from the right, then Moores jumps above Beal at the far post and heads it into the path of Greenhoff who has the simple task of finishing the move.

Ten minutes later it is 2-0 when a one-two between Moores and Hudson sees the playmaker running clear on goal. Naylor gets back to intercept but his back pass is short and Hudson keeps going to flick the ball past Daines in the Spurs goal. Moores continues to add to his growing reputation, winning everything in the air and creating several chances for Hurst, as well as coming close himself. Shilton deals competently with what little threat Spurs muster, and Stoke close out a comfortable win that confirms their revival and extends their unbeaten run to five. Waddington continues to sing Hudson's praises and wonders what more he can do to earn an England call-up. He will play in a World XI before he plays for England, says the manager. Of the team performance as a whole he says, 'We are putting it all together now.'

There is more good news when the players get back to the dressing room and find that leaders Everton have lost at Manchester City and Liverpool have beaten Ipswich. With Burnley winning too, it is once again hopelessly congested at the top. No one can remember a title race like it. There are only around a dozen games to go, but more than half the teams in the division still have the chance to come through if they can create the necessary momentum. In the short term, a win at home to Wolves, when other teams will be in FA Cup action, could be enough to take Stoke back to the top. It is all the more important to get a result, because the game will be followed by a run of five away fixtures out of seven.

Tottenham Hotspur 0 Stoke City 2 (Greenhoff 23; Hudson 32)
Attendance: 22,941

Tony Waddington was pleased that Stoke's emergence as genuine title contenders was at last being reflected at the turnstiles. Gates of more than 30,000 for the West Ham and Manchester City games were well above average.

The manager believed this reflected not only the results, but also the manner in which they were being achieved. 'We have always tried to play the sort of football to attract the public, and it looks as though we could start pulling in about the 30,000 mark regularly,' he said. 'At places like Anfield and Old Trafford this would be regarded as a poor gate, but it is a slow process for clubs like ours to build up big attendances.'

Geoff Hurst had also been ruminating on recent form in an interview with the *Sentinel*. 'We are in with a great chance of topping the league,' he said. 'I think Everton and Liverpool are our dangers, but we have to prove whether we are good enough to stay at the top. No one has yet managed to stay on top for any length of time this season. When we were there before, we found that clubs were really gunning for us, and games became that much more aggressive.

'Personally, I would prefer to keep in the top three until the last four games and then put the pressure on. But we have proved we are good enough to get there and we shall know more about it next time.'

Hurst was happy at the way his partnership with young Moores was working out, 'The extra striker is helping things up front. With just two up in attack we were getting marked out at times, but the present system is giving me that extra space. I am quite happy with my game considering I have played only about half the matches.'

Hurst may not have been quite the player he was, but he still had an eye for goal and an instinct for turning up at the right place at the right time. The loss of Ritchie had put more pressure on him, but the emergence of Moores to reinforce the attack had given him a little more time and space with which to work. His goals had been match-winners on three occasions already.

First Division: Stoke City v Wolverhampton Wanderers

Wolves are in mid-table, neither threatening the leaders nor in danger of relegation. A run of five defeats has just ended with a win over Arsenal. They still represent a threat though, and memories are fresh of the pulsating match at Molineux the day Peter Shilton made his Stoke debut. On that day, Wolves grabbed a point when Kenny Hibbitt stroked home a last-minute penalty. The return game will be just as action-packed.

Up front for Wolves is Steve Kindon, and all the defenders of the time recall what a tough prospect it was playing against him. In Smith's absence through suspension, it is Alan Dodd who has the job of marking him as he comes back after injury. 'I didn't play very well,' he recalls. 'Steve Kindon was a big powerful centre-forward and he dragged me all over the pitch.'

The game picks up where the last one left off, with action at both ends and the Stoke defence looking tentative, with Smith missing and Dodd rusty. Stoke are beginning to find some rhythm, but seem to lose it after about 25 fans run across the pitch and play is halted for a time. Shortly afterwards,

Marsh is adjudged to have grabbed Hibbitt's arm, and the Wolves man has another chance to score from the penalty spot. Shilton almost tips the shot round, but it goes in, and the visitors are in front at the break. Although some of their tackling is questionable, they are playing with more confidence and positivity than Stoke, whose intricate moves are coming to nothing.

Alarm signals sound only two minutes into the second half when an in-swinging corner from Farley beats everyone and is helped into the net by Munro, with Shilton complaining in vain that he is being obstructed. Conroy replaces Hurst to try to add greater attacking threat, but there is no way through, and Wolves threaten again with some good counter-attacking.

With a quarter of an hour to go, Pejic goes down in a challenge with Kindon and is clearly in trouble. He remembers the moment well.

'Steve Kindon was going to take a shot just inside our area in front of the Boothen End,' he recalled in a *Sentinel* column. 'He had a big back lift so I sneaked in, and he kicked the back of my leg. It was an accident, but the pain was … we'll just say excruciating.

'I limped off and our physio Mike Allen said straight away, "Mike, you've broken your leg." There were 15 minutes left so I said, "I'm going back on." He said, "You can't go back on, you've broken your leg!" but I was already on.'

With Stoke having used their substitute, they would have had to play with ten men but for Pejic's determination to continue. This was the kind of devotion to the cause that fans adored. Pejic said, 'It was what I had to do, and nobody could stop me. I remember the noise from the Boothen End and I remember putting in a tackle on John Richards with my bad leg on the halfway line.'

For all his guts, the omens are not good. At 2-0 down and with time ticking away the supporters are drifting out of the ground. They miss a grandstand finish. With three minutes to go a free kick by Hudson is punched out by the keeper, Skeels returns the ball to the middle and Conroy heads home. It is a lifeline but it doesn't look as though there is time to save the game, especially with Pejic barely mobile. But with a minute to go, Conroy returns the favour to Skeels. Hudson puts the winger away and he beats his man before putting in a deep cross that Skeels arrives to nod over the line. He is duly mobbed by his team-mates.

The game ends 2-2 and after several matches in which points have been dropped, this is definitely a point won. Not only that, but the draw is enough to see Stoke return to the top of the table for the first time since December, although it will be tough holding on to top spot as rivals have a game in hand and standards are so high. John Ritchie is a spectator these days as he recovers from his double leg fracture. As he observes, 'To watch Wolves play and realise they are only a mid-table side makes you appreciate how tough it is in the First Division.'

It is a great achievement to hit the top. But it is bittersweet, because it comes at such a cost. Mike Pejic's injury is confirmed as a broken leg. 'I got back in the dressing room and I collapsed. My wife had to drive me up to the hospital, the old A&E in Hartshill, and I was in plaster for the next eight weeks or so,' he reflected.

There is admiration for his refusal to come off in spite of the injury. And there are plaudits for one of the unsung heroes of the team, the veteran Eric Skeels, whose goals are as rare as hen's teeth but he has scored a vital one here. 'Eric doesn't even score in five-a-side games!' says his manager. 'What a player to have at your club. If we want a job done anywhere, just send for Eric. He has been with us 16 years so he is getting on a bit, although there was a mix-up with his birth certificate so we were never sure of his exact age.'

Skeels is actually 35, and this is his first goal since September 1968. His previous one was five years before that. 'I am enjoying life and probably playing as well as ever,' he tells the *Sentinel*. 'It is something new for me to play for Stoke when they are top of the league. You just can't help giving your best.' He will go on to hold the record for the most appearances for Stoke, and this is the last of the seven goals he will score for them.

The suspended Smith was a spectator, but remembers that the feeling was now building that good times lay ahead, 'The Wolves game saw the team display tremendous fighting spirit to claw back a two-goal deficit inside the final five minutes. When you are on a run like that, you think you are going to win every match. You certainly don't think you are ever going to lose. It's great. We were on a real roll and realised we had a realistic chance of challenging for the title. The excitement built within both the squad and the fans as we were finally fulfilling our undoubted potential.' An away trip to struggling Luton will be the next assignment for the new league leaders.

Stoke City 2 (Conroy 87; Skeels 88) Wolverhampton Wanderers 2 (Hibbitt 25 pen, Munro 47)
Attendance: 30,611

HARD NUT: MY TEAM-MATE MIKE PEJIC

ALAN DODD: 'Micky was probably my best mate at Stoke. In some ways we had similar personalities, we were both down to earth. We had similar interests – we loved the countryside. He bought a farm and I used to go up there and help him out. Smithy and Pej would walk through a brick wall for Stoke. Pejic could look after himself. Very aggressive. They might have knocked the ball past him but they didn't get past. That was his motto, "Thou shalt not pass."'

TERRY CONROY: 'Pej had always got a battle to fight – always. He could have a fight in a phone box with nobody else in it. He was just that type of character, aggressive. Not a chip on his shoulder but he would always be thinking someone was trying to get the better of him and he was up for that. We were a humorous bunch, but he was very dry and maybe didn't always see the humour. But he was hard. Maybe not as overlapping as Jackie was. He didn't get forward as much as Jackie. He was a left-winger, then he was cultivated as a back. His strength was phenomenal. When he kicked you, you stayed down. Battles with Summerbee, Tueart, Terry Paine – other lads who were a little bit fiery in their own way – he always seemed to be at war with somebody. There weren't many who could get the better of him, because he was quick as well.'

DENIS SMITH: 'Where Jackie was a laugh a minute, Pej never said anything. Before he came into training each morning, we would lay bets on whether he would speak. There weren't many takers. In would come Pej and all he would say would be "morning" and then when he was leaving he'd just say "see ya" and that was it. That was all you got out of him.

'He would come into training dressed like a gentleman farmer and he sometimes used to turn up to matches in his Land Rover with two sheepdogs sat in the front. For all that, I would trust him with my life. No one was going to go past him. We used to call him "The Claw" because he would grab hold of players when they did manage to best him, and he'd rather give away a free kick than let someone get clear down the wing to do us damage.'

ALAN HUDSON: 'Pejic was his own worst enemy. If only he would listen. Tony never spoke to Pejic because he knew he wouldn't listen. It was his way or no way. He was a hard nut. He was a good player.'

ERIC SKEELS: 'He liked to get forward. He was fast and could deal with a winger who was nippy. There was no messing with Pej – if one of the opposition went in strong, they soon knew that they were up against somebody. You wouldn't want to have a fight with him. He liked beating someone and going on a bit of a run and getting to the byline and getting it across. He was very much his own man.'

GEOFF SALMONS: 'Pej was temperamental, but no problem to play with. He was a good full-back. Tough.'

Waddington was left to rue the addition of another name to his long-term injury list. 'We must be fated,' he said. 'Three broken legs and a broken nose must be some kind of record. We have an entire back four out of action.'

As well as the three broken legs, Alan Bloor had yet to make a start, Smith remained suspended and Mahoney and Bowers were still nursing injuries. Waddington called it the worst injury crisis in his 15 years at the helm. 'We will have to play at Luton with someone who is not 100 per cent fit,' he said. But he ruled out a further foray into the transfer market. 'I have given the matter a great deal of thought over the weekend. Another signing now would not be in our interests in the long run. It would only curb the progress of the younger lads.' It would also put very considerable further strain on the club's finances.

First Division: Luton Town v Stoke City

Luton are mounting a spirited fight against relegation, with an unchanged team taking ten points from their last seven games. Their manager Harry Haslam is planning to take the attack to Stoke. 'It is the way we know best,' he says.

Conroy's contributions to the late show against Wolves have earned him a recall to the starting team, but in the unaccustomed role of centre-forward, with Hurst on the bench. True to their word, Luton do most of the early attacking and Shilton is called into action to make several saves. His huge clearances are causing problems for the Luton defence in turn, and Conroy and Greenhoff both have the ball in the net only for both to be ruled offside.

The talking point of the game comes two minutes before the break. Hudson springs the offside trap, beats the goalkeeper and rolls the ball into the goal. Or does he? Full-back John Ryan scurries back and scoops the ball out before it hits the back of the net, and the referee rules that it has not crossed the line. No goal. Hudson is furious. He is still furious today, 'I played a one-two on the edge of the box, went round the goalkeeper and rolled it in. As I turned away, it was a goal, the full-back had run in and scooped it out, and he disallowed it. It was in! There was no one there, else I would have blasted it. It was two yards over the line by the time John Ryan cleared it.'

Stoke are still complaining as the teams go in for half-time, and come out again with all guns blazing to force two quick corners. Within five minutes the pressure tells. Greenhoff puts Conroy through and he is brought down in the box. Penalty. Step forward Geoff 'just close your eyes and belt it' Salmons. But this time the formula does not work and he rolls the spot kick wide of the post.

By this time, Stoke might be forgiven for thinking that this is not going to be their day. The game continues at the same high tempo. Hurst comes on and immediately misses two chances, and Greenhoff brings a superb one-handed save from the goalkeeper with a darting header. Luton are undaunted and again test Shilton, and both sides are still pressing hard for a winner when the 90 minutes are up.

Luton Town 0 Stoke City 0
Attendance: 19,894

Once again, Stoke are finding it tough at the top, and although they are clinging on it is only by goal difference from the surging Burnley. A goalless draw in the Merseyside derby helps their cause, but Manchester City and Derby County both make up ground. Once again it is impossibly tight at the top.

It is not surprising, then, that Stoke are swiftly dethroned. Everton play one of their games in hand during the week, also against Luton. A 3-1 victory means they leapfrog Stoke and Burnley, and go to the top of the table at the start of the critical month of March.

FEBRUARY 1975		P	W	D	L	Pts
1	Everton	30	12	14	4	38
2	**Stoke City**	**31**	**13**	**11**	**7**	**37**
3	Burnley	31	15	7	9	37
4	Ipswich Town	31	17	2	12	36
5	Liverpool	30	14	7	9	35
6	Leeds United	31	14	7	10	35
7	Manchester City	30	14	7	9	35
8	Derby County	30	13	8	9	34
9	West Ham United	31	11	11	9	33
10	Middlesbrough	31	11	11	9	33
11	Queens Park Rangers	31	12	8	11	32
12	Newcastle United	30	13	6	11	32
13	Sheffield United	30	12	8	10	32
14	Wolverhampton Wanderers	30	10	10	10	30
15	Coventry City	31	9	12	10	30
16	Chelsea	30	8	11	11	27
17	Birmingham City	30	10	6	14	26
18	Arsenal	29	9	7	13	25
19	Tottenham Hotspur	32	8	8	16	24
20	Leicester City	29	6	8	15	20
21	Luton Town	30	5	10	15	20
22	Carlisle United	31	8	3	20	19

16

MARCH

STOKE WERE by now one down and two to go in a run of three consecutive away games. They had sometimes been accused of an excessively defensive attitude on the road, but results had been good. The *Sentinel*'s Stoke reporter, Peter Hewitt, thought it was time for some perspective. 'When Stoke look back on the season,' he wrote, 'they will be reflecting that despite last-minute slips at Chelsea, Wolves and Leicester, and a missed penalty at Luton, it is at home where they have missed vital points, having dropped eight so far.

'Yet in a year when they have maintained their title challenge all the way in the face of three broken leg setbacks, Stoke have scored 19 goals away from home, a total only bettered by Burnley and QPR. They have scored nine more away goals than Liverpool for example and gained as many points on their travels as Leeds. They have already won twice as many away games as in the whole of last season.

'Stoke have been involved in some tremendous away games. Three goals at Chelsea is scarcely negative defensive play, and they went flat out on attack at Everton only to be beaten by defensive errors. They have come a long way this season.'

Hewitt noted that with more teams achieving higher standards and nursing greater ambitions, 'It is hard in the English First Division.' It was a point Tony Waddington had made before, and made again now. 'It is a far harder First Division than it was when we came into it 12 years ago,' he said. 'More teams are acquiring good players than ever before. There was a time when clubs like Stoke just could not afford the sort of players they have.'

Stoke received further encouragement ahead of their trip to Middlesbrough from an unusual source. With his customary candour, Jack Charlton told his Middlesbrough team that they were not good enough to win the league. They had been in the mix for most of the campaign but their challenge had fallen away of late, and they had scored only once in six outings. Although tenth, they were still only five points off the top. Stoke were unbeaten in the league since Boxing Day – a run of seven games, with three wins and four draws.

First Division: Middlesbrough v Stoke City

Although Denis Smith is back after suspension, there is a makeshift look to the back four with Dodd and Lewis at fullback. Hurst is restored up front and Conroy reverts to his usual position on the right wing. But Boro are on the attack from the word go, and Stoke, taking time to organise themselves in defence, are hard-pressed to hold them out. A four-man move after 18 minutes is finished by Hickton from 12 yards. Shilton gets a hand to it but cannot keep it out. The lead is quickly doubled as Foggon latches on to a loose ball and places his shot past Shilton. Stoke cannot get a foothold, and look anything but title challengers as they go in 2-0 down at the break.

In the second half they fare no better against a well-organised defence that chases and harasses effectively and wins the aerial battles. Mahoney, Salmons and Conroy all have shots, and Smith spends some time in attack to try to win something in the air. But Middlesbrough are largely untroubled and run out comfortable winners.

Having dismissed the title prospects of his own team, Jack Charlton gives an equally blunt assessment of Stoke's chances: 'I thought Stoke were a good bet for the title. But after watching them today, I feel they have got to have a few more players prepared to die if they are going to do it. I thought they played too much football, but we confined them well, knowing that if you give Stoke room to play, they can paralyse you. They missed Micky Pejic, who always causes us problems.'

Tony Waddington can only agree, 'We lacked that bit extra up front. We had the chances to have pulled back, but I was disappointed with the way we played. We took too long to get organised.' He ends on a defiant note, 'Having got this far on the title road, we shall not be giving up. We shall be battling on.'

It has been a sobering afternoon and with Everton and Burnley both winning, Stoke have again lost valuable ground. It will be a fortnight before they have the chance to make it up, because their next scheduled opponents, Ipswich Town, are in FA Cup action the following Saturday. Stoke will play a friendly against Bristol Rovers instead.

Middlesbrough 2 (Hickton 18; Foggon 25) Stoke City 0
Attendance: 25,765

The following week, as Stoke and some of the other title contenders sat it out, Everton and Derby both took advantage with wins while Burnley and Liverpool drew with each other. Stoke were now five points adrift and Everton had moved two points clear – as big a lead as anyone had held since the start of the season. They seemed to have timed their run to perfection, and with ten games to go were now favourites.

Stoke fans took their minds off these dispiriting developments by turning their attention to the forthcoming friendly international between England and their old foes West Germany at Wembley – a game in which Alan Hudson would make his debut. Manager Don Revie, who had been slow to recognise the midfielder's sensational performances for Stoke, suddenly could not speak highly enough of him. 'Hudson could be a key figure for the next six or seven years if he goes out and takes control of himself,' he said. 'By then people will be telling lesser players that they could become another Alan Hudson. He has that special kind of talent.'

Hudson himself betrayed no qualms about his biggest test to date, 'I have been waiting six years for this cap, and I always thought I would be nervous about my first England game. But when I saw who I would be playing with, I just felt I was going to play well. The team has the sort of players I like playing with.' He would be alongside Alan Ball, with Malcolm Macdonald, Kevin Keegan and Mick Channon up front.

On the night, he did not disappoint. Hudson overshadowed everyone else on the pitch with a display of artistry, vision and arrogance. At 23, he appeared to have been born for the international stage. England beat the old enemy 2-0 and Revie was pleased with the Stoke man: 'He has set himself a standard now at international level and has to live by it. He has a lot to offer English football.' In the press box, the great German player Günter Netzer said, 'Hudson is the best English player I have ever seen. He has control and style and I think he will be one of the great players.'

From the lush green spaces of Wembley, the next assignment for Hudson would literally bring him down to earth, in the shape of the deep and clinging mud of the Baseball Ground. Derby County's pitch was still notorious, and in the middle of the week was considered unplayable. It was now drying out a little and there would be an inspection before the game.

Derby had been on the fringes of the top group for most of the season, and with three wins on the spin had overtaken Stoke and suddenly emerged as contenders. Stoke's efforts to give new energy and impetus to their own challenge had been hampered by another injury to Conroy, who had been hurt while on international duty in midweek. Smith was playing with eight stitches in his calf, inserted at half-time in the Middlesbrough game – by his standards no more than a minor irritant.

First Division: Derby County v Stoke City

Within minutes of the start, it is evident that the state of the playing surface will be the key factor. The players warm up in about three inches of glue to chants of 'we want a pitch' from the terraces. Short passes quickly come to a standstill in the cloying mud, and Moores is twice frustrated by the bounce as he shapes to shoot. An attritional long-ball game develops but there is still plenty of entertaining action in a first half that produces no goals.

That changes early in the second half when Derby have a stroke of good fortune. A cross into the Stoke box is aimed at Kevin Hector, who is in an obviously offside position. But it glances off a defender's leg on the way through, playing him onside, and the alert Hector prods it past Shilton from ten yards.

Both sides continue to produce a stirring game in near-impossible conditions, with Hudson showing that class can exert itself on any surface, Salmons skimming over the mud and Mahoney tireless at the heart of the action.

Stoke deserve an equaliser, and when it comes it is a superb goal. It follows an almighty let-off which could have seen Derby two up. Shilton can't hold a Hinton cross and Rioch has two shots blocked before the ball is cleared. Danger averted, Salmons, Hudson and Hurst work it upfield to the edge of the

Derby box. The ball is lost and then reclaimed, and Hudson does a reverse back-heeled pass through the mud to Salmons. He hangs a great cross at the far post where Greenhoff comes in at speed and slashes a trademark volley through the narrow gap between Boulton and the post.

Archie Gemmill nearly restores the Derby lead straight from kick-off but his shot is deflected. Great interplay by Greenhoff and Hudson ends in a low cross which Hurst and Thomas reach together, and the ball loops over from six yards.

With a minute to go, Stoke win a free kick on the left, and Hudson manages to find one of the few patches of grass on the pitch on which to place the ball. His kick is cleared to the Derby right-back Thomas, who decides to pass back to his keeper. But Denis Smith has gone up for the kick and is still lurking in the box. He nips in to intercept and slip the ball to Salmons. Another great cross is met by a classic flying header from Greenhoff into the far corner. Greenhoff accepts the congratulations while lying face down in the Derby mud on the penalty spot.

It is a significant result in the context of the title race, with Stoke leapfrogging Derby once again, and denting their hopes. They also gain a point on Everton, who draw at Leeds, but who still manage to extend their lead to three as Burnley lose. Stoke are third, four behind Everton. Most importantly, they are once again back in the hunt.

Derby County 1 (Hector 49) Stoke City 2 (Greenhoff 75, 89)
Attendance: 29,985
Highlights available online

The next match is the rearranged fixture against Ipswich, who have kept their own title hopes alive with a breathless 5-4 win over Newcastle. Two fruitless trips to East Anglia this season have resulted in a league defeat and a League Cup elimination, and Stoke are anxious to make amends and to build on the brilliant result at Derby.

First Division: Stoke City v Ipswich Town

That there is still some residual ill feeling about the John Ritchie injury is evident from kick-off, with tackles flying in and three players booked in a game that will eventually contain 44 free kicks – even more than in the previous outing. There is clearly little love lost between the two teams. Ipswich appear the better capable of handling this sort of game, defending tightly and breaking at speed when the opportunity presents itself. Stoke have repeatedly found it hard to break out of defensive straitjackets over the course of the season, and without Robertson and Conroy, the latter of whom is injured again, they have no one with the guile to get around the stern Ipswich defence.

It comes as little surprise when Ipswich take the lead five minutes into the second half as a cross from Hamilton is met by a close-range header from Whymark. Fifteen minutes later England full-back Mick Mills catches a right-footed rocket that screams past Shilton.

Stoke reduce the deficit within two minutes when Greenhoff evades some scything tackles and shoots left-footed past Sivell. He needs lengthy treatment after scoring, but Stoke are back in the game until the injury jinx strikes yet again.

Denis Smith describes the sequence of events, 'Ipswich's Mick Lambert was sent clear to race through on goal. Mick was quick. I was faced with a choice of letting him race ahead to take Shilton on, or bringing him down. I lunged and tripped him up. It was a fairly cynical professional foul if I'm brutally honest; but I would argue necessary in the context of the game. We were chasing an equaliser and could not afford to go two goals behind with only a dozen minutes left.

'I certainly did not hurt Lambert. In fact quite the opposite. As referee Gow hared over to give me what I can only assume would have been a red card, I told him that it was a waste of time getting his cards out because I'd have to go off anyway. One glance down at my right knee told me that I'd buggered my leg. I hobbled off. Ultimately it didn't help the team either. Our substitute had already been used so we were down to ten men.'

Ipswich hold on to inflict only the Potters' second home defeat of the season and to achieve the dubious distinction of having broken a Stoke City leg in each of their league meetings.

Stoke City 1 (Greenhoff 67) Ipswich Town 2 (Whymark 50; Mills 65)
Attendance: 28,589

IRON MAN: MY TEAM-MATE DENIS SMITH

MIKE PEJIC: 'Smithy scared everyone, didn't he? He even tackled me many a time on the touchline. If I was jockeying someone, holding the play up, he'd come and knock the pair of us into the paddock.'

TERRY CONROY: 'You tended to take him for granted because you knew he would do what you wanted him to do – which was basically to look after the opposition.'

ALAN HUDSON: 'I wouldn't have swapped him for the world. Denis Smith, the "Iron Man" of the Stoke City defence, was one who you definitely wanted in the trenches with you. You felt absolutely secure with him behind you. When there were corners and free kicks, there was only one man going to win them. Denis was our tough guy – not as big as many thought in size, but in self-belief and football fighting terms, a giant. He was first to everything that moved and hardly ever missed a challenge. It gave everybody around him the opportunity to pick up the pieces – which, more often than not, was the opposition's number nine.

'My everlasting memory of Denis will forever be at half-time in the dressing room at Middlesbrough on a cold and blustery day which saw us three goals down, a mountain to climb, and Denis lying there with his head smashed in. As the last stitch was inserted, the buzzer went, and I said to him that it would be difficult without him, but to take it easy as we had difficult games coming up. He growled at me as he jumped off the small table and ran to the door. So he entered the arena like a gladiator, ready for not only the opposition but the lions and all, it was a sight to behold, a challenge he loved and something he wouldn't dream of missing. Smithy loved pain!'

ERIC SKEELS: 'He wasn't frightened of anybody, and he just went in 100 per cent. If someone was trying to go past him even if he missed his tackle, he didn't get out of the way! He was a good centre-half and you could always trust him going up for the ball. When I was wing-half, I used to drop off behind in case the centre-forward headed the ball on but that didn't happen too often. He was broad and muscular so he looked the part of a centre-half – you wouldn't fancy playing against him.'

GORDON BANKS: 'Playing with Denis was wonderful for a goalkeeper like me. I thought he was the strongest, bravest centre-half I ever played behind. He helped me keep clean sheets and build my reputation by risking life and limb to throw himself in front of a volley, at a cross or any shot that was coming my way. Denis was a tiger of a player, and we relied on him to win tackles and headers. He did so ferociously, and often put a centre-forward off by trying to reach a ball that really wasn't his, crashing into his opponent in the process. The striker would then think twice about challenging for the ball again.

'When he flew into somebody in his usual fierce manner, they knew they'd been tackled, and often would be found lying face down in the mud. But he'd lift them up and ask if they were okay. The end of a brutal, physical 90 minutes would see him shake hands and put an arm around his direct opponent. In those days it was a lot more sporting than the modern game.'

ALAN DODD: 'Denis was my ideal partner – he was very aggressive and liked to attack the ball, and I used to like to play like a sweeper. He always gave me advice and told me where I was going wrong. He was quite vocal.'

After the buoyant mood in the dressing room at Derby only three days earlier, the atmosphere was now despairing. Stoke had lost their rock and talisman for the rest of the season. Their injury list was like the log in an A&E department: Ritchie, Robertson, Pejic and Smith had broken legs. Bloor had yet to make an appearance with his long-term injury, though he was now back playing in the reserves. Conroy had been out again. Many of the other players were nursing strains and niggles. Hudson and Salmons would finish the season playing in all 42 league games, but both had long-term injuries that nowadays would rule them out. Salmons had persistent hamstring problems and Hudson a suspect ankle that required frequent attention. 'Injuries are one of the hazards of the game,' said Tony Waddington, but he was at his wits' end. Of the back four on which Stoke's defence had been solidly based for more than five years, Jackie Marsh was the last man standing. Alan Dodd's emergence as a top-class defender had been a major plus, but the squad was not big enough to sustain this level of serious injuries.

All this was bad enough, but the loss to Ipswich appeared to be a near-fatal blow to Stoke's title ambitions. Every up seemed to be followed immediately by a down. Hudson admitted, 'After that defeat, I thought we'd blown it.' There were still eight matches to play, but a widening gap to the leaders and a heavily depleted squad suggested that a valiant effort might be about to run out of steam.

First Division: Stoke City v Carlisle United

Cometh the hour, cometh the man. One ray of hope amid the encircling gloom is the return of Terry Conroy after the latest in a succession of knee injuries. This time he is fully recovered and will feature in every one of the remaining games. So far, he has played in only three league games and one League Cup tie, in which he scored a hat-trick. Thankfully for Stoke, he is now in the mood to make up for lost time.

Stoke deploy virtually all their available defenders in a back line of Marsh, Dodd, Skeels and Bowers. After their sensational start to the season, Carlisle have been on the slide. But they keep raising hopes of First Division survival with the occasional eye-catching win, the latest being against Manchester City at Maine Road in midweek.

Conroy displays his appetite for the fray after only eight minutes when Salmons finds Hurst in the box. Hurst's lob hits the bar and Conroy taps in the rebound. It is just the fillip they need, and they seem to be in control, when they carelessly let Carlisle back in after 20 minutes. A free kick has the Stoke defence in a tangle and Laidlaw fires home from close range.

A much more evenly contested passage of play follows, with Stoke having more possession but surrendering it far too easily. As an hour passes, the crowd gets impatient and the tension begins to show. But then it is Conroy again, timing a run into the box perfectly to head a Salmons cross into the net.

A minute later, Salmons is the provider once more with a corner that Greenhoff nods home. And a few minutes later it is 4-1. The rampant Salmons finds Greenhoff with a long pass. He squares to Moores whose first-time right-footer hits Conroy on its way into the net, allowing the Irishman to claim the goal, and with it his second hat-trick of the season.

Stoke's concentration wavers and they let in Carr for Carlisle's second goal, but it proves only a blip. Two minutes from the end, Conroy finds Salmons and he smacks a 25-yard left-footer into the back of the net. After a long period of edginess, 5-2 is a convincing result.

'Terry Conroy was his bubbling, unpredictable, defence-tormenting self,' says Peter Hewitt in the *Sentinel*. The winger's claims to have deflected the shot by Ian Moores and so recorded a hat-trick are described as 'a touch of Irish blarney'. But the goal is duly credited to Conroy. 'The quickness of the foot deceives the eye,' he says, and he deserves his luck after such a long run of frustrating cartilage problems. His goals partly overshadow the contribution of Salmons, who has become a massive asset to the team. He has laid on four of the goals and smashed the fifth himself.

It is one of the biggest wins of the season, the perfect comeback after the lows of midweek: the title challenge is not dead in the water after all. But the scoreline disguises weaknesses that might have been punished by stronger opponents. The reshaped defence is having trouble sorting itself out, and gets itself into some terrible tangles on occasion. Waddington admits he was relieved to get to half-time on level terms, 'We were moving the ball too short, which was why I brought on Ian Moores. We had Alan Hudson playing a little deeper and began to hit the ball longer. But what a tremendous display by Terry. It was what we wanted after we had sorted things out at half-time.'

He is less happy about the response of the supporters. There are only 20,000 of them, well down on recent home gates, and some jeers could be heard as Stoke struggle to master their lowly opponents. 'We are not looking for sympathy,' says Waddington. 'But we expect supporters to have an understanding of our position and give us extra support. With that backing we might still achieve something this season. It is a great credit to the players to be where they are in the First Division, and they deserve encouragement. We have reached a situation where if you turn up for a game, you play. The situation has been farcical at times, and yet we have pulled through because of the way the players have approached the situation.'

I am pleased to say that I am one of the faithful who do turn up, do not jeer, and enjoy what in the end is a decisive win. Elsewhere, Everton and Ipswich share the points, and with Derby and Liverpool winning, everything is yet again getting squeezed at the top. Kevin Keegan sticks his neck out and says Liverpool will now go on to win the title. 'We are the only side capable of winning our last six matches,' he says. One of those games will be against Stoke on Easter Monday.

Stoke City 5 (Conroy 8, 65, 73; Greenhoff 66; Salmons 88)
Carlisle United 2 (Laidlaw 20, Carr 78)
Attendance: 20,525

Today's managers would have an attack of the vapours and throw a hissy fit about fixture congestion, but back in the day it was routine for clubs to play three games in four days over Easter. That is why results over the Bank Holiday weekend so often decided the destination of the title.

Stoke's travelling commitments over Easter 1975 were reduced by consecutive away games in London – at West Ham on Good Friday and Arsenal the next day. Then it was back to the Potteries for what looked like a highly significant home game against Liverpool on Easter Monday.

The group of players that headed for London contained just about everyone who might be considered for selection.

Alan Bloor was at last back in the reckoning after coming through five games in the reserves, and his commanding presence was much needed in a defence shorn of all of its regulars and showing an alarming degree of vulnerability. Jackie Marsh was the only fit member of the original back four, but even he would miss the next two games through suspension. Waddington called 19-year-old John Lumsdon into the squad as cover. Kevin Lewis and Danny Bowers had done well deputising for some of the injured defenders and were also in contention. 'It is no longer a case of being stretched to the bone,' says Waddington. 'We are down to the marrow.'

First Division: West Ham United v Stoke City

The pitch at Upton Park is a muddy one, but Stoke have shown in their home matches and at Derby that these are their preferred conditions. The patched-up defence shows much more assurance than in recent matches and Stoke's first two shots on goal come from the returning Bloor and stand-in left-back Danny Bowers. Stoke are moving well on a heavy pitch with Hudson and Mahoney to the fore and Greenhoff a constant threat.

Five minutes from half-time, though, West Ham legend Trevor Brooking springs the offside trap, rounds Shilton and puts his team in front. Fortunately the lead is short-lived. Straight from the restart, Hudson breaks quickly on the right and his cross is met first time by Conroy to bring Stoke level.

Five minutes after the break, Conroy pops up again, in the middle this time, and finds Greenhoff. Mervyn Day slips as he tries to close down the threat, and Greenhoff centres the ball for Conroy to score his fifth goal in two games. He misses a couple of good chances to add to that tally before Stoke are caught out once again. A long ball from the back finds Jennings and he runs 35 yards before sending Shilton the wrong way, evading a lunge from Mahoney and slotting the ball home. There are close-run things at either end in the last 20 minutes but 2-2 is the final score.

West Ham United 2 (Conroy 40, 49) Stoke City 2 (Brooking 39; Jennings 69)
Attendance: 29,811

First Division: Arsenal v Stoke City

There is barely time to draw breath before an unchanged team trots out the next day to do battle with lowly Arsenal at Highbury, on another heavy playing surface. Stoke are pleased to see that Brian Kidd, whose goals had won the reverse fixture in December, is suspended, and another danger man, John Radford, is out with flu. Frank Stapleton makes his debut in the forward line.

Stoke are bright in attack, with Conroy, Salmons and Hudson all testing the defence. Mahoney is producing a masterful display in midfield, breaking down all Arsenal's efforts to counter, and he is then closest to scoring with a fizzing shot that Rimmer dives full length to keep out. From a free kick way out, Hudson sees Rimmer off his line and forces him to backpedal and tip over.

Typical quick thinking by Hudson helps Stoke take the lead just after the half hour. Hurst wins a free kick just outside the penalty area and Hudson lifts it perfectly for Salmons to rifle a low shot past the end of the wall and into the net, with Rimmer motionless. Conroy has a great chance to settle things just after half-time when he wins a 50-50 chase to a ball from Greenhoff in the centre circle and finds himself in acres of room. He takes it to the left of the advancing Rimmer but goes a little too far, and the angle is too tight for him to finish it off. The ball hits the post. Three successive corners, and shots from Mahoney and Salmons keep up the pressure and Hudson nearly sets up Hurst.

The Stoke defence is looking much more solid, but it needs to be as Arsenal gradually turn the tables and begin to look threatening themselves. They have a period of sustained pressure and finally break through with only eight minutes left. A goalmouth scramble sees first Brady and then Storey have shots blocked before an attempted clearance rebounds off a Stoke defender into the path of Eddie Kelly, who blasts home from close range. There is time, for Salmons brings a good save from Rimmer with his weaker right foot. Rimmer safely catches Greenhoff's follow-up effort, and it is another draw.

It means Stoke will end the season unbeaten in all five visits to London, but they have had enough chances to win both games. Alan Dodd thinks that is certainly true of the trip to Arsenal, 'We should have won that match. Arsenal weren't very strong at that time, and it was unusual to see Stoke more or less favourites to win that match. Looking at the strength of the team, we were better than Arsenal.'

Two draws represent a reasonable return, especially as there are the usual topsy-turvy consequences of other results. Doomed Carlisle United continue their wrecking operation, thrashing leaders and title favourites Everton 3-0. The rejoicing in the red half of the city is intensified by Liverpool's 1-0 defeat of Birmingham which means they overtake their neighbours and go top of the league. But in spite of Keegan's blithe self-confidence, the job is not done yet. Ipswich and Middlesbrough maintain their challenge with victories, and Stoke are still there, in fifth. Only Burnley are finding the pace too hot and fall away from the leading pack.

Arsenal 1 (Kelly 82) Stoke City 1 (Salmons 33)
Attendance: 26,852
Highlights available online

Alan Bloor came through two games on successive days, but picked up another knock and rejoined the ever-lengthening casualty list. It was further frustration for the big defender, who was such an influential presence in the back line and who had appeared to be returning just when he was most needed. His season was over before it had properly begun. A great servant to Stoke City, he had to watch the bulk of this momentous season from the sidelines.

ROCK SOLID: MY TEAM-MATE ALAN BLOOR

DENIS SMITH: 'Bluto was class, but he never sought the limelight and so was one of those players people often forget about. They are actually vital to the make-up of a successful team. He was a far, far better player than people remember. Alan was always quite happy to just do his job and go for a quiet pint. He didn't want to be a star. He was a very unassuming type of fellow, and he was quite happy for that to be the way it was.

'He was a joy to play with. It seemed to me that he was always there; he read the game so well. When I made mistakes he cleaned up, especially when I was settling in early on. He was born a couple of hundred of yards down the road from me and he was a good guiding light for me. He made sure I understood what was expected. Very strong but very quiet. But when he spoke everybody did listen. You wouldn't argue with Bluto.

'Bluto had got good pace for such a big man, and as I was the one who man-marked and attacked the ball, his role was to clean up the bits and pieces. Often he'd tell me, "Den, go and get your face smashed and I'll pick up the bits!" He didn't go in for the tough guy thing, although he wasn't to be messed with and he could look after himself quite happily, but he didn't get involved as much as I did. The fact that Alan and I were so different meant we complemented each other perfectly and worked brilliantly together as a partnership.'

TERRY CONROY: 'Smith and Bloor had a great understanding – people assume that Denis was the harder man, maybe because he was more physical. But Bluto was solid, very very solid, and he could look after people. Smithy was a little bit more cavalier in his tackling. Bluto was efficient. Smithy would go through the whole gamut – he'd clear you man, ball corner flag, advertising board all at once.'

ALAN HUDSON: 'Alan Bloor was different class for me. I loved Alan Bloor. He lacked that bit of mobility – he was a big boy. The first time I saw him was at Stamford Bridge, I was an apprentice. He was phenomenal.'

ERIC SKEELS: 'The silent killer. He wasn't dirty but he thought things through, and he just timed things well and he read the game very well. He was sturdy, and to go past him you'd have to go through him.'

MIKE PEJIC: 'Bluto was a local lad, a City Boys player and England youth at a time where there were so many good centre-backs around his age. Remember he was competing with the likes of Jack Charlton. And he became a big strong, rock-solid centre-back, a consistent, reliable, dependable performer who read the game so well. He would very rarely be drawn out of that central area; he knew when to pass players on and when to hold.

'In training, he was always complaining about being a hefty player and still being asked to do canal runs down to Trentham. He hated doing endurance runs and he had a point. What he didn't mind was speed work and short, sharp bursting runs.

'He was uncompromising and powerful and even if he wasn't particularly vocal, he would certainly complain if people didn't take notice. He was very opinionated, and he would keep going at them until what he wanted was done – and he was usually spot on. When he gave you instructions, you'd be wise to take them.'

There was a domestic emergency to handle after the Arsenal game, as Geoff Salmons came into the changing room to be told that his wife was seriously ill and had been taken to hospital. 'They never told me until after the game!' he recalls now. 'I went straight home on the train from London to Doncaster.' Val Salmons had been taken ill while staying with her in-laws in Mexborough, and was suffering from life-threatening acute bronchial asthma. She had no history of such problems, and the family's new Persian cat was later identified as a possible culprit. Thankfully she soon recovered.

As the team travelled home from London, Tony Waddington had more fitness headaches to contemplate ahead of the make-or-break match with Liverpool. Apart from the loss of Bloor, it seemed likely that Salmons would miss the game, either because of his wife's illness or his persistent hamstring problems. Worse than that, Stoke faced the prospect of being without their playmaker and inspiration for what was shaping up to be the most important game of the season. Two games in two days had taken their toll on Hudson's problem ankle. The recent weather in the Midlands had been mild, and the Victoria Ground pitch was bone hard for once. On the train home, Hudson told his manager he didn't think he would be able to play.

'I told him, "My ankle's bad, I can't take another pitch like that,"' says Hudson. 'He said, "We'll talk about it when we get back to the hotel." We always used to get off the train and go into the North Staffs hotel and have a few drinks. And Tony said, "Look, when you go home tonight, go straight home. You're playing on Monday. Don't go to the pub tomorrow. You're playing Monday." And I said, "Not if the pitch is like this."'

Hudson was gutted. 'I was choked because it was a huge encounter,' he says. 'I was so disappointed that I would miss the biggest match since my debut – even bigger, as I believed we'd win the title. I knew sitting there watching that dream disappear would be so very hurtful. I was so wrapped up in our season and mine in particular, as since joining Tony, my form had not only returned, but moved up to another level. I was, in my eyes, the complete inside-forward, or number ten.' The thought of missing such a crucial game was agony for him.

But Hudson had reckoned without the resourcefulness of his manager. He wrote, 'He called me the first thing on Sunday morning, a delightful day with absolutely no sign of even an April shower. "You'll be fine tomorrow Alan. I've just spoken to the weatherman and he assures me of rain, rain and more rain."

'The following morning I woke early, and immediately checked out the garden but found it as dry as Dave Sexton's drinks cabinet. "That's me out," I thought straight away. I felt such disappointment missing so crucial a match at such a vital time.'

Hudson told me the rest of the story in an interview, 'On that Monday I walked into the ground still thinking I wasn't playing. At about a quarter past two I went into the dressing room and saw my boots were out and my shirt was out. Tony told me how he used to talk Stanley Matthews into playing when he was injured. So I knew he was up to something. I thought, before I go in to see him, I'll have a look at the pitch. So I doubled back and walked down.

'I remember meeting John Toshack, Ray Clemence and Kevin Keegan coming off the field. They all had mud on their shoes. The look on their faces was a sight to behold. And they said to me, "What's happening here Huddy? We haven't had a drop of rain up the road." I said, "Well boys, this Potteries weather is something else," and I walked out, and I thought, "We're back in business."

'I walked into Tony's office to get my tickets – all my family were coming up. He sat in his office and he didn't flinch. He never said anything. And I took my tickets and I said, "Anything else to mention?" And he went, "No." What a poker player he would have made.'

Waddington had turned rainmaker by playing one of his old tricks, trading on his friendship with the local fire chief, helpfully a Stoke fan. The fire service had spent the previous day turning the hard-baked surface of the pitch into something approaching an artificial lake.

'No rain sighted from Birmingham to Liverpool,' says Hudson. 'It only rained at the Victoria Ground. He had brought in the fire brigade in the middle of a drought and absolutely soaked the entire pitch, not missing a blade of grass.'

They were the conditions Stoke preferred – and crucially, the going was now soft enough for Hudson to risk his suspect ankle.

First Division: Stoke City v Liverpool

Stoke choose the perfect moment to put together their best performance of the season. Liverpool are without the influential Ian Callaghan, but Stoke are a class above them for most of the game, with Hudson dominating just as he had on his Potters debut against the same opposition 14 months earlier. Mahoney is also a titan and it is his precise pass to Conroy in the 20th minute that helps put his team ahead. As Conroy advances on goal, he is clattered by Phil Thompson, and Stoke have a penalty.

It is their fifth of the season. Ritchie has converted one but he is no longer playing. Salmons has scored one and missed one. Hurst, a penalty specialist, has missed one and is not called upon. Instead, the responsiblity is given to the in-form Conroy. He shoots confidently to Clemence's right and Stoke have a reward for their early pressure.

Stoke are still the quicker in thought and execution, and Liverpool can make little impression. Ray Kennedy is getting no change out of Alan Dodd, and the inexperienced Bowers is policing Keegan brilliantly. When Toshack is thrown on at the break, he fares no better.

A corner five minutes into the second half is taken by Salmons. Greenhoff heads it on, and Conroy's shot is blocked by Tommy Smith. Conroy reacts quickly and forces the ball home for 2-0.

Liverpool never look like coming back and Stoke continue to torture their illustrious defence with a series of flowing moves. Mahoney comes close and Greenhoff's shot is cleared off the line. It is a completely dominant performance, and this time, there is a full house there to enjoy it, with more than 45,000 packed into the ground.

Like every other team that has reached the top of the pile in this crazy rollercoaster season, Liverpool have found it impossible to stay there. This time, their reign has lasted only two days. Defeat drops them to fourth, on the same number of points as Stoke. There is a three-way tie at the top, with Ipswich the new leaders, but with the same points tally as Everton and Derby.

After cruising along in the peloton for most of the season, Derby are now mounting a serious threat, brushing aside Burnley 5-2 at Turf Moor. Derby, Everton and sixth-placed Middlesbrough have played one fewer game than the others, and it looks as though the winner should come from these six. But an extraordinary climax to the season beckons with fully a dozen genuine contenders rounding the last bend closely packed together.

Unbeaten over Easter, and with a win over the leaders in the bank, Stoke have managed to add vital impetus to a battered and battle-weary squad. Tony Waddington is excited not only by the victory against Liverpool but the manner of it. 'Magnificent,' is his verdict. 'I have always insisted on the skill factor – and it was there today. Our football was out of this world.'

Although the players insist that they did not discuss their title chances as a group, the result must have given them a burst of adrenalin and optimism. 'When you beat Liverpool your confidence is sky high and I suppose we started dreaming then,' says Alan Dodd. Hudson has also earmarked this game as make-or-break. 'We never spoke about it. But I felt when we beat Liverpool, that was a big match. If they'd won they would have pulled away and won the title. But that win gave us belief. We didn't just beat them, we outplayed them, we really did. It was after that game that as a team we thought, if we can beat the top of the league team here, we can go all the way. Four broken legs and we're still at the top!'

Hudson calls this 'my finest 90 minutes on a football field in a red and white shirt – in fact in any coloured shirt'. He recalls a post-match compliment from former Liverpool manager Bill Shankly, 'As I sat at my locker covered in mud – what a wonderful feeling – a head popped round and it belonged to Shanks. As I took off my right boot he was standing over me with his hand out. This was when he paid me the finest tribute that any footballer can have paid to them. "Son, I thought Peter Doherty's performances would never be surpassed. But you just did it."' Doherty had been a star player on either side of the war for Manchester City and Derby County among other teams, and was one of Shankly's heroes. 'He could not have done it in a better place, right in front of all my team-mates including the ones who were a little jealous,' wrote Hudson. 'It was the sweetest sound my ears have ever heard.' Waddington said that Shankly told him, 'That was the greatest 90 minutes' display I have ever seen from a player.' And to think that but for the fire brigade and his wily manager, he would have been watching from the stands.

Denis Smith *was* watching from the stands, along with the rest of the now-limping wounded, and he was not enjoying the experience. 'All the time I was wishing I was out there. It was so frustrating not to be involved. You sit in the stands kicking every ball, heading away every cross. It's probably worse to be in that position than out there on the pitch involved in the action.' But he thinks the experience helped prepare him for his later career in management. 'During the run-in, my role was to keep spirits up and minds on the job. I'd be in the dressing room before the game, talking to the players who'd be going out there. I tried to take on the job of keeping everybody bubbling yet focused. I suppose it was the beginnings of my managerial career in the sense of dealing with a dressing room packed with nerves, tension and anticipation.'

Stoke City 2 (Conroy 20 pen, 50) Liverpool 0
Attendance: 45,954

	MARCH 1975	P	W	D	L	Pts
1	Ipswich Town	38	21	4	13	46
2	Everton	37	15	16	6	46
3	Derby County	37	19	8	10	46
4	Liverpool	38	17	11	10	45
5	**Stoke City**	**38**	**16**	**13**	**9**	**45**
6	Middlesbrough	37	16	11	10	43
7	Burnley	38	16	9	10	41
8	Sheffield United	37	15	11	11	41
9	Leeds United	37	14	12	11	40
10	Manchester City	38	16	8	14	40
11	Queens Park Rangers	38	15	9	14	39
12	West Ham United	38	12	13	13	37
13	Wolverhampton Wanderers	37	13	10	14	36
14	Newcastle United	37	14	8	17	34
15	Birmingham City	38	13	8	15	34
16	Coventry City	37	10	14	13	34
17	Arsenal	36	11	10	15	32
18	Leicester City	37	10	11	16	31
19	Chelsea	37	9	13	15	31
20	Tottenham Hotspur	37	10	8	19	28
21	Luton Town	37	8	10	19	26
22	Carlisle United	38	11	3	24	25

17

APRIL

AS FOOTBALL followers digested the consequences of the busy Easter period, Tony Waddington put into words what most of them were thinking, 'The team that wins all its remaining matches will win the championship.' He would like Stoke to be that team, 'It is up to us now to do just that, and put the pressure on the others.'

Supporters of the six clubs still with a strong chance of triumphing were now frantically scrutinising the fixture list to see who still had to play whom, and when. Stoke could have few complaints about their last four fixtures. They would avoid facing any of their rivals. Although their next opponents, Chelsea, were in a fight to avoid relegation, the other three games were against mid-table sides with not much to play for, beyond perhaps the distant prospect of a place in Europe: Sheffield United and Burnley away, sandwiching a home match against Newcastle United.

The Chelsea game in particular looked appetising. The Londoners had managed to pick up three points over Easter after losing four times on the run, including a 7-1 pasting at Wolves. Stoke knew all about them from the four league and cup meetings in October, and would have felt that, although doughty opponents, they looked eminently beatable now. Stoke were on a high after defeating Liverpool and had that wonderful feeling that everything was possible. They had put in a great performance, the fans were back in force, and all the remaining games looked winnable. Denis Smith sums up the mood, 'It was a wonderful time. We didn't think we could get beaten. Everybody was buzzing. It's great to go out there thinking you are the best, or believing that you are going to win. There is nothing better. Everybody is relaxed, everybody is smiling. That's when football is simply the best way to make a living. Everybody loves one another. You are all the best of mates. It's always the same if you are winning. When you are winning everybody loves you.' How long could the love affair last?

First Division: Stoke City v Chelsea

Stoke field the same team that beat Liverpool, and are no doubt pleased to note the absence in the Chelsea line-up of Ian Hutchinson, who had so tormented them in the earlier encounters. Once again, the pitch is well watered, and it almost costs Stoke when Conroy skids in the mud while on defensive duty. It is Conroy who comes closest to scoring when he touches on a deft flick by Greenhoff and draws a good save from Phillips. The in-form Irishman has three shots saved in the opening ten minutes. Mahoney forces another smart save from the keeper, and Hurst sends a shot whistling just wide.

Just before the half hour, Hudson wins a free kick on the left touchline and Salmons sends in one of his trademark crosses. Conroy is on the end of it and heads into the roof of the net to keep his hot scoring streak going. Chelsea are mounting a rearguard action, but the nearest they come to troubling Stoke is early in the second half when Houseman heads home a cross. But Shilton has been obstructed and the goal is disallowed.

It is a reminder that another goal is needed to make the game safe, and that security is provided after an hour by the quick reactions and quick feet of Jimmy Greenhoff. He seizes on a Droy back pass that lacks pace, and cuts in between the defender and goalkeeper before shooting home.

Chelsea keep coming, but Skeels and Dodd are solid at the back and Conroy and Greenhoff cause more problems up front. They are now playing within themselves, and wrap up a convincing win in the closing minutes with a classy move. Conroy exchanges passes with Mahoney and latches on to the return before scoring with an angled drive. It takes his tally to nine in five games.

Stoke have done their bit, and as soon as they get into the dressing room they are anxious to know how others have fared. Everton have drawn and Derby and Middlesbrough have shared the points. Ipswich are not playing, and so lose top spot after enjoying it for only four days. The only other team to have advanced is Liverpool, 2-0 winners at Leeds. The upshot is that there are now four teams with identical points. One of them, Derby, still have four games left, while the others have only three. As far as Stoke, Everton and Liverpool are concerned, the Waddington diagnosis is now even more pertinent: they have to win all their remaining matches to stand a chance. Ipswich, also with a game in hand, are far from out of it yet. It looks as though Middlesbrough now have too much to do, but it is still a five-horse race.

Denis Smith remains optimistic and is still busy dispensing encouragement from the sidelines, 'I'm one of those people who forever thinks that if we've got anything going, we're going to do well. If you think it, you've got a better chance of achieving it. If things are going right, build everyone's confidence, try to be positive. If people are not naturally self-confident having confident people round them helps to lift them. So you need your positive people to be there in front. It would have been discussed in the dressing room that we could give it a good shot.'

Stoke City 3 (Conroy 28, 87; Greenhoff 63) Chelsea 0
Attendance: 26,375

	April 5	*Played*	*Points*
1	Derby County	38	47
2	Liverpool	39	47
3	Everton	39	47
4	**Stoke City**	**39**	**47**
5	Ipswich Town	38	46
6	Middlesbrough	38	44

Terry Conroy's return to the team, and to spectacular goalscoring form, could not have come at a better time. It had been a frustrating season for the Irishman, sidelined first by injury and then by the form of Jimmy Robertson, who had made the right-wing position his own in the early part of the season. Conroy had been substitute 13 times. And even when Robertson's injury paved the way for his return, he had had to serve a suspension for being sent off in a reserve match.

But now he had no more cartilages to remove and was back for a prolonged run, his form as red hot as the colour of his hair. Pressed into a more central attacking role than was his wont, he was scoring freely just as others were struggling to hit the target consistently, and it seemed as though he could not miss. At half-time in the Chelsea game, Waddington joked that he was going to ask Conroy to take the goal kicks because everything he hit seemed to go in, 'He could score a hat-trick if he fell out of bed.' The banter seemed to relax the team and they pulled away in the second half.

UNPLAYABLE: MY TEAM-MATE TERRY CONROY

DENIS SMITH: 'He was absolutely unplayable when he was fully fit and in form. He was so quick he used to go past people. They knew what he was going to do but they couldn't stop him. He would drop his shoulder, knock it past the player and then was gone in a flash of ginger sideboard with his skinny white legs pumping. He crossed great balls in too. I must have scored quite a few goals off his crosses and corners, so have a lot to thank him for.

'Terry had a winning combination of brains and pace, which gives any defender a huge problem. If players are merely quick you can catch them offside, but TC had a footballing brain and to ally that with pace at the top level, that's frightening. He had two or three seasons when he was unplayable, before the damage to his knees began to affect his form. As a defender you don't want to come up against somebody that you know will take you on with pace and he could go both sides. TC gave us an extra dimension because all at once people dropped off an extra yard because of his pace. He was a threat. And when you look at his record, he scored as well. We missed him when he was out, without any shadow of a doubt.

'He was fantastic in the dressing room too. A real laugh a minute, he would act as our social secretary, bringing the disparate members of the squad together. He's just naturally funny. He loved taking the mick, and to be honest that was good, because I was too serious. Sometimes I would get a bit too intense, and Terry helped me relax a little bit. You need people like TC to take the edge off tense situations, which is something Waddo understood. He knew the kind of blend of personalities you need to make a good team. On the field,

Terry was just the same. He caused opponents all kinds of problems with his skill, pace and vivacious, irrepressible spirit.'

GORDON BANKS: 'Naturally two-footed, he possessed incredible stamina, lightning pace and one of the best body swerves I ever saw. As Jackie Marsh once remarked after seeing Terry execute a sublime dummy on Arsenal's Ian Ure, "TC, you not only sent Urey the wrong way, the crowd on that side of the ground had to pay again to get back in."'

ERIC SKEELS: 'When he first came to Stoke I couldn't understand what he was saying, with his Irish accent! He was unlucky with injuries. He had a sort of long stride and before you know it, he's gone. He could beat you quite easily because he was pacy. He wasn't a header of the ball but he wasn't frightened of anybody and he'd get round the full-back and either cut in, have a go himself, or cross it. He could play in one or two positions in the forward line.'

Conroy needed to keep his run going at Bramall Lane, graveyard of Stoke City's championship hopes in the final game of the 1946/47 season, when a win would have clinched the title. The Blades had been climbing steadily and now lay just outside the leading pack. A place in Europe was still within their grasp, so they had plenty to play for.

Geoff Salmons was available to turn out against his old club in spite of a harrowing few days. He had been dashing back and forth to Yorkshire to visit his wife, who was recovering from her health scare, but still in hospital. He had plenty of health issues of his own: a persistent hamstring strain, a torn toenail that had left his foot badly bruised, a tooth abscess that had required a dental operation, and a bout of laryngitis that had left him barely able to speak. Any one of these would be enough to floor a modern player, but Salmons was up for the challenge. He was an uncomplicated and companionable soul who required nothing more of life than to be kicking a football or downing a pint.

But his health issues paled into insignificance compared with a shocking brush with death for Mike Pejic. Pejic's broken leg was still healing but he was in light training again. He had a horrific accident near his moorland farm when his car skidded on a bend in a blizzard. The vehicle, with Pejic and his two-year-old daughter Claire inside, plunged 50 feet down a bank and came to rest upside down against a rock – the only thing between the car and a ravine below. Pejic managed to scramble out through the driver's window and help Claire out too. Both were unhurt, but even the hard man of Stoke City was badly shaken by the accident.

'I could not sleep last night for thinking about our escape,' he told the *Sentinel*. 'I have had a right season one way or the other. There must be a jinx on me, let alone the club. It's marvellous to be alive and to see Claire running about the house.'

He gave the paper a graphic account of what happened, 'We were going to the sweet shop near the farm when a blizzard broke. The back wheels of the car lost their grip and we spun over a bank. Before I knew what was happening, we were rolling over and over down this steep embankment. We were not wearing our seat belts and Claire and I were both rolling around in the car. I kept blacking out, but after what seemed an age, we came to rest against a big rock. We were upside down, hanging over the edge of a 30-foot drop. I kept seeing Claire passing me in mid-air, but I came to sufficiently to switch off the engine.

'When we stopped she was lying in a heap and I pulled her to me. The doors were jammed but I managed to wind down the driver's window and scrambled out. We had dropped about 50 feet but the rock saved us going down further. The back was all smashed in. Usually we place Claire in a special seat in the back but fortunately this time she was next to me otherwise she would have been crushed for certain. On this occasion I think the fact that we were not wearing our seat belts also saved us, for the passenger side was all smashed in as well. I don't know how we would have managed to get out if we'd been strapped in. The back of the car was already over the edge. Another foot and that would have been it. It is amazing neither of us are seriously hurt considering what we have been through.'

His jinx theory had plenty of evidence to support it. Apart from the broken legs and other injury woes, he was the third player to be involved in a car accident during the season, this one by far the most serious of the three.

As Pejic was thanking his lucky stars for his escape, Tony Waddington was rallying the depleted ranks for a big effort at Sheffield. 'The championship is in the melting pot,' he said. 'With three matches left, anything can happen. When you think about our troubles this season it is incredible that we are still in contention at this stage. It is a real credit to the players, and they will not be giving anything up now.'

He knew though that the task had become even harder during the week, because Derby had played their game in hand and squeaked home 1-0 against Wolves. Derby were one of the few clubs not to have topped the table at some point but had been quietly biding their time. Now they had suddenly opened up a two-point gap at the top. In his first full season in charge, Dave Mackay was bullish, 'The pressure is on us. We are the target men but this is an ideal time to hit the top and I am confident we can win through.' It was beginning to look as though he might well be right.

First Division: Sheffield United v Stoke City

With a strong wind at their backs, Stoke start the sharper and Salmons uses the breeze to trouble Brown in the Sheffield goal with a couple of in-swinging corners. Salmons is close again after 20 minutes, almost replicating his goal against Arsenal when Hudson touches a short free kick to him and he lets fly. Brown does well to save. Greenhoff's shot strikes a defender but the referee waves away appeals for a penalty. Sadly, the referee takes a different view shortly afterwards, when Shilton comes flying out to close down Dearden just inside the box. Shilton claims he could not have avoided the collision, but the referee doesn't see it that way, and awards a penalty that is converted by Keith Eddy. After that it is pretty much even until the interval, but Stoke are not showing much sign of turning the game around, as they must do to keep their title hopes alive.

After the restart, Alan Woodward's ferocious free kick nearly takes Shilton into the net with it but the keeper manages to push it wide, and then Hurst and Dodd have attempts on the other goal.

The Blades weather the pressure and with almost an hour gone put another massive dent in Stoke's title aspirations. It is smart play by Anthony Field, who picks up a through ball, nipping past Dodd and Skeels and placing a left-footed shot out of Shilton's reach. It is going to be an uphill struggle now, and Tony Currie plays to the gallery by beating one man and taking a bow to the crowd before repeating the trick. The home fans love it, but the travelling Stoke faithful give a derisive cheer when Currie ends up running the ball out of play.

Conroy and Greenhoff have good efforts on goal and Salmons produces three testing corners one after the other before himself drawing a good save from Brown with one of his left-footed specials. But the home defence stands firm with some well-timed tackles and the game is running away from Stoke. Eric Skeels is booked for the first time in his 16-year career for what looks like an innocuous challenge. With at least two goals required, probably three, the weight of expectation suddenly seems too much and the game ends in a dispiriting defeat.

Once in the dressing room, it is time to find out how their title rivals have fared. The result that matters is at the Baseball Ground, where Derby have eked out another 1-0 win, this time over West Ham. They have 51 points, which is the maximum Stoke can now register, assuming they win their last two matches. Ipswich still have that game in hand, and their 2-1 win over QPR means they are still in the hunt. Liverpool and Everton both win so are still contenders too. But the title is now Derby's to lose. Stoke's chances are mathematical, and rely on a series of unlikely results and complicated calculations of goal averages. To all intents and purposes, their race is run.

Sheffield United 2 (Eddy 25 pen; Field 57) Stoke City 0
Attendance: 33,255

	April 12	*Played*	*Points*
1	Derby County	40	51
2	Liverpool	40	49
3	Everton	40	49
4	Ipswich Town	39	48
5	**Stoke City**	**40**	**47**

The players knew that it was too much of a long shot. 'We knew we weren't going to win after Sheffield United,' says Alan Dodd. 'There was a lot of publicity about that match. But it was one of those days. Nothing went right.'

There was still that slender thread of hope, and – more realistically – a place in Europe to play for. Waddington needed to galvanise his tired troops for a final effort. Remarkably, two days after the Sheffield United match, the team flew to Norway to play a Norwegian Select XI. It was hardly ideal preparation for the last two league games, but the need to keep the cash rolling in was a constant backdrop.

After his triumphant international debut against West Germany, Alan Hudson was selected for a friendly against Cyprus and lined up with Malcolm Macdonald. They would be on opposing sides come Saturday. Hudson put in another assured performance but it was Supermac who stole the headlines by scoring all the goals in England's 5-0 win. Although Newcastle's promising start to the season was by now a distant memory, and they had lost six of their last eight, it was clear that Macdonald would represent a considerable threat.

First Division: Stoke City v Newcastle United

Heavy rain during the week has put the last home game of the season in doubt. After spending most of the last few months watering the pitch to create soft going, Stoke groundsman Len Parton and his team now find themselves pumping hundreds of gallons from the playing surface so that the match can go ahead. The pitch passes muster, but the players struggle to put any moves of any substance together on the sticky surface. Chances are at a premium, and the nearest thing to a goal comes when Hurst meets Conroy's cross, and Newcastle's newly signed goalkeeper Mike Mahoney manages to touch it over the bar.

The second half is a slight improvement. Macdonald is being well handled by Dodd, but he does manage to get away and beat Shilton, only to hit the post. Then Hibbitt volleys wide. Stoke are the more positive going forward and there is a comedy of errors in the Newcastle goalmouth as the ball splashes around while first Dodd, then Mahoney, then Hurst and finally Conroy try to get a shot away. Greenhoff finally succeeds, only to shoot straight at the keeper. In the end it is one-way traffic, but Newcastle hold out for a draw and Stoke finish their home campaign and leave the field to sustained applause.

Once again, the news in the dressing room is depressing. Derby have drawn 0-0 with Leicester, which means even that mathematical sliver of hope is gone. Stoke cannot catch them. There are defeats for Liverpool and Everton, both of whom had looked good bets at various junctures. Their chances have gone too. Only Ipswich, with a game in hand, can deny Derby.

The mood is sombre. 'It was like letting a balloon down,' Hudson recalls. 'It was deflating. I still say today that we had the best team. We had four lads from Stoke at the back and we played the best football, and I knew in my heart of hearts that we were the best football team in that season. It would have been incredible for Stoke to win the championship.'

'We were very disappointed,' says Salmons. 'We were flat. We had to be, because it was there for the taking.'

'That result was the defining moment,' says Conroy. 'We knew we'd blown it, and there was a feeling of despair. That's it, it's gone.'

Stoke City 0 Newcastle United 0
Attendance: 25,784

It seems utterly bizarre that in these circumstances and at this stage in the season, Stoke and Derby played an extra game – against each other. It was a testimonial match for Derby goalkeeper Colin Boulton. Derby, potentially only 48 hours from a chance to win the title, played a full-strength side and won 4-1. Both sets of players must have been wondering what on earth they were doing being involved in such a game at that point. Their hearts can hardly have been in it.

Peter Shilton took the time to reflect on his first season in the Potteries. He had just moved into his new home in Newcastle, and talked to the *Sentinel*. 'I feel I can play better than I have been doing,' he admitted. 'I would say I have played just above average since I came to Stoke, but I would love to be able to say that my form has been brilliant in every game. That is what I shall be striving for next season.

'It seems to have been a long season for me. Being out of the Leicester side early on, then the move to Stoke in November has not helped me hit my best form. We are only now in the process of settling into a new house after renting accommodation, and that too has not helped.

'I have had some good games for Stoke, but in my own mind I know I can do better. The fact that the side has had to be changed around in defence has not made that much difference. I fancy Stoke to win something big next season. We are good enough to win the league.'

Before the final game of the season, it was awards time. Greenhoff received a Golden Boot for the best goal scored in televised games during the season – his opener at Birmingham in December. Alan Mullery, who had captained Second Division Fulham to the FA Cup Final, was named FWA Footballer of the Year. Colin Todd of Derby was second with Alan Hudson third. Meanwhile, Tony Waddington confirmed that the full playing staff would be retained for the following season.

The last match of a long, wearying, exciting but ultimately unsuccessful campaign would be at Burnley. A mid-season surge had taken Burnley right into title contention, but they had won only once in their last nine and now had nothing to play for. Stoke, however, did: a place in Europe. They had assumed that this place had already been secured, but had had a rude awakening. There were only four slots, but the FA operated a rule that only one club per city could qualify – which would eliminate either Liverpool or Everton, leaving Stoke with the final spot, even if they finished fifth. Now, however, came the disturbing news that Everton intended to contest the rule, and appeared to have a decent chance of success. A further threat emerged in the shape of Sheffield United, who had a game in hand and whose late run up the table meant they could possibly overtake Stoke and claim fifth spot.

Compounding these worries were doubts about the fitness of Hudson, who had not missed a league match all season but whose ankle was still troubling him. He also had a thigh strain. Waddington went to work on him. He persuaded his star to travel to the game and 'see how you feel when you get there'.

Hudson knew what that meant, because Waddington had already told him previously that he used to pull the same stroke with another of his star turns, Stanley Matthews. 'Stan said he wasn't fit one day. Tony says, "At least come up to the game – it's good for team spirit." He still hadn't named his team. And they were going up the M6 and Tony sat next to him and told him to have a look out of the window. "What do you see?" he said. And Stan said, "I can see all these cars with red and white scarves hanging out of the window and tooting." And Tony said, "Well what do you think they're doing it for?" And Stan said, "They're coming up to watch the game." "No Stan, they're coming up to see you. You can't let the fans down. You've got to play." And Stan played. And this is what he did with me at Burnley. He said, "Give it a go, and if you need to come off then it doesn't matter." He had no intention of bringing me off.' So Hudson played, and so did Salmons, making them ever-presents in the league programme for the season.

First Division: Burnley v Stoke City

Stoke need both points to have a chance of fourth place and be sure at least of fifth, and they set off at a cracking pace with Greenhoff and Hurst testing the goalkeeper. Next it is Shilton's turn to show his prowess, saving point-blank from Hankin after a rapid Burnley counter, a save that even the Burnley players applaud. Shilton is then at full stretch to keep out an effort from Flynn.

Stoke take the initiative after the break, with Marsh coping well with Leighton James, whom he sees as one of his trickiest opponents. He does well enough to persuade James to go and try his luck on the other wing. Conroy, Salmons and Greenhoff all come close to opening the scoring, and even the Burnley manager later concedes that Stoke should have had a penalty when Hurst is barged by Waldron. Hudson almost settles the game with a rasping drive but it is just too high. It remains a good, open and attacking game, but neither side can score, and for the second time in successive games Stoke finish with a goalless draw.

It's an unsatisfying result for the Burnley faithful too. They have had an exciting season, scoring more goals than any other team but only conceding fewer than two others. After Conroy's electric burst of scoring, Stoke have not found the net in any of their final three games. Led by Hudson and Greenhoff, the players trot over to salute a large group of travelling supporters, and then disappear down the tunnel for the last time.

The other results settle a raft of issues. Derby have already been confirmed as champions and end with a 0-0 draw against Carlisle, relegated after a single season in the top flight. Everton's draw with Chelsea means the Toffees pip Stoke to fourth place by a point, and condemn the Londoners to relegation. Spurs escape the same fate by one point and Luton are the third club to go down. Sheffield United beat Leicester 4-0, and if they win their last game at Birmingham in three days' time, they can overtake Stoke and take that fourth European place.

'Whatever happens, we have given a lot of pleasure with our football,' says Tony Waddington as he prepares to sweat it out on the Blades' result. 'And we have gained an extra bonus in the performances of Alan Dodd and Ian Bowers. John Mahoney has become a world-class player this season. He was tremendous again today and Alan Hudson still managed to do the job we wanted, even on one leg.'

Burnley 0 Stoke City 0
Attendance: 19,191

Sheffield United's last game also ended goalless, so Stoke clung on to fifth, and the last European place. The Football League duly nominated them for the fourth spot, but Everton were preparing an appeal to UEFA. Waddington's mood was a lot less benign now. 'You cannot change a situation that everyone appreciated right from the start of the season,' he raged. 'Any change now would make the whole thing farcical.' Yet that is exactly what happened. UEFA insisted that clubs be admitted 'on merit', which meant that Everton were in and Stoke were out. It was the final shattering blow at the end of an exhausting season.

Hudson's ankle woes forced him to withdraw from the England squad after two appearances. The man for whom many had predicted a ten-year career and a century of caps would never represent his country again.

	FINAL TABLE	P	W	D	L	F	A	GA*	Pts
1	Derby County	42	21	11	10	67	49	1.367	53
2	Ipswich Town	42	23	5	14	66	44	1.538	51
3	Liverpool	42	20	11	11	60	39	1.500	51
4	Everton	42	16	18	8	56	42	1.333	50
5	**Stoke City**	**42**	**17**	**15**	**10**	**64**	**48**	**1.333**	**49**
6	Sheffield United	42	18	13	11	58	51	1.137	49
7	Middlesbrough	42	18	12	12	54	40	1.350	48
8	Manchester City	42	18	10	14	54	54	1.000	46
9	Leeds United	42	16	13	13	57	49	1.163	45
10	Burnley	42	17	11	14	68	67	1.015	45
11	Queens Park Rangers	42	16	10	16	54	54	1.000	42
12	Wolverhampton W	42	14	11	17	57	54	1.056	39
13	West Ham United	42	13	13	16	58	59	0.983	39
14	Coventry City	42	12	15	15	51	62	0.823	39
15	Newcastle United	42	15	9	18	59	72	0.819	39
16	Arsenal	42	13	11	18	47	49	0.959	37
17	Birmingham City	42	14	9	19	53	61	0.869	37
18	Leicester City	42	12	12	18	46	60	0.767	36
19	Tottenham Hotspur	42	13	8	21	52	63	0.825	34
20	Luton Town R	42	11	11	20	47	65	0.723	33
21	Chelsea R	42	9	15	18	42	72	0.583	33
22	Carlisle United R	42	12	5	25	43	59	0.729	29

* GA stands for goal average, which was how clubs on equal points were separated before 1976. It was calculated by dividing the number of goals scored by the number conceded. The higher the number the better. If you had scored and conceded the same number, your GA was one – as with Manchester City and Queens Park Rangers in the final table above. It was a ridiculously complicated system, and everyone heaved a mighty sigh of relief when the much simpler goal difference was adopted instead.

The *Sentinel*'s Stoke City reporter Peter Hewitt offered readers his verdict on the 'Nearly Men', beginning with a bit of statistical analysis. The first ten games had yielded 11 points and the next 11 brought 16 – enough to take Stoke to the top of the table. There followed a relative slump of ten points from 11, and 12 from the last ten games. It added up to a reasonable degree of consistency. The goals for and goals against columns bore comparison with the performances of the other top teams. The 18 points gained away from home was a good return, but too many points had slipped away in draws at the Victoria Ground.

'Stoke City can look back on a season of challenge and despair,' Hewitt wrote. 'They know they were good enough to have finished up as champions – but four pairs of crutches in the treatment room indicate where it all went wrong. Just how many more points they might have had with a full squad available is something that supporters will be arguing about over the summer.'

He could hardly have predicted that supporters would still be arguing about it half a century later. Some of us, anyway.

'Big John Ritchie looked to be heading for his best year when his season ended on September 24,' said Hewitt. 'Yet the strongest squad in years, good enough to overcome the setbacks, still topped the table on February 15 – the day Mike Pejic became the third broken leg victim. But it meant that players were turning out not quite 100 per cent fit. Stoke really had to rely on experience with so much to play for. But events caught up with them at the end, with Denis Smith joining the casualty list from mid-March.

'Yet Stoke will surely look back with pride rather than anger. They took three points off the new champions and produced two England under-23 players in the midst of their troubles in Alan Dodd and Ian Moores. They showed the extent of their ambitions by going into the red for Peter Shilton, while another notable landmark was an England place for the talented Alan Hudson, who is always thinking about his game on and off the field. Hudson has just been voted Player of the Year by a national sports weekly after taking third place in the covered Football Writers' awards.

'The way in which Stoke overcame so many obstacles until they all piled up near the end was a tribute to the team spirit, and there was obvious understanding from supporters as they acclaimed their efforts.'

Hewitt was a fair man, and it was a balanced verdict. He was a journalist of perspective and proportion too. After giving his assessment of a momentous campaign, he went on to report that a 42-foot-long club scarf, knitted by the staff of the Edith Beddow Old Peoples' Home at Trentham, had been auctioned for £40 at a Stoke City Social Club fundraiser. Hewitt knew it was only a game.

Alan Hudson also wrote an end-of-term report for the paper. 'We perhaps missed Alan Bloor most of all,' he said. 'I am sure we would have finished ahead of Derby if Bluto had been around in the early part of the season, when the back four were in the process of getting together.

'Alfie Skeels was our saviour. He came in to do a vital job in whatever position he played in. Everyone though has done his bit – especially John Mahoney who never quite believed in himself when he started this season, but knows now he was wrong to have any doubts. He had such a fine season, establishing himself on the international scene and must feel he can face up to anything in the game now.

'Sammy has had a good settling-in season with us but we have not seen the best of him yet, while Terry Conroy's form looks to be on the up. Our injuries gave young players like Danny Bowers and Kevin Lewis a chance and they proved good enough to take it when it came. It took a lot of character to come in when so much was going against us, but they both did splendidly, while Alan Dodd can only get better.

'I fancied Stoke to win something this time, so after the way events have exploded around us I am not going to forecast anything at the moment. But the future has to look pretty good. You can never tell with any certainty in this game. You start off with high hopes and then all the planning suddenly has to be altered to cope with injuries. The boss spent all that money on the team, only to be hit by a series of body blows. Yet he never once showed that he felt sorry for himself, but just battled on. We backed him up the only way we could – on the field.'

It would be easy to pick through the season's results and identify where crucial points went begging or were dropped. Easy to find the five extra points that, in the event, would have been enough to deliver the title. Easy, but pointless. Given how tightly packed the table was right until the end, there are maybe a dozen clubs who could engage in the same fruitless exercise. Each of them could muster enough 'if onlys' and 'might-have-beens' to argue that, with a little bit of fortune, the title could have been theirs. Supporters of any club in any league can play this game at the end of any season, or at any point during the campaign. It is always a waste of time. All you do is make yourself miserable.

It is worth taking a broader look though at the factors that, in the end, conspired to make Stoke fall short at the sharp end of the season. Hewitt's analysis is at once the most obvious and the most compelling: a talented squad of players put themselves in contention, but a series of unlucky breaks – literally – stalled their progress, and in the end they didn't quite have the resources to get over the line.

Broken legs were not uncommon in those days of sliding thigh-high tackles, but to suffer four in one season must be some kind of record. On top of that, Alan Bloor missed all but two games of the season, and utility man Eric Skeels started the season recovering from a broken leg himself, and was not available until the end of November. Terry Conroy's dodgy knees meant his appearances were spasmodic, and the impact he made when he returned to the action for the run-in showed how sorely he had been missed. His absences were intensely frustrating to him, 'I was champing at the bit. I'd have fitted into that side the way they were playing. I scored ten goals that season and if I'd been able to do that in the first half of the season, that's the league won isn't it?'

Greenhoff had also underlined how integral he was to the team: he missed two games after breaking his nose. Stoke were short of ideas and options without him, and lost both of them. Several key players turned out regularly when not fully fit – that applied in particular to Hudson and Salmons for the last dozen games of the season. No wonder Waddington was pulling out what remained of his hair by March, and was calling it the worst injury crisis of all his years in charge. Smith, Pejic, Marsh and Conroy all served suspensions. In the days when senior squads were half the size they are now, the team simply did not have the depth or quality to sustain that level of absence and maintain their challenge for the title. It was asking too much. As Denis Smith wrote, 'Just when we really needed to rise to the challenge, the boys could not find it within them to raise their game.' And as Tony Waddington said, it was massively to their credit that they kept the challenge up for as long as they did.

There were some bright points, as junior players were blooded to fill the gaps. Alan Dodd missed only three games and emerged as a versatile and mobile defender potentially of international class. But he was only 21, was often played out of position and lacked self-confidence. Danny Bowers made ten appearances and belied his lack of experience with a number of mature displays. Ian Moores began to make a name for himself as a tireless target man, strong in the air and able to score with either foot. But valiant though their efforts were, these were boys taking the places of men.

When they reflect today, the players believe the number of injuries to key personnel undoubtedly cost them the title. 'I guarantee that if we had not lost those players, we would have won those last three vital games and lifted the title,' says Terry Conroy. Denis Smith agrees – and blames himself and his self-inflicted injury, 'The defence needed me to get in there and pull people together and keep it tight when necessary. My job was to organise and do the talking because that's what I'm good at. So in the end, the reason we didn't win the league championship could come down to me making that rash tackle.'

Mike Pejic goes back to an even earlier injury – that to Gordon Banks. 'We had a fantastic team but finished fifth when we should have been number one,' he wrote in his column. 'We went toe to toe with some of the best teams. I know we would have completed the job if Banksy hadn't got injured. It still eats away at me that we didn't.' Hudson and Pejic did not always see eye to eye, but on this they are as one. Hudson says, 'I truly believe that if Banks hadn't had his accident – and if Terry Conroy hadn't had his ongoing injuries – we'd have won the league.'

The players have two other theories about what went wrong. We have already looked at the ongoing debate about Waddington's decision to break the transfer record for a goalkeeper and sign Peter Shilton in November. Shilton was sensational on his debut. And although, as we have seen, he does not think he was at his absolute best, he made many other important and spectacular saves, while his mighty clearances regularly caused all sorts of problems for opposing defences.

The Stoke back four, however, as we have heard from Smith, were accustomed to playing in front of Banks and Farmer. They had some difficulty adjusting to Shilton, who tended to stay on his line much more than either of his predecessors.

This led to a few tangles and misunderstandings at the back, which occasionally proved costly. No one doubted Shilton's ability or commitment, but somehow he was not the perfect fit for which Waddington – the man who loved goalkeepers – must have hoped.

'It is odd that Shilts's signing didn't work out well,' says Terry Conroy. 'But there it is. It didn't. It just didn't happen. He trained hard, and in the winter, when there was sludge on the training ground he'd come in and you wouldn't recognise him – he was full of mud. He was a perfectionist. He couldn't get enough of training. But his performances weren't as consistent as you would have expected from a world-record signing. I genuinely think it was a lack of understanding with the defenders. He made sure his own position was right, and that everything was right with himself. But good goalkeepers also consider the defence. Banks could see the game in front of him and was able to manipulate the defenders into the positions they needed to be in. Shilts didn't have that same skill.'

The argument was not really personal to Shilton. It was about whether Stoke really needed a new goalkeeper at the very time their all-time leading goalscorer had just sustained a season-ending injury. With Ritchie gone, the target men left in the squad were Geoff Hurst, who was still effective but much less so than in his pomp, and Ian Moores, who was raw and untested. The players felt the dumping of John Farmer was not necessary, and that what the team needed was reinforcement up front and not at the back.

'If you'd asked most of the players who played with him, they would have felt that Farmie was good enough,' says Conroy. 'But Waddo didn't have the confidence in him, and he went out and spent all that money on Shilton. But if he'd have spent it on a forward and given Farmer another chance, the results would have been a lot different.'

Smith says that was particularly evident when the players ran out of steam at the end of the season, 'Both the last two games ended goalless. We really should have been beating 15th-placed Newcastle at home at that stage. That decision to invest in Peter Shilton and not a striker came home to roost.'

The other theory advanced by the players to explain the near miss is that the manager was not proactive enough in the final stages. To be at the top of the league with three games to go was a new experience for all of them, and they perhaps needed some help in handling it – a strategy to win those games and bring the title home.

This was not really Tony Waddington's style. He was a hands-off manager whose policy had always been to assemble good players, give them the minimum of instructions and advice, and trust them to deliver on the pitch. But perhaps this was the moment for intervention, for more detailed team talks and a three-match strategy to seal the deal.

Views are mixed among players looking back on this with the hindsight of so many years. Let's hear first from Terry Conroy, who believes the manager should definitely have been rolling up his sleeves at this point and providing greater leadership: 'When we defeated Chelsea with three games remaining, we should have come together to discuss exactly how we were going to get maximum points from those three matches. But that meeting never happened. And that to my mind was a fault. They should have sat us down and said, "Listen, here's the plan, here's how we prepare." I suppose in one way we'd got to that stage without doing that, so why change a winning formula?

'Waddo's theory was that because we'd had success playing off the cuff, we should stick to our guns. Pej wanted us to be more professional and clinical, with less being left to chance, but then he'd been banging on about it for years. What do you do as a manager, though? Put doubt into players' minds by suddenly changing your approach? Waddo clearly didn't believe that was the way to go. Looking back now – and hindsight is a wonderful thing I know – we were the best team in the league, but we didn't go on and win the league because we didn't talk through how we were going to get three wins from those last three games. I just think that if we'd approached them with more forensic detail and had been given a bit more guidance, maybe we'd have emerged victorious.'

Conroy acknowledges that this was new territory for Waddington too. But Pejic clearly took the same view, and Jackie Marsh also has some sympathy with it. 'TC feels we carried on in a cavalier style and thought Waddo should've reined us in and said, "We're within touching distance here. Let's not go mad,"' said Marsh. 'Maybe he's right. That was our big chance.'

Smith is not so sure that changing horses in midstream would have been such a good idea. 'I can't see it,' he says. 'We'd got that far because of the way he allowed people to play. He wasn't going to change his mind with half a dozen games to go. It wasn't in his make-up as a manager and it wasn't in the make-up of the players he'd got either. The attacking players wouldn't have wanted to sit behind the ball. It wasn't going to happen with the players he'd got. As a manager you look at the players you've got before you decide what you're going to do. And the players Waddo had, to ask them to sit and defend would have been a total waste of time. He hadn't enough players of that mindset, so they'd have possibly lost those games anyway.'

His defensive partner Alan Dodd agrees, 'We were doing it right, and you don't fix it if it isn't broken. So we just went along and did what we'd been doing previously. We never sat down and discussed it. Even when we almost did it. We didn't have long discussions, we just prepared ourselves for the next game. We didn't talk about it as regards winning the league, we let other people do the talking.'

Geoff Salmons agrees that changing course would have been completely out of character for the manager. 'I don't think it was in him, Tony Waddington. He let the lads do what they do, and play to their ability. That was his way.'

Conroy sees this side of the argument too. 'We'd achieved what we'd achieved up to the Liverpool game by playing in an off-the-cuff cavalier devil-may-care style that was pleasing on the eye. There was no strategy. That was the way Waddo looked at it – he trusted the players and he let them get on with it, and team talks were a bare minimum. So maybe if he'd started coming on strong during the last month of that season who knows if it would have worked or not.'

And that's the point of course. Nobody knows, and no amount of talking about it down the decades has made us any the wiser. Though the frustration lingers, over the years the disappointment has given way to resignation and a pride in what had been achieved. Mike Pejic summed it up in one of his columns: 'We had a superb team. It frustrates you knowing we came so close, but it was also a privilege to be part of such a team with a wonderful team spirit and connection to the fans, the Boothen End. We could compete with anyone.'

Hudson agrees, 'We were a terrific football team, and if we'd have won the league we'd have been worthy champions. My family came up week after week and said, "Even with all the time you were at Chelsea this is the best football you've ever played." It wasn't to be, but I am proud to have played in the best team Stoke have ever had.'

It's all history now, and every club has its stories of heroic failure. As Smith says, 'It's football.' That's life. But it can be hard to let go. Alan Hudson is musing yet, 'I still wonder what would have happened if that goal had counted at Luton.'

SEASON 1974/5	Apps			Goals		
	League (+ sub)	Cups (+ sub)	Total	League	Cups	Total
Bloor	2		2			
Bowers	10		10			
Conroy	11 + 5	3 + 2	14 + 7	10	3	13
Dodd	39	8	47			
Farmer	17	7	24			
Greenhoff	39	8	47	14	1	15
Haslegrave	18 + 1	4 + 1	22 + 2	1		1
Hudson	42	7	49	4		4
Hurst	30 + 5	6	36 + 5	8	3	11
Lewis	5	1	6			
Mahoney	39	8	47	4		4
Marsh	37 + 1	7	44 + 1	1		1
Moores	10 + 7	1	11 + 7	4		4
Pejic	28	8	36			
Ritchie	7		7	4		4
Robertson	9 + 5	3 + 3	12 + 8	3	2	5
Salmons	42	8	50	8	1	9
Shilton	25	1	26			
Skeels	22 + 1		22 + 1	1		1
Smith	30	8	38	2	2	4
Total 20						

18

GONE WITH THE WIND

ON THE windswept morning of 2 March 1976, the players assembled at Stoke railway station to catch the train to London. They were playing Tottenham Hotspur in the third round of the FA Cup the following day. Soon after leaving the station, the railway line passed by the Victoria Ground. As the train picked up speed, those members of the party looking out of the right-hand window would have glimpsed a scene of devastation.

The great gale of January 1976 – 'the storm of the century' – was the most severe storm to have hit the British Isles in the 20th century. Few areas of England and Wales escaped widespread damage, and more than 20 people were killed. A gust of more than 100mph was recorded in Cambridgeshire. Part of the tower of Worcester Cathedral crashed through the roof. A tree fell on to the elephant house at Longleat Safari Park: the two resident elephants were unhurt, and helped drag the branches from the wreckage of their home. The storm also caused massive disruption in Ireland and across western Europe.

The damage just visible from the London-bound train was another legacy of the gale. Peter Shilton remembers that the ground looked as though a bomb had hit it, and that there was debris by the side of the line. He said wreckage from the stand had littered the practice pitch, 300 yards from the ground, where they had trained that morning.

The Victoria Ground was the oldest football stadium in the country, and it had been no match for the fury of the storm. The barrel-shaped wooden roof of the Butler Street Stand, down the long side of the ground backing on to the railway, had been ripped off by a gust, and now lay in ruins. No one knew it at the time, but that fateful day set in train a series of events that would end with the destruction of the title-chasing team of the previous season, the peremptory sacking of the manager, relegation from the First Division and a long period of decline. There was to be no calm after the storm.

All this lay ahead as the players fought out a tough draw against Spurs the following day to bring the Londoners back to Stoke. But would the Victoria Ground be fit to stage the replay? Or be playable in time for the next home league game against Middlesbrough, only two weeks away? At first it looked as though things could be made ready in time for the replay. But a few hours before the game, there was a further collapse as more of the roof gave way, and the ground was declared unsafe.

The Boro game was moved across the Potteries to Vale Park, the home of local neighbours and occasional rivals Port Vale. Their ground was only 25 years old and had once been dubbed 'the Wembley of the North'. No one knows why. Stoke won a scrappy encounter with a late goal and were able to return to the Victoria Ground for the FA Cup tie a week later, when they beat Spurs 2-1 thanks to a late Salmons penalty.

While the team battled on, a huge row and a financial crisis were looming. The row was with the insurers, who were willing to pay out for the damage caused by the gale, but not for the subsequent collapse. The stand would now have to be entirely demolished and the repairs would be much more extensive –

and expensive. Maybe the stand was underinsured in the first place. Whatever the rights and wrongs of it, Stoke were faced with a bill of around £250,000. This was a problem. The big signings of 1974 had cost £750,000 and had been paid for by loans. The new financial burden would be hard to bear. Income in those pre-sponsorship days came mainly from gate money, but crowds had been diminishing. The banks started getting jumpy. The club would have to liquidate some of its assets and players would have to be sold.

A good run in the cup was now essential, although having overcome Spurs, a tough tie at home to Manchester City lay ahead. How Stoke must have rued their failure to win those heated arguments over European qualification that had been played out over the previous summer. For all Waddington's furious remonstrances, he had been unable to overturn the decision. With the unexpected loss of a UEFA Cup place went a potential source of what, as things turned out, would have been very valuable income.

The team's run in the FA Cup was not a bad one, but fell short of what was needed in financial terms. Manchester City were dispatched 1-0, but in the fifth round, Sunderland earned a 0-0 draw at Stoke and won the replay 2-1. Now there was nothing to do but salvage as much as possible from the season and hope to regroup in the summer.

At the time of the great gale, Stoke were going reasonably well after a patchy first half of the campaign. Any thoughts of another shot at the title had swiftly evaporated in a poor start that saw the team down in 18th place by mid-September, with only a couple of wins and a couple of draws. A home defeat to Fourth Division Lincoln City in the League Cup did nothing to lift morale. That loss proved a low point, however, and seven wins in the next ten games lifted Stoke back up into the top ten. Progress might have been even better but for an irritating tendency to lose games from winning positions. By the time the roof fell in, they had 27 points from 24 games and were sitting comfortably enough in mid-table.

Not surprisingly in the pressured external environment, things did not go so well after the storm. The team won only five of the remaining 18 fixtures to finish 12th in the table. It was a bit of an anticlimax after the heroics of 12 months earlier, but matters off the pitch were now the focus of attention as the financial crisis became ever more acute. The pressure to sell players to help balance the books could no longer be resisted.

Waddington tried to limit the damage by holding on to his stars and sacrificing some of the younger players he had developed. Sean Haslegrave went to join Waddington's old mate Brian Clough at Nottingham Forest in July 1976 for £50,000. The gangly striker Ian Moores went to Tottenham a month later for £75,000.

After such a poor finish to the previous season, 1976/77 began with a sense of crisis still hanging over the club. The fans shared the sense of foreboding, and gates continued to fall as the new season got under way. Over the first couple of months the team were on mid-table form in spite of long-term injuries to Smith and Mahoney. But another storm was about to break. The creditors were at the gates, and something more drastic needed to be done. The cost of the new stand had risen to £1m. The board decided to build another new stand at the Stoke End while they were at it. But the club was still in debt. The sums didn't add up. More players would have to go.

The club captain, Jimmy Greenhoff, was as aware as anyone of the impending crisis. But he felt his own position at least was secure. He loved Stoke, and Stoke loved him. He had absolutely no thoughts of going anywhere else. Then, one day in November, he was told that Tony Waddington wanted to see him out on the pitch. He found the boss surveying the building site that had taken the place of the Butler Street

Stand. He recalled their conversation in two interviews in 2019 – a podcast with a fans' website and an interview with the Stoke fanzine *Duck*. This account is an amalgam of the two:

'We were in the Social Club at the ground for lunch, as usual. We were a close bunch and always ate together. I got a message that the gaffer wanted to see me on the pitch. I found it strange as we didn't have a game.

'So I walked out down the tunnel and there Waddo was – in the centre circle, looking up at the Butler Street Stand. I said, "Crikey gaffer, what a mess that is, eh."

'"Yes it is. And it gets worse Jimmy."

'I said, "In what way?"

'He said, "We had an emergency board meeting last night, and they informed me that it's not fully insured."

'I said, "You're joking."

'He said, "It gets worse."

'"What do you mean it gets worse?"

'"We've got to sell someone to pay for it. And it's you, Jimmy."

'I said, "It is not! I'm going nowhere." And I went on like that, and I was using expletives and saying you can so-and-so off.

'He said that Billy Bingham, manager of Everton at the time, was on his way down the M6 to try to sign me.

'I said, "He's wasting his journey. Watch my lips: I am going nowhere."

'He said, "I've also had a phone call this morning and it was from Sir Matt. It went like this Jim, 'Hi Tony, Matt here. I've just had Tommy Doc on the phone from The Cliff and he said Matt, will you do me a favour? Will you ring your mate Tony Waddington up, 'cause the lads have heard a rumour here at the training ground that Stoke are going to sell Jimmy Greenhoff. Can you find out if it's right? And if it is right, will you get Jimmy over here as soon as possible?'"

'Man United wanted me to go to speak to them that afternoon. I was all confused and so I went over to them on the Monday. I didn't sign on the Monday, didn't sign on the Tuesday, didn't sign on the Wednesday ... that tells you something.

'So I called an Extraordinary Board Meeting at Stoke and we were all sat there: the gaffer, me and the directors. I told Waddo and everyone I didn't want to leave.

'"So what's this all about, Jimmy?" asked someone.

'"It's about me telling you that I don't want to leave," I replied.

'After a while someone got up and said, "To be honest Greenhoff, we think you're past it."

'I was only 30. They didn't mean it, but it was a way of getting me to go. So I stood up, looked at Waddo and said, "I'm really sorry gaffer, I'm signing for Manchester United."

'I never wanted to go. It doesn't take much looking into, does it? I still live in Stoke – that's how much the club, the people and the area mean to me. I'd already thought that I would finish my career at Stoke. I'd like Stoke fans to know that everything I have said about how I love the club is true. I mean every word.'

Waddington's memory of those events chimes with Greenhoff's in most of the material details. It fills in some of the financial background, and makes it clear how reluctant he was to sell such an influential and popular player. 'Greenhoff was a firm favourite with supporters and I felt we needed him to help bring on younger players like Sheldon and my own son, Steve,' Waddington recalled for the *Sentinel*. 'At the time in 1976 the government had a credit squeeze which compelled banks to make their clients reduce their overdrafts. We were under pressure constantly and were getting letters from our bank manager at every weekly board meeting. The implication was that we had to sell a player quickly. The five directors helped by putting £10,000 each into the account and the bank agreed to increase the overdraft to £50,000. The pressures were still intense.

'We had just drawn at Leeds, where Greenhoff had been outstanding. At our next board meeting I was asked if there had been any offers and I replied that there had been just a few inquiries. But the Everton chairman had made an approach directly to Albert Henshall about Greenhoff, and later Billy Bingham the manager approached me. I said it would be discussed, and the board told me that in the circumstances they had no choice. I pointed out his popularity at the club and felt he probably would not leave the club anyway, but I was left with little alternative. Everton had offered £100,000. I told the board that there was only one club Greenhoff would wish to join, and that was Manchester United.

'I told Matt Busby about the situation. He suggested that I contact Tommy Docherty who was manager at Old Trafford and had tried to sign Jimmy during his spell at Aston Villa. We agreed on a £130,000 fee and I then had the thankless task of explaining the situation to the player.

'Greenhoff did not want to leave us and was not very happy with the episode. In the meantime, the Doc rang me to say that his chairman and Matt Busby, who still had the last word on transfer matters, would not pay more than £100,000 for a 30-year-old. That suited me fine. It meant the deal was off, and I told the board that Man U had reduced their fee.

'Greenhoff wanted a meeting to know where he stood. At that meeting it was accepted that he would be staying with us. Then one director said, "There is no way we can turn down six figures for a player who is 30." Greenhoff said quietly to me, "That's it boss." And he actually signed for Man U for lower wages than he was getting at Stoke.

'The futility of the Greenhoff transfer was even more evident when on receiving United's fee, the directors took out the £50,000 they had contributed, whereupon the bank withdrew their £50,000 facility. We were back to square one and no Jimmy Greenhoff.'

Older Stoke fans are only half joking – or not joking at all – when they say they can remember where they were and what they were doing when they heard that the club was selling Jimmy Greenhoff. I certainly do. I was visiting friends, and one of them told me they had heard the news on the radio. I couldn't believe it. I went into a state of what can only be described as mild shock. I had an empty soft drinks can in my hand and I kept squashing and twisting it. Eventually it gave way, and a jagged edge carved a deep cut in my finger. I had to go to hospital and have stitches in it. The faint scars I still bear are a reminder of The Day Stoke City Sold Jimmy Greenhoff.

All the supporters were in a similar state of shock and disbelief. The older heads remembered the last time the club had sold its best and most popular player, when Stanley Matthews went off to Blackpool in 1947. That hadn't ended well. They didn't blame Waddington personally – they knew the sale had been forced on him by the board. Even at £100,000, the fee was not a bad one for a player of his age – it was what Stoke had paid Birmingham for him seven years, 338 appearances and 97 goals ago. Given their financial plight, the board clearly felt it was too much to turn down for a player of his age. But it was a sad day – the saddest in my 50 years plus of following Stoke; worse even than losing those FA Cup semi-finals, or being edged by Ajax, or any of the relegations and years in the third tier. Jimmy Greenhoff, like Denis Smith, Terry Conroy and the others *was* Stoke City. The feeling was like one of bereavement. The soul seemed to go out of the team. Half a century on, there are many who still think the sale was unforgivable and hastened the decline and fall that was now looming ever nearer.

Greenhoff's career enjoyed an Indian summer at Manchester United, and no Stoke fan would begrudge him a moment of his success there. He played 123 times for United, often alongside his brother Brian, and scored 36 goals for them. He played in two FA Cup finals, and finally got his winners' medal in 1977, scoring a goal in United's 2-1 defeat of Liverpool. The following season he was United's Player of the Year.

Greenhoff's disappearance left a vast and unfillable hole at Stoke, but as Tony Waddington might have said, 'it gets worse.' Within a month, Alan Hudson had followed Greenhoff out of the door. Although Hudson insists that he never fell out with Waddington, he became frustrated that the club's ambitions no longer seemed in tune with his own. He went to Arsenal for £200,000 and this time it did not even look like a good piece of business. In his time at Stoke, he had matured from gifted but wayward wild child to a cultured and dominant player for whom a lengthy England future seemed guaranteed. Yet Stoke got £40,000 less for him than they had paid.

Denis Smith took over the captaincy. 'Waddo knew he was being forced to sell his best players, and he parted company with Alan Hudson, who had been like a son to him,' he wrote. 'It was obvious that not only had the heart been ripped out of the side, but it had also been ripped out of our manager.'

For Smith, the loss of Greenhoff was the hardest to bear, 'Jimmy's sale was pivotal to the downfall of the club in my opinion. He had been the fulcrum of all that was good and exciting at Stoke City for eight years and he still had two or three more years at the top in him. Jimmy never wanted to leave Stoke. He loved it at the club and cried when he was told by Waddo that he had to go. Waddo cried too.'

It is not a sign of disrespect to those who remained to say – as Smith himself did – that with the loss of Greenhoff and Hudson the heart had gone from the team. Smith, Bloor,

Dodd, Conroy, Mahoney and Marsh all went on to give further sterling service to the club. But none of them was getting any younger. The form – and the flair – of earlier years could not be sustained in the absence of two such influential players.

Again, 'it gets worse'. Early in the new year, the most durable member of an exceptionally durable defence, Mike Pejic, was off too. Like Hudson, he could see which way the wind was blowing. He knew Everton wanted him and he went to the board to ask them to let him go. Again, Waddington was powerless. He threatened to resign if Pejic was allowed to leave. His bluff was called. In a matter of weeks he had lost three of the most important members of the side he had spent years assembling, the team he hoped would win the title. The end would not now be long delayed.

Performances on the field inevitably began to suffer. Terry Conroy wrote, 'As each sale was announced, it felt as if a little piece of us was being cut away.' Tony Waddington, he said, 'had spent a lot of money assembling the best squad the club had ever had, but now his lads were being sold from underneath him, one by one. How was he supposed to replace them? They were demigods as far as the people of Stoke-on-Trent were concerned. The simple truth was that he couldn't. There were no more rabbits to be pulled out of hats.'

What made matters worse as far as the players were concerned was that no one took the trouble to keep them informed of what was happening. They had to rely on the media and the rumour mill to try to keep up. It was not a situation that would help their morale, confidence or sense of security. They spent a lot of time wondering if they were going to be the next to go in what amounted to a fire sale. Smith says he began to think that soon he would have no one to play with.

Although the supporters knew the departures had been forced on the manager by financial necessity – and that he was as upset about them as they were – Waddington now became the target for their frustration and anger. Many stayed away from the games. Crowds that had been in the mid-to-high 20,000s when things were going well now fell into the teens – several gates were as low as 12,000. The club went straight out of the FA Cup, going down 2-0 at Everton.

Even with a bad trot of results in January and February 1977, Stoke were still several points clear of the danger zone when the dam burst. The final straw was a home match against Leicester, settled in the last minute by a Shilton howler and a Frank Worthington winner. The cries of 'Waddington out' rang out around the ground.

The next day there was an emergency board meeting to discuss Waddington's position. On the Monday there was another. Waddington entered that meeting as the manager and left it out of a job. Did he jump or was he pushed? After the meeting, he called Denis Smith, who says Waddington told him, 'They want me to go. What do you think?' Smith replied, 'It's simple. If you go, we'll go down. You have got to stay. Convince them that you have got to stay. Don't you resign. If it's got to happen, then make them sack you.' And that, he believes, is what happened. The final humiliation was that Waddington was not even able to drive home to Crewe. His car belonged to the club. After his 17 years of service, during which he had given the club more success than any in its history, and delivered its first major trophy, Stoke City sent their manager home in a taxi.

Two days later, with assistant manager George Eastham in charge, the team managed a home draw against Arsenal. It was perhaps not a great idea to select Waddington's son for the team. Steve Waddington had made a scoring debut in November, but on this day he vented some of the frustration he must have felt at the treatment of his father with a thigh-high tackle on Arsenal playmaker Liam Brady. Waddington was booked and Brady was sent off for retaliating.

There were 12 matches remaining, but by now the events of the previous months were taking their toll. A victory against Leeds would be the only other win they could muster for the rest of the season. There was a smattering of draws, but mostly it was one defeat after another. From a position of relative safety, relegation was now a real threat. Even so, they travelled to Villa Park for the last match of the season knowing that their fellow strugglers Bristol City and West Ham both had tough fixtures themselves, at home to Liverpool and Manchester United. If they both lost, a point against Villa would be enough to keep Stoke up. It didn't pan out that way. Bristol City and West Ham both won, while an early penalty was enough to see Stoke go down 1-0. It meant relegation to the Second Division.

Denis Smith reflects on that tumultuous time, 'I felt less devastated than nonplussed by what had gone on. I just couldn't square it all. It was enormously frustrating, and it is only when I think back to what went on that I fully understand the tornado that literally and figuratively had pulled the club apart. If the loss of Gordon Banks was a major blow, then the storm which demolished the Butler Street Stand was the straw that broke the camel's back. It arguably cost Stoke City 25 years of development. The worst thing in the world had happened as far as I was concerned. The place was just in total disarray. To all intents and purposes, my beloved Stoke City were broken.'

Relegation marked the end of a miserable year and a half since the fateful storm that had destroyed the stand and exposed the fragility of the club's financial position. It was the end of the team that Waddington had assembled with such skill and flair, the team he believed was good enough to win the league title. It was the end of Waddington's 17 years at the helm – years in which he had more than made good on his ambition to put Stoke City back on the map. It was the end of a 14-year stay in the First Division. Stoke were back a couple of years later, but then relegated again in the mid-1980s and twice slipped into the Third Division for a while. There were to be many long years of mediocrity before a revival of interest in Stoke during their ten-year sojourn in the Premier League, beginning in 2008. Those years in the wilderness serve only to add lustre to the achievements of the early 1970s, and the conviction that Waddington's team was the finest ever to represent the club: the team that won the League Cup; the team that appeared in successive FA Cup semi-finals; the team that – nearly – won the league.

19

THE BOYS OF '74

Tony Waddington

Waddington left the Victoria Ground in 1977 after 25 years with Stoke as youth coach, assistant manager and then manager. He was only 51, but he was so closely associated with the club that his managerial career seemed to be over. One person who kept faith with him was Brian Clough, who had never forgotten Waddington's kindness in taking him to the Ajax game soon after he had been sacked by Leeds and was out in the football wilderness. When Clough's star rose again at Nottingham Forest, and they reached the 1979 European Cup Final against Malmö in Munich, he returned the favour. He called Waddington and told him, 'You're coming with us. The tickets are in the post. See you at East Midlands Airport.' When Forest won the cup, Waddington was sitting in a place of honour next to Clough and his assistant Peter Taylor on the touchline.

After two years out of the game, Waddington returned to Crewe, where he had spent seven years as a player after the war. Crewe had just finished 92nd out of 92 – bottom of the Fourth Division. Waddington stayed there as manager for two years, showing something of his old flair for eye-catching transfers by recruiting several of his former Stoke players, including Terry Conroy and Jimmy Greenhoff. An attempt to snare Alan Hudson was thwarted only by red tape. Waddington also blooded a promising young goalkeeper from Zimbabwe who had been playing in the United States. As soon as he saw Bruce Grobbelaar, Waddington knew he had a player capable of playing at a much higher level, and he alerted both Manchester United and Nottingham Forest to his new discovery. Neither was interested, so Waddington picked up the phone to Bob Paisley, who was more receptive. Grobbelaar went on to make more than 400 appearances for Liverpool.

Crewe finished bottom again. They fared a little better the following year, but not well enough for Waddington to avoid the sack in July 1981. He returned to Stoke in 1991 when he was made an associate director of the club that had shoved him out so unceremoniously 14 years earlier. It was a magnanimous gesture by Peter Coates, then in his first stint as chairman. Coates appreciated Waddington's achievements. 'He deserves a special place,' he said. Tony Waddington died in 1994, at the age of 69. Some of his former players were coffin-bearers at his funeral.

Alan Bloor

Having been restricted by injury to just two appearances in 1974/75, Bloor roared back the following year with a total of 37 games and a personal best season's tally of five goals, including – within the space of four days – one at Anfield and another at Old Trafford. After 17 years at the Victoria Ground and just shy of 500 appearances, he moved in 1978 to Port Vale as a player and youth-team coach. The following year he became manager, with Gordon Banks on his coaching team. But the quietly spoken Bloor soon found that management was not for him. 'I don't have what it takes,' he said, on resigning in 1979. He later became a carpet salesman and still lives in the Potteries.

Ian 'Danny' Bowers

Bowers came through the youth and reserve teams at Stoke and made his debut in November 1974 against Wolves. He was somewhat overshadowed by Peter Shilton, who was also making his first appearance for Stoke that day. After Mike Pejic broke his leg, Bowers had an extended run at left-back, playing in the last eight games of the season. He played a further 29 times over the next four seasons before his former manager Tony Waddington took him to Fourth Division Crewe, where he notched up nearly 200 appearances.

Terry Conroy

Conroy was not part of the exodus of 1976/77 and played through the relegation season that followed. His appearances over the next couple of years were limited, and he left Stoke in 1979 after 12 years and more than 300 appearances. A brief and unhappy spell with Bulova in Hong Kong followed, and then he rejoined Tony Waddington at Crewe. He finished his career playing for Waterford and Limerick in his native Ireland, which he combined with a part-time role coaching the Republic of Ireland national team.

After his retirement from the game, Conroy returned to Stoke to live, and established his own insurance business in Ashton-under-Lyne. He later supervised industrial cleaning contract work at exhibitions and shows. He rejoined Stoke City to work in the hospitality department at the new Britannia Stadium, and still works as a matchday host in the Waddington Suite. In 2011, Conroy survived a near-death experience with a vascular aneurysm and was given the last rites. He recovered, and published his autobiography *You Don't Remember Me Do You?* in 2015.

Alan Dodd

Dodd was the last of the 1974/75 regulars to part company with the club, when he joined Wolves in 1982 for just £40,000. It was the end of ten years and 400 appearances, during which he had experienced the highs of the title tilt in 1975 and promotion in 1978/79 and the lows of relegation in 1977. Although at one stage he made 102 consecutive appearances, he was increasingly disenchanted with the tactics of managers Alan Durban and Richie Barker. He left with mixed feelings, 'I was surprised that I went so cheaply, but I was relieved to go. I couldn't see a future at Stoke under Richie Barker, but leaving the Victoria Ground was the most upsetting day of my footballing life.'

He was promoted to the First Division with Wolves and although he was their Player of the Year, they went straight back down again and suffered three consecutive relegations. Dodd came back to Stoke, only to see them drop back down to the Second Division. There followed six years in Sweden during which he played for three different clubs, finally retiring at the age of 39.

Dodd went on to fulfil his teenage ambition to work in the building trade, doing up rundown properties – in one of which he still lives, just outside the Potteries. He told the Wolves Heroes website in 2009, 'I have always enjoyed renovating old properties and building extensions, so it was obvious what I would go into. I set out working on one derelict property which was literally falling down and it took me two years to make it habitable. I have four or five terraced houses now around the Stoke area which I've worked on and rented out.'

He retained his love of heavy metal music – and also his prodigious fitness. He gave up running marathons only in his 50s. 'I have run about ten marathons and around 20 half-marathons and have had some fun doing them,' he told the website. 'But those days are behind me now. I'm content to just keep a level of fitness by running up and down the hills near where we live.'

John Farmer

Farmer was an ever-present for the first 17 games of the 1974/75 season, but once supplanted by Shilton he did not regain his place. The process was grimly familiar to him, since he had been shouldered aside in the same way seven years previously by the signing of Gordon Banks. He had remained loyal to Stoke, and served as Banks's understudy before reclaiming the jersey after the England keeper's car accident and enforced retirement. After that, he barely missed a match until the signing of Shilton. The debate about whether or not Stoke needed another keeper, and whether the money would have been better spent on a goalscorer, is one that continues to this day. But once Shilton was installed between the posts, Farmer never appeared again for Stoke, and left in 1975 to play for Northwich Victoria. Over ten seasons at Stoke he made just under 200 appearances. He later ran a crisp factory in Cheadle. His hobby is writing poetry.

Jimmy Greenhoff

We've already described how fans' favourite Jimmy G was dragged kicking and screaming from his beloved Victoria Ground, and went on to have a superb late-career flowering at Manchester United. Old Trafford took to him as warmly as the Boothen End had done, and he was named Player of the Year by United supporters in 1979, having finished the season as their top scorer with 17 goals.

In 1980, in common with some of his other former Stoke team-mates, he was reunited with Tony Waddington at Crewe Alexandra. After a season there, and a stint in Toronto playing in the North American Soccer League, he finished his playing career at Port Vale and Rochdale, joining them as player-manager at the age of 36. He played a total of 749 games and scored 202 goals.

Greenhoff's post-football career was clouded by a failed business venture that put him in dire financial straits. The story is recounted at The Mighty Mighty Whites – a website for fans of Leeds United, where he had made his debut at the age of 16. 'A so-called friend of mine wanted to go into insurance and I was silly enough to go with him,' said Greenhoff. 'I did that for about eight or nine years, but unfortunately I found out he had been doing the dirty on me since day one. I ended up losing everything that I'd worked for in my 23-year playing career. I really did lose everything, including my house. It was absolutely shocking. I had always expected to be comfortable but that was snatched away from me.

'I had to now make sure there was food and drink on the table. Because I needed the money, I ended up taking the first job that came along. I was in a warehouse pulling trucks and trolleys around and collecting wallpaper. A lot of people have to do it, and I had to do it to bring a wage in. People ridiculed me for working in a warehouse but it had to be done. I began working for a pharmaceutical company. They were absolutely wonderful towards me and knew the predicament that I'd been in. It was a job that was obviously completely different from football. I'd be dressing up putting my overall, mask and hood on and manufacturing respiratory products for hay fever and asthma. After what I'd done in the warehouse it was wonderful!'

Greenhoff is now retired and lives just up the road from Terry Conroy.

Sean Haslegrave

A local boy, Haslegrave was a midfield terrier who made his first-team debut in 1970 and was in and out of the team for the next six years. In 1974/75 he played 19 league games, most of them in the early part of the season when he wore the number seven shirt. He was angry at being substituted during the away leg of Stoke's UEFA Cup tie with Ajax, and exchanged words with the manager as he came off the pitch. The watching Brian Clough admired his competitive spirit, and signed him for Nottingham Forest in July 1976 for £50,000. He was part of the reluctant exodus in the wake of the Butler Street Stand disaster.

After little more than a year, during which injury and the arrival of Archie Gemmill limited his opportunities, he went to Preston, then Crewe and York City, where he was reunited with his old team-mate Denis Smith, by then York manager. His last club was Torquay, with whom he became a coach once his playing days were over after a total of 599 games. Coaching later took him back to Preston and the English Colleges team.

In 2012 he completed a 1,200-mile charity walk to Spain, which raised £15,000. Interviewed by the *Sentinel* in that year, he recalled his early time at Stoke, 'I remember after training at Stoke, Gordon Banks would tell us to meet him behind the ground at 2pm. It was for shooting practice and we couldn't shoot in the 18-yard box and we couldn't go home until we scored. I would be there until 4.45pm; I used to tell him my tea was ready and I needed to go!'

Sean Haslegrave died in 2019, aged 68.

Alan Hudson

Considering his impact at the time and subsequently, it is remarkable that Hudson was at Stoke for less than three years, during which he made 120 appearances. He didn't even spend that long at Arsenal, where disagreements with manager Terry Neill limited his appearances. Arsenal sold him to the North American Soccer League side Seattle Sounders for £100,000, and he spent four years playing in America. After a brief return to Chelsea, during which he didn't feature in the first team, it was, amazingly, back to Stoke. At Tony Waddington's recommendation, manager Bill Asprey brought him back to the Victoria Ground for £22,500 in January 1984 – exactly ten years after his first arrival. The effect was just the same, as a team seemingly doomed to relegation from the First Division went on a strong run and just managed to stay up. They couldn't beat the drop the following season, however, and although Hudson was named captain for the next campaign, a knee injury forced him to retire just a handful of games into the 1985/86 season. He had played nearly 500 career games in all, with more than 300 of them in the First Division.

Hudson's life after retirement was just as eventful as his career on the pitch had been, as he battled problems with money and drink. In December 1997 he was seriously injured when hit by a car while he was walking along a street in London. He was in a coma for weeks and has since undergone more than 70 operations. Although there were fears that he would not walk again, he is able to do so with the help of crutches.

Hudson has enjoyed a late-blossoming career as a writer. The title of his autobiography, *The Working Man's Ballet*, is a nod to the man who coined the phrase, his old friend and mentor Tony Waddington. Hudson paid further tribute in *The Waddington Years* in 2008, a detailed account of the unique and enduring relationship between player and manager. He was at Waddington's hospital bed the day he died. *The Tinker and Talisman* is also autobiographical but reflects on the more philosophical side of the game, as well as giving Hudson's take on the recent history of his first club, Chelsea. Hudson still writes and talks about football and is an active pundit on social media – and still goes to Stoke City games. His son Anthony has coached and managed in the United States, the Middle East and New Zealand, where he was for three years manager of the national team.

Geoff Hurst

No sooner had the dust settled on the disappointments of April 1975 than Hurst was off to West Bromwich Albion, where new manager Johnny Giles was trying to build a team to get out of the Second Division. But at 34, Hurst acknowledged that he was too old to lead the line, and after only a dozen games for the Baggies he was off to the United States and a successful swansong with Seattle Sounders.

A career in coaching now beckoned, and Hurst was for three years player-manager at Southern League club Telford United and part of the England coaching team under Ron Greenwood. In 1979 he became Danny Blanchflower's assistant at Chelsea, and took over when Blanchflower was sacked. A poor finish to the season dashed the club's hopes of promotion back to the First Division, and when the same thing happened the following year, Hurst lost his job. After three years managing in Kuwait, he quit football to work as an insurance salesman. Over the next 20 years he enjoyed a successful career in the insurance business before retiring in 2002. Since then he has done much charity work and public speaking, and toured the country with his *An Evening With Sir Geoff Hurst* show. He was knighted in 1998.

Kevin Lewis

Lewis made just 15 appearances for Stoke during a four-year stay, five of them in 1974/75. He spent three years out of the game before joining Crewe, where he was a regular for three seasons. He was manager of Leek Town in 1985/86.

John Mahoney

After relegation in 1977, Mahoney joined Middlesbrough for £90,000. Like most of the leavers he was not keen to go, but saw little future for himself in the Second Division. 'I didn't want to leave, but when I looked at the fixture list and Stoke were away at Mansfield, while Middlesbrough were at home to Liverpool, I knew I had to go.' He had played more than 300 times for Stoke.

After two seasons as a regular at Middlesbrough, he dropped a division, joining Swansea City, with whom he gained promotion in 1981. Mahoney's playing career was ended by a heavy tackle in early 1983 that left him with a permanent limp. He was 36 and had played nearly 600 league games. He went into management with Welsh clubs, with two stints at Bangor City and spells at Newport County and Carmarthen Town. He lives in Swansea.

John Marsh

John 'Jackie' Marsh was a one-club man. He joined as an apprentice in 1962/63, at the height of Matthews Mania, and after making his debut in 1967 racked up 444 appearances. He was given a free transfer in 1979, and after following Terry Conroy to Hong Kong, played his final games for Northwich Victoria. He worked as a sales rep and has remained a diehard Stoke fan, continuing to attend games when his health permitted.

Ian Moores

A Staffordshire boy, Moores played for Stoke's youth team as a left-winger but switched to centre-forward, a position better suited to his imposing build and muscular presence. He made his debut in April 1974. The injury to Ritchie gave him more chances in 1974/75 and he scored four times in ten outings. Tall, blond and bearded, Moores was talked of as a possible England prospect, reflected in a £75,000 fee when he was sold to Tottenham in 1976, another victim of the post-storm money-raising clear-out. After two years there he went to Leyton Orient, and enjoyed the most successful run of his career playing for APOEL in Cyprus in the mid-1980s.

He retired after scoring in the final of the FA Vase to help Tamworth win the trophy. He returned to the Potteries and worked in personal finance, but developed lung cancer and died in 1998 at the age of 43.

Mike Pejic

As we've seen, Pejic's Stoke career was another that came to an end as the result of the 1976 storm, and he joined Everton for a fee of £135,000. He missed only a couple of games in the 1977/78 season, when Everton finished third in the table. He suffered another broken leg in 1978 and the following year joined Aston Villa. Injury kept him out of the team, and he retired in 1980. Various management and coaching jobs followed at Leek Town, Northwich Victoria and Port Vale – where he won a case for unfair dismissal – and Chester City. He taught on FA coaching courses and coached in Malaysia, Zimbabwe and Kuwait.

Pejic kept himself super-fit, which was a great advantage when, in his 60s, he took up the martial art taekwondo. In 2012 he opened the Pejic Taekwondo Academy in the Chesterton area of the Potteries where he grew up. In 2019 he became the over-65 European champion. He has been a matchday radio commentator at Stoke and wrote a weekly column in the *Sentinel*. His brother Mel appeared just once for Stoke, in 1980, but had a 12-year career at Hereford United and also played for Wrexham.

John Ritchie

Big John's career came to an end on the September evening in Ipswich in 1974 when he was flattened by Kevin Beattie. The tackle left him with a double fracture of the leg, and sparked half a century of never-to-be-resolved debate about whether Stoke would have won the title if he had stayed fit – or if he had been replaced. He never played for the first team again.

Ritchie was sufficiently recovered to have a few outings in the reserves in 1975, but after breaking his nose he decided to call time on his long, goal-studded career. He was 34. In his two spells at Stoke he had scored 176 goals in 347 games – almost exactly a goal every other game. He is Stoke's all-time top scorer.

Ritchie turned his back on football and established his own pottery company. He was a wholesaler of china, earthenware and giftware, before later moving into the catering business, and died in 2007 at the age of 65 after a battle with Alzheimer's. He is immortalised in the Potteries with a road named after him on the site of the old Victoria Ground, and a bust outside the bet365 Stadium. Part of the lengthy inscription says, 'His brave performances elevated him to cult status and he would go on to score a remarkable number of goals … He is Stoke City's top marksman of all time and lives on in our hearts as one of Staffordshire's greatest sporting heroes.'

Jimmy Robertson

Robertson's broken leg on Boxing Day 1974 signalled the beginning of the end for his career at Stoke. When he recovered, he found it difficult to command a regular place, and played only a handful of games in the next two seasons before deciding to try his luck in the United States with Seattle Sounders. He returned to the UK and finished his career with short spells at Walsall and Crewe. After football, he worked in the Potteries as the director of a computer insurance company and later a financial services company in Newcastle-under-Lyme.

Geoff Salmons

After relegation in 1977, Salmons briefly rejoined Sheffield United on loan before being sold to Leicester for what seems like a paltry sum of £45,000. He was only 29. After one season there, he dropped down two divisions to join Chesterfield, where he played for four years before retiring in 1982. He went on to realise his ambition of running a pub. Indeed, he built a pub – not once but twice: first the Manor in Old Denaby, and later Pastures Lodge in his native Mexborough. He is now retired.

Peter Shilton

Shilton was one of the few members of the team who went on to greater things as a player after the 1974/75 season – though sadly not in a Stoke City jersey. Although no one doubted his quality, his time at Stoke did not see him performing at his best. But his departure was the start of a long period of excellence during which he took his tally of England caps to 125 – still a record. It's hard to believe that for some of the time Ray Clemence was preferred in goal, and Clemence himself won 61 caps. Shilton also holds the world record for the most appearances in competitive matches – an astonishing 1,387 over a career that spanned 30 years. His three years at Stoke therefore form only a small part of his CV.

In the enforced clear-out resulting from the storm damage, Stoke agreed to sell Shilton to Manchester United in the summer of 1976, but United would not meet his wage demands. So he stayed at the Victoria Ground for another year, and after relegation joined Brian Clough at Nottingham Forest for £250,000. Forest won the league title in his first year and he was named PFA Player of the Year. Two European Cup winners' medals followed, but then things turned sour because of the keeper's well-publicised problems with gambling and alcohol.

There were five-year spells at Southampton and Derby County before a brief stint in management at Plymouth Argyle. Shilton played his 1,000th league game for Leyton Orient and finally retired at the age of 47. He later became a motivational after-dinner speaker, and announced in 2020 that he had overcome his gambling addiction with the help of his second wife, Stephanie, formerly a senior NHS manager. They live in Essex and run a consultancy providing advice in the fields of public service, healthcare and football.

Eric Skeels

The 1974/75 season was the last in which Eric 'Alfie' Skeels made a significant number of appearances. He played 23 times and scored once – only his seventh goal in his long career in the top division. It had been 16 seasons since he had made his debut in a home defeat by Charlton Athletic in March 1960. He was the sole survivor of the side that played in Stanley Matthews's famous second debut for Stoke in October 1961. Skeels had joined the club as an inside-forward, but Waddington converted him into a hard-tackling half-back.

Mr Dependable was also Mr Versatility, playing in every outfield position to fill gaps as required – always consistent, always reliable. His preferred position was midfield, as he told the *Sentinel* at the time of his 80th birthday: 'That's because I was a grafter, and in midfield you're working all the time. I used to enjoy man-marking, which was something we would do if we weren't playing so well and were up against a good team. I remember doing that on Jimmy Greaves and Denis Law, the goalscoring stars. As long as I'd kept them quiet, I'd done my job.'

Skeels passed the club record for appearances in 1975 and turned out 597 times in all. He was given a free transfer in 1976, and after brief spells in the United States and with Port Vale, he became a publican, first running the Hare and Hounds in Glossop, in the High Peak. Later he came back to the Potteries to run the Noah's Ark in Hartshill, and in his 80s is still a regular at the bet365 Stadium. In spite of his records and achievements, he could still be described as an unsung hero. He is a modest man. 'All that mattered for me was playing in games and doing my best for the team,' he said.

Denis Smith

Of all those who tried their hand in management once their playing days were over, Smith was the only one to stay the course, and enjoyed remarkable success over a long period. He began coaching Stoke's reserves when injury prevented him from playing at all in the 1980/81 season. He played his last game in the red and white stripes on the final day of the 1981/82 season, featuring in a 3-0 win that kept Stoke in the First Division. It was 14 seasons and nearly 500 games since his bluff had persuaded Tony Waddington to give him a contract. He was given a free transfer to Fourth Division York City, for whom he had played seven games while on loan a few weeks earlier.

He joined York as player-manager, and played 30 games in his first season before hanging up his boots for good. Some shrewd signings – including former team-mate Sean Haslegrave – and the overhaul of a training regime he described as 'a shambles' when he first arrived saw York begin to climb the table. They won the Fourth Division title, and initially did well in the Third Division, as well as beating Arsenal in the FA Cup and then holding Liverpool to a draw at home.

In May 1987, Smith moved to Sunderland, who had just been relegated to the Third Division for the first time in their history. The team won the Third Division, and in their second season in the Second Division they reached the play-offs, losing 1-0 to Swindon Town. But Swindon were denied their place because of financial irregularities, and it was Sunderland who went up. They lasted for only one season in the top tier. In the summer of 1991, Smith was offered the manager's job at

Stoke, but felt it would be too much for him to return to the club. His loyalty to Sunderland was rewarded with the sack a few months later.

Within a couple of months he had found another manager's chair, this time at Bristol City, who were threatened with relegation. Smith hauled them out of trouble but their form remained variable and he had several disagreements with the board over transfers.

He was soon on the move again, first to Oxford United and then to West Bromwich Albion, both in the Second Division. Finishes of tenth and 12th at Albion were not considered good enough though, and he was dismissed only a week before the start of the 1999/2000 season. After that it was back to Oxford for a short period before his sixth and final club as a manager, Wrexham.

Wrexham were already deep in relegation trouble when Smith joined in October 2001, but he brought them back up at the first attempt, winning the Third Division Manager of the Season award in the process. His managership now became mired in political and financial issues. He refused to support a campaign by fans to unseat the club's chairman, but the club went into administration and were docked ten points – which condemned them to relegation. Smith stayed loyal, in spite of an offer to manage Blackpool, and eventually Wrexham came out of administration. But off-field events had taken their toll, and with relegation again threatening, Smith's time at the club came to an end early in 2007.

By then, Smith had joined an elite group of managers to have been in charge for more than 1,000 professional games. He managed six clubs over a period of 25 years, leading to a final tally of 1,195. Smith returned to Stoke to live, and published his autobiography in 2008. He has worked as a radio pundit and match delegate, and worked part-time for Stoke as a mentor for academy players.

The Victoria Ground

The Vic had a record all its own – as the oldest ground in English football. It was the home of Stoke City for 119 years, beginning long before they even *were* Stoke City. The first recorded game there was in March 1878, with the first league fixture the following year, the inaugural year of the Football League. The ground took its name from the Victoria Hotel nearby. It was originally used by the local athletics club, with the ground surrounded by an oval running track. Even in those days there was a Boothen End, a stand with a capacity of 1,000. A main stand was not built until the 1920s, the Boothen End was covered in 1931 and the Butler Street Stand was opened in 1935. The stand served as an army munitions store during the war. In those less safety-conscious days before all-seater grounds, the official capacity was about 45,000, although 51,373 packed in to watch a game against Arsenal in 1937. They were rewarded with a goalless draw!

The Victoria Ground was never a byword for luxury – remember Waddington's comments about the state of it when he arrived, and again when he took over as manager. A new main stand was built in 1960, with the terracing concreted in 1963. Some of the players helped to build it in the summer, being paid a shilling an hour for their labours. The storm of 1976 meant the Butler Street Stand had to be rebuilt, and a new stand was also built at the Stoke End. The Taylor Report of 1990 required all First and Second Division club grounds to be all-seater by 1994, and although Stoke were by now languishing in the third tier, plans for a major refurbishment were drawn up. The club decided instead to build a new ground at Trentham Lakes. The Britannia Stadium, now the bet365 Stadium, was the result.

The last game at the Victoria Ground was on 4 May 1997 against West Bromwich Albion, who had also been the opponents in that first league match in 1878. Gates in

1996/97 had averaged only 12,000, but there was a capacity of 22,500 for an emotional farewell to the Potters' old home. Graham Kavanagh scored the last Stoke goal at the ground in a 2-1 win. Before that match, there was a 30-minute game between teams of former players from the two clubs. Stoke's team included Adrian Heath, Gordon Banks, Ian Cranson, Peter Fox, Alan Hudson, Eric Skeels, Mickey Thomas and Alan Dodd. Cyrille Regis, Ally Brown and Jeff Astle lined up for Albion. Sir Stanley Matthews kicked the match off.

For 20 years the site stood empty but for the ghosts of matches and footballing heroes of yore. Some of the fixtures and fittings were sold to supporters. In 2019, the Victoria Park housing development was built there, with some streets named after former players. Those names – John Ritchie Street, Frank Soo Street, Bob McGrory Street, Paul Ware Street and the name of Victoria Park itself – are all that remains of the famous old ground.

ACKNOWLEDGEMENTS

FROM THE start, I wanted this book to be less a straightforward narrative, more a story told as far as possible through the memories and reflections of the players themselves. A powerful attraction when embarking on the project was the prospect of meeting some of my boyhood heroes in person. Sadly, as the book was written during the coronavirus pandemic, this was not possible: interviews had to be conducted by phone or video link.

They say you should never meet your idols, as they will inevitably disappoint. I am happy to say that this was not my experience at all. I found the ex-players who kindly agreed to speak to me to be thoughtful, modest and highly accessible. If anything, I now hold them in even higher regard than before. So my particular thanks to Terry Conroy, Denis Smith, Alan Hudson, Alan Dodd, Eric Skeels and Geoff Salmons, whose first-hand accounts form such an important element of the book.

Conroy, Smith and Hudson have all written their own books, and with their permission, I have drawn freely from them as well. I have usually tried to indicate whether a particular quotation comes from a book ('he wrote') or an interview ('he says'). Details of those books appear in the list of sources.

Many of the quotations from Tony Waddington come from a series of interviews he gave in retirement to the *Sentinel*'s Stoke City reporter of the 1970s and 1980s, Peter Hewitt. They appeared in the *Sentinel* between October 1988 and January 1989. I am grateful to Reach plc for permission to quote from these and from other archive material in the *Sentinel*. Chris Adams, syndication editor at Reach, was particularly helpful in tracking down photographs from the archives.

I owe a further debt to Terry Conroy for agreeing to write the foreword, and for putting me in touch with other players. I also received help and encouragement from Simon Lowe, himself the author of many books about Stoke, and from John Leonard, John Ruggiero and Cris Reynolds. Anthony Bunn gave me permission to quote from interviews conducted by him for *Duck*, the magazine for Stoke City fans.

I am grateful to Paul and Jane Camillin at Pitch Publishing for agreeing to publish the book and guiding me through the production process, and to Duncan Olner for his brilliant design work.

I regret not being able to include Stoke City Football Club in the list of those who have helped me. I had hoped to be granted access to club records, in many cases simply to check basic facts such as transfer fees of those arriving or leaving, club appearances and so on. The club historian has left and apparently not been replaced, and the press office politely told me that the archives were in a poor condition and that they could not help. This is a sorry state of affairs for the oldest league club in England.

Where figures were disputed or in doubt, and could not be checked against an official record, I have used those that seemed to me to be the most authoritative. I apologise for any inaccuracies that may have resulted.

SOURCES

Evening Sentinel archives

Banks, G., *Banksy* (Michael Joseph/Penguin Books, 2002)

Conroy, T., *You Don't Remember Me Do You?* (Pitch Publishing, 2015)

Hudson, A., *The Working Man's Ballet* (London Books, 2017)

Hudson, A., *The Waddington Years* (Snide Press, 2008)

Hurst, G., *1966 and All That* (Headline, 2001)

Kernick, D., *Who the Hell was Dudley Kernick?* (Crossley Publications, 1986)

Leonard, J., *Tony Waddington: Director of a Working Man's Ballet* (Pitch Publishing, 2018)

Lowe, S., *Match of My Life: Stoke City* (Pitch Publishing, 2012)

Lowe, S., *Stoke City, the Modern Era – a complete record* (Desert Island Books, 2000)

Lowe, S., *Stoke City: 101 Golden Greats* (Desert Island Books, 2001)

Matthews, S., *The Way It Was: My Autobiography* (Headline, 2000)

Matthews, T., *The Legends of Stoke City 1863–2008* (DB Publishing, 2008)

Matthews, T., *The Encyclopaedia of Stoke City, 1868–1994* (Lion Press, 1994)

Miller, D., *Stanley Matthews: the authorised biography* (Pavilion, 1989)

Pettigrove, J., *Huddy: the Official Biography of Alan Hudson* (Ashley Drake, 2017)

Shilton, P., *Peter Shilton: The Autobiography* (Orion Books, 2004)

Smith, D., *Just One of Seven* (Know the Score!, 2008)